Cyber Warfare

Recent Titles in the

CONTEMPORARY WORLD ISSUES
Series

Books in the **Contemporary World Issues** series address vital issues in today's society such as genetic engineering, pollution, and biodiversity. Written by professional writers, scholars, and nonacademic experts, these books are authoritative, clearly written, up-to-date, and objective. They provide a good starting point for research by high school and college students, scholars, and general readers as well as by legislators, businesspeople, activists, and others.

Each book, carefully organized and easy to use, contains an overview of the subject, a detailed chronology, biographical sketches, facts and data and/or documents and other primary source material, a forum of authoritative perspective essays, annotated lists of print and nonprint resources, and an index.

Readers of books in the Contemporary World Issues series will find the information they need to have a better understanding of the social, political, environmental, and economic issues facing the world today.

Cyber Warfare

A REFERENCE HANDBOOK

Paul J. Springer

 ABC-CLIO

Santa Barbara, California • Denver, Colorado • Oxford, England

Library of Congress Cataloging-in-Publication Data

Springer, Paul J.
  Cyber warfare : a reference handbook / Paul J. Springer.
    pages cm. — (Contemporary world issues)
  Includes bibliographical references and index.
  ISBN 978–1–61069–443–8 (hard copy : alk. paper) — ISBN 978–1–61069–444–5 (ebook) 1. Cyberspace operations (Military science) 2. Cyberspace—Security measures—History. 3. Cyberterrorism—Prevention. 4. Computer crimes—Prevention. I. Title. II. Title: Cyberwarfare, a reference handbook.
  U163.S66   2015
  355.4—dc23   2014038753

ISBN: 978–1–61069–443–8
EISBN: 978–1–61069–444–5

19 18 17 16 15   1 2 3 4 5

This book is also available on the World Wide Web as an eBook.
Visit www.abc-clio.com for details.

ABC-CLIO, LLC
130 Cremona Drive, P.O. Box 1911
Santa Barbara, California 93116-1911

This book is printed on acid-free paper ∞

Manufactured in the United States of America

Contents

Preface

The importance of cyberspace to the modern human environment cannot be overstated. Computer networks have become a fundamental part of society, influencing virtually every aspect of life for much of the planet's population. Even individuals who have never sat before a computer screen are affected by computer networks, whether they realize it or not. Computers have revolutionized the function of the world. Unfortunately, computers do not have the power to reform human nature, or at least not yet, and thus conflict remains a common part of the human experience. Computer networks play an increasingly important role in conflicts of the twenty-first century, and the cyber domain touches almost all elements of human conflict. This work explores the current state of affairs in cyber warfare, including what can be done now, and what is likely in the near future.

The cyber realm is unique in terms of warfare, primarily because it is an entirely manmade domain of conflict. There are no rules within cyberspace that cannot be changed, through physical changes to the architecture of the environment or programming changes to the systems that control it. Thus, the challenge of developing a national strategy for cyberspace becomes increasingly difficult as the rules of engagement change with the nature of the conflict zone. Cyber assets offer enormous potential for enhancing the communications, economic partnerships, and knowledge sharing of nations. In this regard, the cyber domain might serve as the great unifying force of the twenty-first century, in part because it is not bounded by the geographic delineations that dominate the thinking of political leaders around the world. However, computer networks are also prone to abuse, as they offer enormous potential for new forms of criminal activity, for the propagation of terrorist ideologies, and for the facilitation of attacks within the physical world.

As Dr. Jonathan Coopersmith, one of my mentors at Texas A&M University, often stated to his students, technology is not good or evil, nor is it neutral. Essentially, most technological innovations can be put to limitless different uses, some of them unfortunately of a nefarious nature. The challenge, then, is for the developers and users of cyberspace to find ways to encourage, or even compel, the use of computer networks for the greater benefit of humanity, rather than allowing them to become just another zone of human conflict and never-ending struggle. Likewise, national and international leaders must strive to facilitate this goal, both by supporting international accords on the acceptable uses of cyberspace, and by encouraging the positive uses of cyberspace to improve the standard of living for the entire population of the planet.

No work of this nature is created in a vacuum, and the current volume is certainly no exception to that rule. I naturally owe particular thanks to Major Heidi L. Dexter, U.S. Air Force; Dr. Martin Libicki, RAND Corporation; Dr. S. Michael Pavelec, Joint Advanced Warfare School; Dr. Nick Sambaluk, U.S. Military Academy; and Major Brian Tannehill, U.S. Air Force, for their important contributions to this work. Each brings decades of experience within their field of expertise into their discussions, and all made valuable contributions to other aspects of the book throughout its production.

I also owe thanks for the tireless efforts of Pat Carlin and Robin Tutt of ABC-CLIO, both of whom maintained faith in this project even during the darkest hours of its creation. You did an amazing job of offering support, encouragement, and prodding, as each was required. I am extremely thankful for your assistance and look forward to decades of future collaboration. This is our second book-length work together, but it will not be our last. Suba Ramya of Lumina Datamatics did excellent work in moving the manuscript through the editorial process, and I appreciate all of her efforts.

My colleagues at the Air University provided a wonderful sounding board for some of my thoughts on cyber warfare, and are no doubt sick of hearing about my fears regarding computer networks, even if they will not publicly admit it. All of the officers named are members of the U.S. Air Force, unless otherwise noted. In particular, I derived significant assistance from Dr. Michael Allsep; Lieutenant Colonel Paul Clemans; Brigadier General Thomas Deale; Dr. Everett Dolman; Lieutenant Colonel Mack Easter; Major Brian Erickson, Canadian Air Force; Dr. Mary Hampton; Lieutenant Colonel Paul Hoffman; Dr. Kenneth Johnson; Dr. James Kiras; Lieutenant Colonel Paul Kirmis; Lieutenant Colonel Benjamin Kruggel; Colonel Robert Lass; Dr. Sebastian Lukasik; Dr. Michael May; Major John Merrill; Lieutenant Colonel Robert Miller; Lieutenant Colonel Shannon Mosakowski, U.S. Army; Colonel Ray O'Mara; Major Steve Quillman; Dr. John Reese; Dr. Chris Rein; Commander James Selkirk; Major Tony Silvera; Lieutenant Colonel Mark Sloan; Colonel Robert Smith; Dr. John Terino; Dr. Ryan Wadle; and Dr. Jacqueline Whitt. I look forward to many years of continuing collaboration with them all.

Of course, no one in my life deserves more thanks for undying support and love than my wife, Dr. Victoria Springer, who continues to inspire me with her insights, gracefulness, and never-ending patience. I am quite certain that if she never hears another paranoid rant about the future of cyber warfare from her husband, it will still be far too soon.

I am of the generation of Americans who has always had computers as a part of life, but whose early years were not dominated by cyber networks. Computers have certainly developed much faster and further than I have personally done, but they continue to be tools rather than a way of life for someone my age. Of course, being a historian, it is possible that I am simply too stuck in the past to truly accept the nature of the present, much less the future. That said, it is the next generation of Americans, and citizens around the world, who will truly deal with the ramifications of the cyber revolution. Within my family, that means that my dear nieces and nephews will probably be far more affected by the changes that computers have brought, and thus, it is to Alex, Allissa, Kendall, and Sean that this volume is humbly dedicated. May your generation handle the power and responsibility of computers with wisdom and kindness, and use them to make a better world.

Cyber Warfare

1 Background and History

Many elements of the history of human conflict have combined to create the cyber warfare environment. Long before the invention of the computer and the ability to interact on the Internet, certain precursors established the norms of conflict that still apply to the cyber domain. This chapter serves to examine the importance of information in the history of human conflict, both the attempt to garner knowledge about the enemy and the need to protect such information from foes. As cyber operations have become more common, the constant need for new and accurate information has influenced every aspect of conflict through computer networks.

Information as a Tool of War

For as long as humans have engaged in anything that might be characterized as "warfare," they have engaged in information operations to obtain advantages in war. Classical information campaigns included attempts to observe enemy troop dispositions, or deception operations to hide one's own forces in an ambush position. The successful military commander might rely upon a massive network of spies for collection of

---

Union telegraphers at the Battle of Fredericksburg on December 13, 1862. The telegraph allowed almost instant communications between field armies and U.S. Army headquarters in Washington, D.C. (Library of Congress)

intelligence about the enemy's resources and intents. Such espionage might be conducted by uniformed scouts, or it might be provided by a camouflaged insider, posing as a loyal member of the enemy's service. Of course, information had value only if it could be accurately communicated in a timely fashion, and the transmission of information created inherent vulnerabilities. A courier might be intercepted by the enemy, with the message lost and the information turned over to the opposing commander. Thus, it might be necessary to transmit the message in only a verbal fashion, under the assumption that the courier would not reveal the information, or in an encoded script, which hopefully could not be broken by the enemy. Perhaps false messages might be deliberately leaked to the enemy, to interfere with the decision-making and cloud the information available to an opponent.

Information campaigns are a vital part of virtually every classical text on the proper conduct of warfare, as well as a number of religious and social treatises that document military operations without offering advice for their conduct. Thus, the Bible tells the tale of Joshua, who sent spies into the city of Jericho to ascertain the state of its defenses. Sun Tzu, China's ancient author of *The Art of War*, admonished commanders to use spies as a mechanism to develop foreknowledge of an enemy's intentions. In India, the successful military leader might have read the *Arthashastra* by Kautilya, which recommended disguising spies as ascetics and sending them in groups into the enemy's territory. During the Second Punic War, Carthaginian commander Hannibal used subterfuge to hide his entire army near Lake Trasimene. When his less-aware opponent blithely advanced his troops in a long, indefensible column, Hannibal's troops attacked, annihilating the numerically superior Roman force at almost no cost to themselves. The Mongols proved extremely adept at denying the enemy information about their location and capabilities, while maintaining a close watch upon opposing forces. This practice helped the Mongol Horde seem to appear from nowhere, to fall upon defenseless enemy cities while the enemy army combed the frontier for an opponent that had long since bypassed the defenses. By the end of their expansion, the Mongol Empire was the largest land empire in world history, spanning from the Pacific Coast of Asia to the Middle East. The raw size of their holdings was awe-inspiring but also presented a fundamental problem, in that communication technology had not improved to allow the governance of such a vast empire. A rider attempting to travel from one end to the other of the Mongol Empire required months of hard riding, making anything but the most broad and strategic orders practically worthless (Arquilla and Ronfeldt 1992, 9–13).

In the early modern era, the art of espionage became a despised, if indispensable practice. Uniformed troops engaged in surveillance operations might claim the right of being taken prisoner and exchanged, but spies, who used deception to move among their enemies, could expect no quarter if captured. Although George Washington was known to operate a large network of spies, he maintained utter secrecy about their identities, knowing that their lives would be forfeit upon discovery. When Benedict Arnold attempted to sell West Point to the British, his contact, Major John André, was captured before the deal could be completed. His decision to cover his uniform with civilian attire sealed his fate. Despite personal pleas from Sir Henry Clinton to release André, or to exchange him for any American in British hands, Washington ordered André's execution as a spy. Even André's plea for death by a firing squad, as befit a soldier, went unheeded, leaving him to hang from the gallows.

The acclaimed Prussian theorist Carl von Clausewitz popularized the notion of the "fog of war," using the term to refer to all of the pieces of information that might assist a commander, if they were only made available. Clausewitz saw such a fog as both a physical phenomenon, in the form of the clouds of smoke caused by gunpowder weapons, and as a metaphorical tool, as a commander could not directly observe every movement of an enemy and thus could make decisions only upon the information possessed. Military leaders acknowledged the advantages of a greater battlefield awareness, searching for any solution to cut through the fog, ranging from signal towers and observation platforms to the use of hot-air balloons to extend visibility for miles. Of course, for every new innovation in observation, a counter was quickly devised, whether it was deliberately targeting the balloons or creating a false picture for the observers, such as by the emplacement of "Quaker Guns," logs cut and painted to look like artillery pieces from a distance. Seeing hundreds of unexpected cannons could give any nineteenth-century commander pause, and on occasion, it turned the course of a war by deterring an attack that might have succeeded.

The Role of Communications in Modern Warfare

Communication technologies gradually evolved over the course of the nineteenth century. Napoleon employed a semaphore system that allowed a message to pass from the coastline of France to his headquarters in Paris in a matter of a few hours. Unfortunately, the messages passed via the signal towers could also be observed by any enemy in sight, and the slow speed of the communication technique meant that only the simplest of messages could be passed. The creation of steam-powered railroads made for a much faster potential means of transmitting not just messages, but also the armies that were needed to engage in the massive battles of the nineteenth century. However, the railroad was an inherently defensive movement system—the location of the tracks was fixed, and any enemy with even a small bit of sense could easily tear up sections of track or destroy a small bridge span, preventing the transportation of armies. Thus, only lines completely under the control of friendly forces could be counted upon for rapid transit, making advancement against enemy-controlled territory more difficult.

In the realm of nineteenth-century communications, the telegraph system allowed the possibility of a centralized command system to direct a war that spanned a continent. British and French political leaders in London and Paris sought to send orders to their military counterparts in the Crimean Peninsula. President Abraham Lincoln reportedly spent many sleepless nights in the White House telegraph office, frantically hoping for news from the far-flung fronts of the Civil War. Cavalry forces made cutting telegraph lines a key portion of any raid behind enemy lines, under the assumption that such actions might trigger a loss of centralized control and coordination of the opposing armies, which might in turn lead to paralysis or indecision by the field commander who had become accustomed to external control. A more effective strategy would have been to tap into the telegraph wires at any point along their length, and intercept the signals being sent. Still more devastating, such a tap might have been used to send false signals to the enemy, under the guise of military orders. The commander who trusted information supplied by the telegraph was inherently at risk of a devastating loss due to an enemy information campaign. The only available means to counter this possibility was to create an encryption system, allowing messages to be delivered in a code that could then be decoded at the receiving end. Such codes tended to be fairly tedious and time-consuming, and might still be broken by an enemy given the time and materials necessary. As a result, encryption tended to be reserved for only the most secret information, and there were volumes of useful information transmitted in the clear to anyone along the line (Rosenzweig 2013, 130–36).

As armies became more dependent upon communications and centralized control, they also became more vulnerable to communication disruptions. The logistics requirements of early modern armies made for either very slow advances or a reliance upon foraging, a practice that essentially required armies to remain in constant motion lest they exhaust the surrounding countryside. Most military commanders of the early nineteenth century relied upon a magazine system, pre-placing depots of supplies along their intended route of march, rather than trying to organize enormous pack trains back to a central

supply depot. The railroad made this system somewhat unnecessary, as it could be used to transport enormous masses of supplies in a very short period, as long as the army remained within
the reach of a rail line and the commander could transmit a list
of which supplies were needed. Of course, in losing efforts,
even the most basic information operations can break down,
as was the case in April 1865 during the last gasps of the U.S.
Civil War. Robert E. Lee's Army of Northern Virginia aban-
doned its defense of Petersburg, ensuring the fall of the
Confederate capital of Richmond, and began to fall back west-
ward, toward a nearby rail junction. General Lee sent orders to
the nearest supply depot that his troops were in dire need of
food, and that trainloads of rations should be sent to the
Appomattox Courthouse rail station, where he would march
his troops. Upon arrival, they would embark upon the trains,
consume the rations, and fall back into the Confederate
interior, daring the Union troops to follow. When Lee's van-
guard reached the station, they saw an entire train stocked full
of supplies, the potential salvation of their army. Imagine their
surprise when the found each of the stock cars filled with
ammunition, the only thing that his army had in ample supply!
The communication system had broken down completely, and
his quartermasters had sent the supplies they had in abundance,
not knowing that their error ended his last hope and forced him
to surrender his entire army, lest it starve.

The creation of the telephone, which allowed for a back-and-
forth transmission of information through verbal conversations,
offered an entirely new avenue of military communications.
It was almost instantaneous and could eliminate much of the
potential ambiguity of telegraph messages. Of course, telephone lines could be tapped, as well, but spoofing a political
leader's voice presented more problems than the idea of faking
a telegraph message. Of course, this rule worked only if both
sides of a conversation actually recognized their counterpart's
voice, and the connection was clear enough to allow such recognition. Like the telegraph, telephone wires could be cut, and

their production was expensive. It became a high priority to run telegraph and telephone wires as close to the front lines as possible, to further enable centralized control, but bringing the wires within enemy reach almost guaranteed that a connection would not be stable.

The wireless telegraph and the radio solved some of the problems associated with earlier communication methods, in that they did not require a physical network of wires in order to transmit information. Instead, they emitted signals that could be picked up by anyone holding a receiver on the correct frequency. This created a new vulnerability, because the wireless signals could not be sent on a direct line; they could only be broadcast, readily available to anyone within range with the right equipment to receive them. Efforts to encrypt these signals proved every bit as frustrating, but effective, as the methods used for telegraphs and telephones. Switching frequencies for radio devices also might throw off a potential eavesdropper, although probably not for as long as the users might hope or require. Speaking in code, or in a foreign language, might work for a while, unless the enemy possessed sufficient linguists to translate the signals. Mechanical encryption devices, such as the famous Enigma machine utilized by Germany during World War II, offered the illusory promise of an unbreakable code, at least until the enemy captured a decoding machine.

Early Attempts at Encryption

As communication systems advanced, so too did mechanical means of conducting mathematical computations. In 1822, Charles Babbage designed the Difference Engine, a mechanical calculator that could automatically compile complex mathematical tables in a fraction of the time required by human mathematicians. In 1856, he offered a theoretical design for an Analytical Engine, a project that, if completed, might have been the world's first true computer. It was designed to employ punch cards for the input of information, and when coupled with a printer for its output, it would have been capable of running rudimentary programs. Unfortunately, the British government saw little utility to his concepts and withdrew funding for the project. Babbage's designs have been the source of recent experimentation, with a replica of the Difference Engine completed in 1991 at the London Science Museum. In 2010, British computer programmer John Graham-Cumming began a public campaign to raise funds for the construction of an Analytical Engine using the remaining designs from Babbage's papers.

The Allied possession of their own Enigma machine, which was copied and put into use decrypting German signals, was one of the most closely held secrets of the war. German overconfidence in their own "unbreakable" code led to major strategic blunders, in part because Allied signals gathering operations were soon decoding German signals faster than the intended recipients. Had the Germans realized their codes were being intercepted and decrypted, they might have devised a different communication method, but their arrogance and assumptions about technological superiority did not allow them to realize the truth until it was far too late. Little did the Germans know that the Allies had built an enormous electronic computer, Colossus, dedicated solely to breaking enemy codes using brute-force mathematical calculations to resolve even the toughest cyphers.

Direct Observation Techniques

Just as the technology associated with communications continually improved, so too did the technology dedicated to the direct observation of the enemy and collection of information. Ancient scouts might ascend an elevated terrain point, or climb a tree to improve their vantage point. Nineteenth-century scouts used balloons to ascend high above the battlefield, and a variety of signaling methods to communicate what they saw, including dropping weighted messages to their comrades on the ground. Of course, hot-air balloons remained at the mercy of winds, and while they could be tethered to the ground, this also created an obvious vulnerability point that might be targeted by artillery pieces. Further, the balloon, or its inhabitants, became an irresistible target for sharpshooters. The use of observation balloons provoked the creation of deliberate smokescreens to block visibility, but such countermeasures created problems for their developers, who cut off their own view of the enemy by the same device.

When the Wright Brothers demonstrated that heavier-than-air flight was possible, they opened up an entirely new domain to information collection and exploitation. Within a decade, military forces had not only adopted their first aircraft for observation, they had also begun using fixed-wing airplanes to directly attack the enemy, using small bombs and firearms. Aircraft could be used to fly over enemy lines and note their dispositions, to assess the accuracy of indirect artillery fire, or to harass tightly bunched enemy formations. In the first months of World War I, observation aircraft tended to be unarmed, due to weight restrictions, and pilots had to land their planes before they could report their observations. Soon, engines became stronger, designs became more aerodynamic, and lift capacities rose. Some observers carried wireless tele-graph equipment, and later radios, to directly report what they saw. Other aircraft carried bombs to attack troops on the ground, who usually retaliated through small-arms fire. A third class of aircraft was designed to stop the enemy's intelligence collection efforts. Dubbed pursuit aircraft, these early intercep-tors were created to shoot down enemy observation planes, either by destroying the aircraft or simply killing the relatively unprotected pilots. Pursuit airplanes made reconnaissance a far more dangerous occupation, and led to observation aircraft being escorted by pursuit planes that might engage the enemy interceptors, allowing the intelligence-collecting airplanes to continue their mission.

By the end of World War I, after four years of brutal and bloody combat, airplanes had advanced from rickety, slow, wood-and-canvas designs to sleek, speedy, all-metal construction, with heavier armaments, bigger bomb loads, and much greater speed and range. They could be outfitted with wireless telegraphs or, in some cases, short-range radios that made transmission of their vital information to ground controllers feasible. In the decade after the war, many of the nations of the world assumed that no such conflict could ever happen again, and yet they continued to research and improve upon aircraft designs, such that war planners could envision a future conflict conducted entirely in the air. Visionaries like Billy Mitchell of the United States, Hugh Trenchard of the United Kingdom, and Giulio Douhet of Italy all argued that wars would consist of bomber aircraft attacking enemy cities, using high explosives and poison gas. No modern society could absorb such punishment for long, and all of the early airpower theorists assumed that there was no effective defense against such attacks.

Soon enough, though, military theorists had begun to devise methods for countering the envisioned fleets of bomber aircraft. The most prominent was the creation of high-speed fighter aircraft capable of shooting down the slower bombers long before they could reach their targets. Of course, to attack a bomber, a fighter pilot needed to know its location, which meant solving an entirely new problem—how to arrange for the interception of inbound attackers. The speed of aircraft in the 1930s meant that flying patrols over threatened areas, hoping to acquire targets via visual means, was a ludicrous approach to defense. A network of observation stations offered a potential method, but not a very attractive one. However, British engineers devised an entirely new methodology, utilizing the reflective nature of metal aircraft bombarded by radio waves. Their invention, radar (radio detection and ranging) allowed a ground station to acquire and track inbound formations of enemy aircraft. Through radio signals, a radar station could then vector intercepting craft on a course intercepting the aggressors, turning the tables on enemy bombers and putting the defenders at a distinct advantage.

The Germans failed to grasp the importance of the radar stations during the aerial Battle of Britain (1940), and lost the battle despite having a significant advantage in aircraft and trained pilots. Rather than developing their own radar technology, the Germans placed a much greater emphasis upon the development of more capable interceptors, with the result that by 1945, they fielded the first jet interceptors in the world, the Me-262. The German jets were too little, too late by the time they entered the war, although their appearance certainly surprised and terrified the Allies, who did everything they could to capture and copy the technology as quickly as possible at the close of the war. They also sought to capture the German scientists and engineers who had made the jets possible, as well as the developers of rocket engines and other advanced technology that would soon prove important in the Cold War against the Soviet Union.

The Creation of Cyberspace

During the war, American engineers developed a new technology that underpinned the entire future of information warfare. They created a rudimentary computer, capable of rapidly performing the calculations necessary for ballistic trajectories. This early machine was enormous, and could only be sent into conflict onboard a battleship, where it could be used to quickly produce firing solutions that made the ships' heavy guns far more accurate. Very few other practical military uses were initially envisioned for the computer, providing a solid example of a technology's developers massively underselling its utility. Computer technology advanced slowly at first, as the machines tended to be extremely expensive, difficult to operate, and reliant upon very fragile components that broke even without any external stress. Early standalone computers occupied entire rooms and produced an enormous amount of heat that had to be bled off lest the machines literally cook themselves. The vacuum tubes that powered the earliest models could be easily shorted out; many sources attribute the modern computer term "bug," meaning a coding error that leads to malfunctions, to the occasional short-circuits created by insects interfering with the vacuum tubes. However, in 1958, Jack St. Clair Kilby invented the integrated circuit, the basis for all modern computer technology. It not only miniaturized the key component, allowing for a vastly greater computing power in the same-sized machine; it also eliminated many of the heat problems and reduced the cost to construct computers. At the time, even the most optimistic proponent of the new technology expected it to create a machine capable of raw mathematical calculations, rather than a communication system that would revolutionize the world.

When the concept of the Internet was first envisioned, even its wildest promoters had no idea of the transformative power it would have upon human society. While the Internet's creators certainly expected to develop an information-sharing system that would allow researchers in a wide variety of locations to work together on challenging projects, they never expected the system to be used for entertainment, for commerce, and to support the basic communications needs of billions of users. They also had not the faintest clue of the massive infrastructure construction program that their invention would require, an effort costing billions of dollars and creating millions of jobs around the world, as engineers and technicians literally connected the world through wires and fiber-optic cables.

Unfortunately, the pioneers behind the Internet also tended toward optimism and devoted little thought to securing the network. It simply did not seem possible that such a strange invention might one day facilitate the misdeeds of criminals and terror organizations, much less be used as a tool of national aggression and military conflict. As such, they decided upon designs that facilitated information transfer and reliability, but also created inherent vulnerabilities that might be exploited by malicious actors. In this regard, they mirrored the behavior of software programmers, who also placed functionality and reliability at the top of their priorities, and gave little thought to how security flaws might be used to seize control of individual computers and direct them to nefarious purposes.

The structure of the Internet first began to take shape thanks to both the efforts and the needs of the Advanced Research Projects Agency (ARPA). That group, founded in the immediate aftermath of the Soviet Sputnik launch, sought to prevent strategic technological surprises by driving revolutionary innovation. To do so, ARPA provided funding and resources to the brightest minds in the country, bringing them together to solve the thorniest problems on a series of projects. In many ways, ARPA resembled the largest military innovation program of World War II, the Manhattan Project.

The Manhattan Project, the code name given to the combined U.S.-UK effort to build an atomic weapon, involved the intellectual cooperation of dozens of the top scientists in both countries, thrown together in austere conditions during the wartime crisis. Without the looming specter of a Nazi Germany armed with atomic weapons, it is extremely unlikely that the brilliant physicists, chemists, mathematicians, and engineers of the project could have cooperated upon anything —as it was, the squabbles and intellectual disputes were the stuff of legend. For all intents and purposes, the military had an unlimited budget to gather any resources needed for the project, including personnel, and many of the members considered it their patriotic duty to get involved. Even before the bombs destroyed Hiroshima and Nagasaki, though, some of the members began to express reservations about their contributions; many pushed for the bomb to be used in an offshore demonstration rather than against a defenseless city. As soon as the war ended, the temporary cooperation ended as well, and the participants quickly resumed their roles in academic and industrial positions.

The U.S. government could naturally marshal resources that such researchers could not dream of gathering on their own, through any private grants or other forms of sponsorship.

As such, working with ARPA dangled the prospect of unlimited budgets and hence amazing breakthroughs in science and technology. On the other hand, most of the top minds balked at the idea of working directly for the federal government or the military, either of which might restrict their freedom to act or try to control their innovations. ARPA offered a perfect solution to the problem by supplying goals, resources, and a potential collaborative network. Academics could remain in their esteemed positions and continue to enjoy the professional prestige that accompanied their faculty slots, while getting everything they needed to speed their technological innovations.

In principle, the ARPA model created a perfect opportunity to speed research. The participants could operate with a substantial level of freedom and unbounded creativity, both of which were considered advantages over the command-driven approach taken by the Soviet Union. In practice, ARPA required its researchers to either communicate by means that could not be fully secured, or to spend inordinate amounts of time traveling to meet with one another. The collaborative nature of the projects was simply too complex to be performed without substantial interaction. Further, while telephone conversations worked for discussions of theoretical concepts, the actual exchange of data required constantly sending materials back and forth, creating delays that offset many of the advantages of the system. Thus, the need for a new mechanism for sharing information soon became evident to many of the members, and a few began to work on a potential solution.

One of the primary hurdles for how to connect computers over great distances was a conceptual issue. The ability to connect local computers and allow them to communicate with one another was simple and followed the same principle as the telephone system, specifically, creating a direct link between them. Unfortunately, while such a connection allows the two computers to communicate, it also requires a dedicated line that can provide no other services while it is in use. Thus, connecting a network of computers over a large area would require a prohibitive number of such physical links. It might be possible to create a central connection station, akin to a telephone operator bank, but such a concept would only allow each computer to speak with one other computer at a time, and the process for making each connection would be tedious at best.

Three individuals are collectively given credit for solving the data connection dilemma faced by ARPA. Paul Baran, Donald Davies, and Lawrence Roberts developed the idea of "packet switching," essentially, collecting data streams into a single message that could be routed along a single data link whenever there was bandwidth for the data. In this fashion, the data links could be used continuously without being dedicated to specific machines—as space became available, more packets could be sent. As long as the packets had a standardized protocol, in this case developed by Vinton Cerf, Robert Kahn, and Louis Pouzin, they could be sent by virtually any type of computer capable of accessing the network. The protocol allowed the intended address of any packet of data to be read by an "interface message processor," usually called a router in modern terminology. Messages could be broken into smaller packets, which could be transferred through the links much more easily, and each packet could follow its own path to the intended recipient. Each router along the line passed the packet on to the next node based upon the protocol address the packet carried. This simplification of the data stream revolutionized the ability of computers to connect to one another and enabled the creation of the first distant computer network, dubbed "ARPANet."

Initially, ARPANet included only four routers and four computers, with one each at Stanford University; the University of California, Los Angeles (UCLA); the University of California, Santa Barbara; and the University of Utah. The first message on the system was sent on October 29, 1969, from UCLA to Stanford, and was intended simply to log in to the distant machine. As such, it was a command, "login," and the system crashed after only the first two letters had been transmitted.

After this auspicious beginning, the researchers continued to work to establish the network, finally having all four systems permanently connected in early December 1969. Despite its early weaknesses, the logic and utility of the system was quickly evident, and within a year, the size of the network more than tripled, with further connections being established on a monthly basis. In 1973, ARPANet was extended via satellite link to the Norwegian Seismic Array and via a transatlantic cable to London. The earliest ancestor of the Internet had become operational, and information quickly began to flow between its nodes (Singer and Friedman 2014, 16–18).

Of course, the pure data-sharing period of the early Internet could not last forever. While the network remained largely a research and government communications system for the first two decades of its existence, the powerful notion of what information-sharing could potentially achieve was not something that could remain the province of academics and officials forever. Likewise, the sole use of the linked computer systems for positive ends was an impossible pipe dream. Within a decade of the initial links of ARPANet, a rudimentary computer worm had been developed, although such a malicious program was not released upon the network until 1988. That year, Robert Morris, a student at the Massachusetts Institute of Technology, released the Morris Worm, which quickly self-replicated onto thousands of computers, a significant percentage of the total number of systems connected to the network. This accidental release amply demonstrated the lack of any security protocols on the network, and the naivety that permeated its users (Rosenzweig 2013, 22). That same year, Donald Burleson was convicted of deliberately placing a logic bomb on the computer network of his former employer, in a successful effort to destroy their payroll data. These two incidents showed how much devastation even a single programmer with basic skills could inflict on a wide basis, due to the very nature of the network.

In 1989, British computer scientist Tim Berners-Lee announced his concept of how to create a global Internet suitable for the public, dubbed the World Wide Web, by linking hyper-text documents through the Internet. Berners-Lee's idea set off a wave of Internet expansion, as home computer users realized that their systems not only could serve to produce documents and run programs, but they could also be used for research purposes. Within a few years, web browsers had been created by a number of companies and academic institutions, making the Internet accessible to computer users without any programming skills or specific knowledge.

The Cyber Attacks Begin

In 1994, two hackers, one a British teenager, the other a 22-year-old Israeli, managed to penetrate one of the U.S. Air Force's most classified systems, the Rome Laboratories net-work. In doing so, they not only revealed the technical vulner-abilities of many government and military systems, which could be penetrated by relatively unsophisticated means, but they also showed that international and domestic laws had not yet con-fronted the nature of computer attacks. The teenager received a light fine after prosecution for computer crime; the Israeli citi-zen did not violate any laws of his nation and thus was not held accountable at all, beyond having an arrest warrant issued in the United States. The following year, the U.S. Congress demanded an information infrastructure policy as part of the Defense Department budget for 1996. This certainly pushed the issue forward and also essentially handed the responsibility over to the armed forces for protecting government and even private computer systems from hostile activities, but it did little to achieve even a rudimentary level of Internet security (Blane 2002, 49).

As the Internet rapidly developed and became increasingly accessible to ordinary citizens, it quickly emerged as a new avenue for commercial activities. Some online retailers largely followed the patterns of brick-and-mortar businesses, merely using the Internet as a means of expanding their advertising and service area. Amazon.com, for example, began as an online source of book sales, but soon expanded to offer a much wider range of products for consumers. Although it took more than a decade to show even a hint of profit, Amazon quickly became a catch-all household name for almost any type of tangible product, which could be purchased from the comfort of home and quickly shipped directly to the consumer. EBay, another early Internet pioneer, took a much more radical step, creating an online auction house where buyers and sellers could reach one another without any physical interaction. The founders of the company needed only to provide a site for auctions with a server capacity to run millions of such sales at once, and to create a feedback system so that customers and sellers could essentially contribute to policing the entire community. For each transaction, and even each item listing, eBay collected a small fee to cover the costs of the convenience that they provided.

While the private sector exploded onto the Internet, the government did almost nothing to enhance the security of the network's structure. Unfortunately, many citizens had, and still have, a very unrealistic expectation of privacy on the Internet, which has made cyber crime the most rapidly expanding form of illegal activity in the world, costing tens of billions of dollars per year. In 2000, the FBI began to investigate the "Moonlight Maze" series of hacking attacks against academic, corporate, and government networks. The deeper they looked at the problem, the more disturbing it became, in part because they could not identify the culprits who had penetrated hundreds of sensitive servers and exfiltrated an unknown amount of information. They tracked the attacks back to a server in Russia, but the Russian government stonewalled any further attempts at investigation, inadvertently suggesting that the culprits might have been operating in conjunction with the state. Of course, it is also entirely possible that the Russian government refused to cooperate due to other provocations, real or imagined, from the United States (Carr 2009, 162).

While the Moonlight Maze attacks were underway, possibly with national backing, an entirely different campaign of cyber intrusions began, eventually code-named Solar Sunrise. In 1998, two teenagers from California and one from Israel, who met through an Internet chat room, managed to collaborate in compromising more than 500 computer networks, including servers belonging to the U.S. Department of Defense. The three seemed to be engaged merely in one-upping one another, seeing who could sneak into the most secure sites, and there is no evidence that they actually removed any classified information. Nevertheless, despite the fact that they did no harm, the fact that three high school students using commercially available computers could access some of the most sensitive computer files in the nation gave pause to cyber security experts (Blane 2002, 6–7; "Solar Sunrise" 2011). While the Clinton administration did react by creating the President's Commission on Critical Infrastructure Protection, the government's primary focus in the cyber realm was on efforts to combat digital piracy through the passage of the Digital Millennium Copyright Act. This demonstrated a lack of seriousness about the true threat being demonstrated by cyber attacks, and an almost single-minded focus upon the economic aspects of the Internet revolution.

In 1999, the United States joined other members of the North Atlantic Treaty Organization in the conduct of an aerial bombardment campaign designed to force Serbian president Slobodan Milosevic to remove forces from the breakaway province of Kosovo and to remand himself to stand trial in the Human Rights Court at The Hague. Two important cyber events occurred during the attacks. When NATO airplanes began bombing Serbian ground troops, Serbian hackers infiltrated the NATO web and e-mail servers, knocking both offline and complicating the command-and-control process for the air campaign. When an errant "smart bomb" programmed with incorrect GPS coordinates landed in the Chinese embassy compound in Belgrade, Chinese hacker militias immediately swung into action. They launched massive distributed denial of service (DDoS) attacks against U.S. government and military websites and shut down or defaced hundreds of them in the weeks after the incident. Two years later, a Chinese fighter jet collided with a U.S. aircraft engaged in collecting signals intelligence off the coast of China. The fighter pilot was killed, while the American aircraft had to make an emergency landing on the Chinese island of Hainan. The airplane's crew was interned while Chinese technicians swarmed over every inch of the aircraft. In the meantime, nearly 100,000 Chinese hackers launched coordinated attacks against U.S. government websites, again demonstrating the power of motivated citizenry armed with even obsolete computer equipment (Brenner 2011, 123–25; Stiennon 2010, 12–14).

The most economically and socially devastating computer attacks have largely been indiscriminate attacks through the creation of viruses and worms. Unfortunately, there is a certain degree of notoriety and fame within the hacker subculture that comes from creating a particularly elegant, and hence potentially destructive, software virus. The more machines that are infected, the more successful virus creators will be considered within the hacker community. Warnings about such viruses have become all too common within Western society, leading some cyber experts to argue that such warnings actually make users less security conscious. When the Morris Worm was released from an MIT laboratory in 1988, it showed the lack of protections on the Internet. Sadly, despite efforts to combat such software, they have only proliferated in the subsequent decades. A multibillion-dollar industry has developed for the creation of antivirus software and computer security, but the companies offering antivirus software often only become aware of a potential breach when it has already infected thousands or millions of computers. In 2000, the "I-LOVE-YOU" virus, created by Reonel Ramones and Onel de Guzman of the Philippines, spread so quickly that it caused more than $10 billion in damages in a matter of a few days. Cleaning up the virus proved extremely difficult, as it managed to resurrect itself from seemingly cleansed machines by hiding in a variety of locations. The following year, the far more sophisticated "Code Red" and "Nimda" worms exploited software vulnerabilities to create backdoor access for knowledgeable hackers, essentially allowing an infected computer to be remotely seized (Bowden 2011, 77–79).

The power of destructive worms has only continued to grow. In 2003, the "SQL Slammer" worm spread so quickly that it managed to shut down the entire global Internet for more than 12 hours. After more than a decade, Slammer is still one of the most commonly detected viruses in the world, in part because billions of computer users in the world use pirated copies of operating system software, such as Microsoft Windows, that are not eligible for security patches. That same year, the "MS Blaster" worm followed shortly after Slammer and had nearly the same level of success, a fact that not only exposed yet another software vulnerability, but also showed that fixing one problem will do nothing to protect against the next exploit discovered by malicious programmers. In 2004, the "MyDoom" virus attacked computers using recent versions of Microsoft Windows and caused $2 billion in damages before it could be contained. Critics of Microsoft accused the company of rushing its products to the market, leaving them vulnerable to such attacks.

In 2008, several cyber security experts detected a new worm spreading rapidly through Internet-connected computers. The program used a flaw in the Microsoft Windows operating system that allowed it to quickly spread, copy itself, and propagate to other computers connected to the original victim. The various antivirus companies each tagged the malware within their own naming schemes, but to the public, the worm was simply called "Conficker." The creators of the program remain unknown, although it proved to be an extraordinarily sophisticated piece of malware that used many techniques to hide on an infected host and to resist elimination (Carr 2009, 12; Singer and Friedman 2014, 72–73, 196–97). Machines hit by the Conficker worm were integrated into one of the largest botnets in history, with millions of computers definitely infected. Conficker defeated most of the common means of prevention and detection and managed to enter the computer networks of military and government forces around the world. The French military was forced to ground many aircraft because they could not download their flight plans. In Britain and Germany, military computers across the respective nations reported hundreds of computers that showed signs of the virus and had to be quarantined from the network. Strangely, despite showing a remarkable ability to propagate, the Conficker botnet is not known to have launched any significant attacks, even though some estimates placed 15 million machines within the network, plenty to take down virtually any website, server, or network, and possibly enough to knock an entire nation off the Internet. Instead, the fifth major variant of Conficker attempted to spread a spam-generating program and to download a bogus antivirus program onto host computers (Bowden 2011, 122–25, 190–91).

Conficker went through a number of versions, upgrading itself by contacting a control server and requesting instructions. This sophisticated attempt to maintain the utility of the worm, and to patch its vulnerabilities to antivirus and antimalware programs, led researcher Mark Bowden to dub the fight against Conficker "the first cyber world war." Conficker's rapid spread caused Microsoft to take the unusual step of releasing a patch outside of their normal update cycle. It also triggered the creation of an international industry group to fight against its spread and try to prevent any cyber attacks by its controllers. Representatives from Microsoft, ICANN, several antivirus companies, the China Internet Network Information Center, academic institutions, and some of the largest Internet service providers pooled their knowledge and resources to outmaneuver the Conficker programmers. While the authors of Conficker have not been publicly named, the "Conficker

Cabal" organized to counter it have suggested that it originated in Ukraine, based upon a number of digital clues contained within the Conficker programming (Bowden 2011, 218–33).

While many of the most destructive viruses and worms launched attacks indiscriminately at any vulnerable system, over the first decade of the twenty-first century, tailored viruses became a key part of the cyber arsenal. Such malware is designed to spread itself through an enemy's computer network, without requiring a direct link back to the original attacker. It might be used to search for sensitive data, but it might also be used in a sabotage fashion. The most well-known such virus, Stuxnet, designed to attack the Iranian nuclear program computer network, is discussed later in the chapter. In 2011, the "Georbot" worm began to spread through Georgian government systems, allowing attackers to conduct espionage of sensitive files. In a rare victory for cyber defenders, the Georgian Computer Emergency Response Team managed to plant a phony file for the botmaster to collect and open. This executed a program that allowed the Georgian team to seize control over the root file of the attacker's computer and turn on his web camera, as well as trace his location in Russia. Not surprising, the attacker was using a server owned by the Russian Business Network, a massive Russian cyber crime ring, to carry out his activities.

In 2012, the Saudi national petroleum corporation Aramco was the victim of a fairly straightforward brute-force cyber attack, with a twist. Rather than defacing websites or stealing sensitive corporate data, the "Shamoon" virus simply propagated itself as quickly as possible through the computer network, and then executed a file destruction command that rendered more than 30,000 computer workstations completely useless (Leyden 2012). There was no means of recovering any of the files or repairing the systems; they had become "bricks that could not even be booted up" (Rid 2013, 55). Although Aramco had the financial ability to quickly replace the entire network and had it back up and running in under two weeks, the attack was still a powerful economic strike against the nation controlling the largest oil reserves in the world. The attackers, who referred to themselves as the "Cutting Sword of Justice," still had not been positively identified as of this writing.

Around the same time that Shamoon was discovered, Iranian computer experts began alerting antivirus and computer security companies about a new malware program that they had detected within the Iranian petroleum industry computers. Dubbed "Flame" or "Wiper," depending upon the investigating agency, the new virus was enormous by malware standards; at 20 megabytes, it was too large to spread via e-mail or other traditional means. Instead, it was masked as a legitimate security patch for Microsoft Windows, and thus security professionals essentially loaded the worm onto the machines under their administration. Flame had capabilities far beyond any piece of malware seen to date, including the ability to record audio using a computer's microphone, a keystroke logger, and the ability to turn on a computer's camera and use it to capture images. In short, Flame was the ultimate cyber espionage tool, enabling not just the capture and removal of files on an infected computer, but also the ability to spy upon users and build an accurate map of the physical surroundings of a network. Perhaps most disturbingly, investigations into the Flame code showed that it had probably been created in 2006, meaning that it had quietly operated for more than five years before being discovered. Not surprisingly, it shared certain coding elements with Stuxnet, suggesting that it was probably the work of the same nation and possibly the same design team. As of this writing, responsibility for Flame had not been determined, although the list of nations capable of creating such a sophisticated piece of software was extremely short (Rid 2013, 94–95).

Cyber Enabling in the Nuclear Middle East

On June 7, 1981, the Israeli Defense Force launched Operation Babylon. In this military action, a combined strike force of F-15 and F-16 aircraft took off from Israel, flew near the southern border of Jordan and across Saudi Arabian airspace, and penetrated Iraqi airspace along a pre-identified gap in Iraqi air defenses. While flying near Jordanian and Saudi territory, the Israeli pilots spoke only Arabic, using falsified accents to simulate patrols from Jordan and Saudi Arabia that had accidentally penetrated the others' territory. Not only did this provide a plausible explanation for their radar signature, it also explained why they were not using any form of radio frequency that would identify them as friendly forces to air traffic controllers in either country. In this manner, they managed to approach the Iraqi border without creating any alarms. The Iraqis knew that their air defenses had areas of limited or no coverage, but saw little reason for worry along their western and southern frontiers, and concentrated most of their forces in defensive positions to counter any Iranian incursions. The Israelis were flying a massive preemptive strike against the Osirak reactor complex, a nuclear facility that they claimed would be used to develop nuclear weapons. The strike was an overwhelming success from the Israeli perspective, heavily damaging the reactor without the loss of any Israeli assets. While Iraq complained to the United Nations about the attack, its preoccupation with the Iran-Iraq War prohibited any attempt to restart the nuclear program, and the reactor at Osirak remained unfinished until 1991, when it was destroyed by an airstrike during the Gulf War (Clarke and Knake 2010, 9–11).

The attack demonstrated that the Israeli government would not tolerate the idea of a hostile, nuclear-armed nation in the Middle East, and followed an earlier-established precedent that Israel would not wait to be attacked if it foresaw an impending threat. Most Middle Eastern nations have shown little interest in pursuing nuclear weapons, perhaps in part due to the fear that any investment in a nuclear program would be likely wasted due to an almost inevitable Israeli attack. However, not every regime in the region remained content to drop any nuclear ambitions, and those who chose to pursue nuclear weapons certainly learned a great deal from Iraq's inability to protect its facility. Any nation within airstrike range of Israel would need to either keep its nuclear ambitions secret, a particularly difficult task given the skill demonstrated by Israeli intelligence services, or would need to protect the site in such a way that an Israeli attack would be unlikely to destroy it. Two nations, in particular, decided to develop nuclear weapons in defiance of Israel's stated position regarding preemptive attacks on nuclear facilities, Syria and Iran.

The Syrian government's nuclear program dated at least as far back as 2004, when direct links between Syrian and North Korean scientists proved the Syrian interest in developing nuclear power, and possibly nuclear weapons. Of course, given the previous history of conflict between Syria and Israel, including three previous full-scale wars and countless border skirmishes, the Syrians knew that the Israelis would not tolerate a nuclear weapons program on Syrian soil. Thus, they purchased a state-of-the-art integrated air defense system (IADS) from Russia capable of defending the whole of Syrian airspace against an Israeli incursion. To attack such a massive IADS would impose massive losses on the attacker, unless it could somehow be countered; any attack on the facility would need to be conducted on the ground. Naturally, the Syrian army established a major presence in the vicinity of the Deir ez-Zor region, the construction site of the reactor. The Israelis used every intelligence asset they possessed to confirm that the site was indeed a reactor, and may have even launched a commando raid to recover nuclear material from the site to confirm its purpose. However, to destroy the position would require much more firepower than that possessed by a small raiding party, and thus Prime Minister Ehud Olmert turned once again to the Israeli air force to strike the site.

Unlike Iraq in 1981, the Syrians had not left any obvious gaps in their radar coverage of the area. Further, the Israelis would still be flying the same type of aircraft as they had 26 years earlier, albeit in upgraded configurations. They certainly wanted to take every precaution possible to avoid losing any aircraft or pilots in the attack, as such losses would preclude any efforts to deny responsibility for the strike. Thus, they placed a substantial amount of trust in an untested form of offensive action: a cyber attack designed to prevent the Syrian IADS from detecting or engaging the Israeli aircraft. Israeli cyber warriors penetrated the Syrian IADS cyber network and spoofed it, essentially telling the radar systems that there was nothing of note in their vicinity, and preventing any targeting activity. On September 6, 2007, the Israeli Defense Force launched the simultaneous cyber and kinetic attacks. The first indication of the attack that the Syrians received was the sound of bombs detonating in the complex, completely destroying it (Clarke and Knake 2010, 1–9; Stiennon 2010, 54–55).

In the aftermath of the attack, the Israeli government maintained its characteristic silence, neither confirming nor denying that it had launched the strike. For their part, the Syrians accused the Israelis of violating Syrian airspace and bombing Syrian territory, first claiming that the bombs fell on empty desert and later stating that the Israelis had struck an unfinished army barracks. However, subsequent inspections by the United Nations and the International Atomic Energy Association (IAEA) determined that the site, which was completely dismantled and bulldozed by the Syrian government in the aftermath of the attack, had indeed been an incomplete nuclear reactor site. The Israeli government eventually released its intelligence data showing that the site had the same design as a North Korean nuclear reactor and would have been capable of producing enough processed material for the construction of a few nuclear weapons per year.

The possibility of an Iranian nuclear program also terrifies the Israeli government, due in no small part to the repeated Iranian threats to destroy the Jewish state by any means possible. Of course, Iran and Israel have no common borders, and any Iranian site is well beyond the flight endurance of Israeli aircraft to reach without aerial refueling. Thus, a direct attack on such a site would require a circuitous route, as tanker aircraft cannot be used to penetrate hostile airspace with any degree of survivability, or a ballistic missile attack. Any Israeli strike force would need to fly through the Red Sea and around the Arabian Peninsula before crossing into Iranian airspace from the Persian Gulf, unless permission could be obtained from the hostile states between Israel and Iran. Like the Syrians, the Iranians have constructed a first-rate air defense network, and they also possess a substantial air force that might be capable of intercepting any attacking aircraft. Thus, repeating the Osirak and Deir ez-Zor attacks would probably not work on an Iranian nuclear program, and yet, leaving such a program in place would create an existential threat for the Israeli state.

The Iranian nuclear site at Natanz utilized specific industrial machinery produced by the Siemens Corporation. A key aspect of the machinery running the uranium enrichment centrifuges was the Programmable Logic Controllers (PLCs) that automated the systems. These PLCs, in turn, were controlled by a specific program, the Siemens Step7 software, which ran on the standard Microsoft Windows operating system. An unknown nation or nations developed an extremely specific computer worm, nicknamed Stuxnet, that deliberately searched for supervisory control and data acquisition (SCADA) systems produced by Siemens that could be used for certain industrial processes (Brenner 2011, 102–5). While the worm propagated itself through as many computers as possible, it took no action beyond what was needed to spread itself unless it detected the specific target software on an infected machine. In that case, Stuxnet rewrote the control software to change the frequency of centrifuge speeds, inducing a fatal flaw in the industrial machinery. Over time, this change caused the fast-spinning centrifuges to self-destruct. Not only did this ruin a substantial number of the centrifuges at Natanz, it also caused Iranian nuclear scientists to shut down the entire enrichment process until the root cause of the process could be discovered (Poroshyn 2013, 48–50; Rosenzweig 2013, 2–12).

Iran, a relatively advanced cyber power, had not made the foolish mistake of connecting its nuclear program to the global Internet. However, their competence led to overconfidence, and they made the fatal assumption that air-gapping the industrial network from the World Wide Web would keep it safe from any hostile actors. The Iranian Stuxnet incident demonstrates a number of key lessons regarding cyber security and cyber war. First, the greatest vulnerability in the system is always the human user. Although the Iranian system was not connected to the Internet, its terminals within the nuclear network were connected to one another, and once a piece of malware was introduced to the system, it was able to quickly spread throughout the entire Natanz network. It might have been introduced by one of the Natanz technicians on a flash drive or through some other form of removable media, or it might have been uploaded by a human agent. Second, the Stuxnet experience demonstrates the enormous resources that a nation-state can devote to cyber war. Programming such an attack, which very selectively targeted the exact industrial machinery being used at Natanz, required massive planning, extensive intelligence collection, and months of coding by a dedicated team of specialists. It was certainly not the work of a lone hacker attempting to attack the Iranian nuclear program. Third, and perhaps most frustrating to the as-yet unknown attacker in the Stuxnet case, it demonstrated the transitory effects of even the most sophisticated cyber attacks. While it temporarily shut down the production at Natanz, it did not destroy the facility in the same manner as the airstrikes against the Iraqi and Syrian nuclear programs had done. Further, the creators of Stuxnet utilized an unusually large number of vulnerabilities to deliver the worm, with at least four previously unknown zero-day exploits used in the code. Using such vulnerabilities exposes the weakness in a computer's operating system, and typically means that those exploitable coding errors will soon be patched and no longer available (Singer and Friedman 2014, 114–18).

Israel is widely considered as one of the most likely culprits behind the Stuxnet attack, although the United States has also been suggested as a possible source of the worm (Reveron 2012, 152; Rosenzweig 2013, 10). While it was undoubtedly the work of a national cyber force, there are at least a dozen nations with both the capability and the motive to hinder Iranian nuclear ambitions, and thus, it may never be definitely proven which nation or nations was responsible for the attack. There is evidence that suggests the attack was probably launched by a Western democracy, in part because the Stuxnet worm was instructed to delete itself from infected machines on June 24, 2012, a nicety not normally included in the malware designs of non-Western nations. The fact that each infected computer could spread the virus to only three uninfected machines, and that any machine that did not have the target software was not affected by the virus, suggests that the developer went to additional lengths to prevent any collateral damage to unintended victims. Had the worm not been mysteriously detected by a previously obscure Internet security company in Belorussia, its existence might have remained a mystery to the Iranian government. When news of the Stuxnet program first began to spread, a massive DDoS attack struck several servers that distributed industrial cyber security updates, suggesting that Stuxnet's creators tried to prevent the Iranians from learning the cause of their centrifuge problems (Poroshyn 2013, 23–31).

Preparations for Infrastructure Cyber Attacks

Attacks against the critical infrastructure have long been a key aspect of warfare. Transportation networks and communications systems have long been regarded as legitimate military targets and might include physical attacks against critical choke points, such as bridges and railroad junctions, or might include electronic warfare attempts to jam or otherwise disrupt communications. During the American Civil War, one of the key functions of cavalry forces was to bypass enemy infantry armies and attack railroad lines in the rear areas. These attacks disrupted the flow of supplies and reinforcements to the front lines and caused no end of problems for commanders on both sides of the war. Because telegraph wires typically followed the path of railroads, they were also subject to disruption, typically by cutting the wires or destroying the poles that elevated them. When Major General William T. Sherman led his famous march through Georgia, his troops paid special attention to attacks upon the rail lines. Not content merely to tear up the tracks, they built large bonfires of the wooden ties and then piled the steel rails on top of the fires, causing them to warp and require a complete replacement. During World War II, Allied aerial commanders commenced a massive campaign against the German and French rail networks prior to the Normandy landings. For all intents and purposes, it destroyed the German ability to resupply their front-line units, making the amphibious assault much more likely to succeed. During the Persian Gulf War, Tomahawk cruise missiles loaded with a special "Kitt-2" package flew over Iraqi cities, dispensing thousands of microfilaments that shorted out electrical grids. Without electrical power, many of the Iraqi air defenses became completely worthless.

Modern electrical grids and transportation networks rely upon computer systems for their function. Computers are used to track inventory and determine shipments that need to be made from regional distribution centers to point-of-sale terminals. They are also used to regulate traffic on the nation's rail and road networks, and to shift electrical power drains from one station to another to prevent regional blackouts. These innovations make for more efficient systems, so long as they function, but they can also trigger serious cascade effects when they fail. Thus, while they are extremely useful, they can also make a small problem into a catastrophe under the right circumstances. There has been a disturbing trend of evidence pointing to the emplacement of backdoors and logic bombs in the U.S. infrastructure controlling the electrical grid, suggesting that one or more potential enemies have taken steps to facilitate cyber sabotage should a war erupt (Brenner 2011, 99–113; Singer and Friedman 2014, 167–68; Siroli 2006, 37–39).

Russian Hacktivists and National Pride

The nations of Russia and Estonia have a long history of conflict, albeit in a very lopsided fashion. After centuries of Russian domination, the republic of Estonia proclaimed its independence in 1918 and achieved international recognition as a separate nation in 1920. In 1940, the Soviet Union invaded Estonia but occupied the country for only a few months before being driven out by Germany, who held the territory until 1944, when the Soviets again conquered the region. In the aftermath of World War II, Estonia was forcibly incorporated into the Soviet Union as a Soviet socialist republic and remained a part of the USSR until its collapse in 1991, when Estonia once again proclaimed independence. In 2004, the small Baltic republic joined both the European Union and the North Atlantic Treaty Organization, two moves that irritated the Russian government, which saw its previous hegemony in the region in continual decline. In 2007, the Estonian legislature passed the Forbidden Structures Law, which required any public vestiges of the Soviet occupation of Estonia to be removed from public lands. This included a massive bronze statue of a Soviet soldier, erected in the capital city, Talinn, at the end of World War II. The statue symbolized the Russian determination to defeat Nazi Germany, and was surrounded by the graves of Red Army soldiers. Any attempt to remove it might upset the significant Russian minority in Estonia as well as the Russian government in Moscow. Nevertheless, the Estonian government chose to move the statue to a new, less prominent location in the national military cemetery, a move that absolutely infuriated citizens of Russian heritage and Russian nationalists throughout the much-larger neighbor (Clarke and Knake 2010, 11–16).

The statue's removal did not provoke a full-scale invasion by Russian forces, a move that might trigger a much larger conflict with NATO forces. Instead, the entire nation of Estonia was hit by a series of massive DDoS attacks, primarily originating from Russia. Tens of thousands of botnet computers began to flood the Estonian computer servers with requests for information and website access. The result was essentially a massive cyber traffic jam, which knocked hundreds of Estonian government and financial servers offline. Unlike a typical DDoS attack, which might be considered a nuisance and which might last only a few days, the DDoS attacks on the Estonian cyber system continued to increase in intensity and soon began to have a significant effect upon the Estonian economy. Estonia is one of the most Internet-dependent societies on earth, with an enormous percentage of the population relying upon the Internet for information, banking, and employment, and the massive attacks against Estonian servers essentially brought the entire Internet to a nationwide halt. Every attempt to reset the servers brought a renewed flood of DDoS attacks; soon, over a million computers were included in the attacks, most of which were probably being used without their owners' knowledge or consent (Brenner 2009, 1–6; Stiennon 2010, 85–90).

The Estonian government reached out to its new economic and military partners for assistance, including a complaint to the North Atlantic Council, the governing body of NATO. Cyber experts rushed to Talinn to offer assistance, but could do little to halt the unprecedented flood of DDoS attacks. Attempts to trace the attackers demonstrated that the botnets were being reprogrammed to counter any efforts to stop the attacks. Unfortunately, the cyber security technicians could not definitively prove the original source of the attacks, even though some evidence showed that much of the coding for the attack programs had been produced on Cyrillic-alphabet keyboards. Entreaties for help from the Russian government fell on deaf ears; not only did the Russians adamantly deny any responsibility for the attacks, they also refused to participate in any investigative attempts or to allow any cyber investigators access to Russian systems. Even when evidence demonstrated that the botnet controllers were in Russia, the government suggested that Russian patriots might have attacked on their own volition, for which they would not be punished by the Russian government.

Eventually, the diplomatic crisis faded, and so did the attacks upon the Estonian infrastructure. The bronze statue remained in its new location, although the Estonians did deign to engage in some beautification projects in the area to give it more prominence. NATO also created a cyber defense center in Estonia, which opened in 2008 (Stiennon 2010, 138). Of course, in the cyber domain, the location of such a center is largely irrelevant, but its presence on Estonian soil served as a symbol of NATO's resolve to defend the nation, whether against physical or cyber attacks.

In the year after the Estonian cyber attacks, the Russian government turned its attention to a different former Soviet vassal, the tiny republic of Georgia on the Black Sea. Like Estonia, Georgia had attempted to take advantage of the chaos caused by World War I and the Bolshevik Revolution to declare independence from Russia. Its attempt proved far less successful, and once the Russian Civil War concluded in 1921, Soviet troops crushed the breakaway republic and brought it firmly back into the Soviet fold. When the Soviet Union collapsed, Georgia was one of the first republics to proclaim its independence, and like Estonia, it sought to join NATO in the aftermath of the Cold War, although its application was rejected due to issues of autocratic governance and corruption. In 2008, Georgia became embroiled in a conflict with two of its semiautonomous provinces, South Ossetia and Abkhazia, each of which had a Russian-majority population.

A Georgian invasion of South Ossetia provoked an immediate Russian military response, which quickly drove out the Georgian armed forces and threatened to overwhelm the entire Georgian nation (Singer and Friedman 2014, 111–12).

Russian cyber forces acted decisively in support of the Russian invasion of Georgia. Massive DDoS attacks sought to isolate the Georgian population both from the Georgian government and from the rest of the world. Not only did the attacks seek to disable Georgian government servers and media outlets, but they also sought to spread pro-Russian propaganda (Stiennon 2010, 95–104). Targeted attacks went after the Georgian banking system, and when Georgian banks cut their Internet connections in the hope of protecting their clients' information, Russian botnets began sending false messages simulating cyber attacks from the Georgian banks, aimed at the European banking system. This, in turn, triggered a host of defense mechanisms that only served to further isolate the Georgian banking system as well as shut down any ability to process credit card payments in Georgia. Shortly afterward, the entire Georgian mobile phone network was taken offline by DDoS attacks, effectively cutting off the small nation from most of the outside world.

Faced with overwhelming military and cyber force, the Georgian government was forced to sign a humiliating peace accord with the Russian government, dropping all claims to South Ossetia and Abkhazia, both of which soon voted to be annexed into Russia, and allowing Russian forces to retain control over a "buffer zone" until relieved by UN peacekeeping forces that never arrived. As in the Estonian case from the year before, the Russian government denied that it had ordered any form of cyber offensive against Georgia and suggested that any such attacks must have been conducted by patriotic Russians on their own volition. In both cases, the cyber methodology was relatively crude, in that it involved a brute-force DDoS approach that required enormous botnets to continually evolve and continue their attacks. Despite the primitive approach, though, both attacks were remarkably effective and demonstrated the willingness and capabilities of the Russian government and its compatriots to use cyber attacks as a major force-enabler to complement physical violence.

The Chinese Approach to Irregular Warfare

In 1949, the Chinese Communist Party emerged from a decades-long civil war and seized control of mainland China. The remnants of their opponents, the Nationalists, fled to Taiwan, where they established a rival government under the aegis of American protection. The escape to Taiwan allowed the United States and its allies to maintain the legal fiction that the Taiwanese government still controlled China and, perhaps most importantly, should still hold the permanent seat on the United Nations Security Council. Unsurprisingly, the Soviet Union, the only communist power on the council, rejected this notion and in protest decided to launch a boycott of the United Nations until the situation changed. The Chinese communist victory in the world's most populous nation terrified many Western political leaders, who feared that communist insurgents were determined to seize power around the globe and create a world government under the domination of the Soviet Politburo in Moscow. In 1950, the United States adopted an official policy of containment, seeking to block the expansion of communism anywhere in the world. This policy was first challenged on the Korean Peninsula in 1950, when North Korea invaded South Korea in an attempt to unify the two nations under communism. When the North Korean military surged across the border, the South Korean government requested immediate assistance from the United Nations, and a measure deploying UN troops to Korea quickly passed the Security Council. The Soviets could have vetoed the measure, had they not been boycotting the organization, but their absence prevented such a maneuver.

UN forces, under the command of General Douglas MacArthur of the U.S. Army, soon stabilized the lines in Korea and began a counteroffensive with a daring amphibious landing at Inchon in September 1950. However, MacArthur tried to take advantage of a collapsing North Korean army, and soon rolled across the 38th parallel in an invasion of North Korea. The Chinese government, fearing that an anti-communist army on its border might trigger uprisings by remaining Nationalist sympathizers, warned MacArthur to stay away from the Yalu River, the border between China and North Korea. When UN forces approached the border despite the Chinese warning, a massive Chinese counterattack of more than 300,000 infantry troops swarmed over the border and quickly overran UN positions. Despite their generally inferior technology and logistical systems, the Chinese were able to push the UN forces back, primarily due to the raw size of the armies that they could send into the peninsula. It took nearly three years of grinding, attritional warfare to gradually push the Chinese back across the 38th parallel and negotiate an end to the conflict, with an armistice that essentially restored the status quo antebellum.

The Korean War is an excellent example of the Chinese way of warfare, which calls for the use of Chinese asymmetrical advantages in unconventional operations. The Chinese knew that they could not prevail against the U.S.-led UN forces unless they adopted a strategy that maximized their own advantages, such as an almost inexhaustible supply of manpower, and refused to follow the Western way of warfare. This strategy continually frustrated MacArthur, who at one point openly threatened the use of nuclear weapons against Chinese cities. Such a use was unsanctioned by President Harry S. Truman, who eventually removed MacArthur from command for insubordination. In the end, the Chinese political leadership, which was unfazed by MacArthur's threat, demonstrated a much better understanding of American political realities than their opponents held of Chinese motivations. They considered MacArthur's threat a bluff, in part because they did not believe he had operational control of nuclear weapons, and in part because they did not believe the international community would allow the use of nuclear weapons in the conflict. To use atomic bombs only a few years after the attacks on Hiroshima and Nagasaki would almost guarantee that all future conflicts would include some degree of nuclear warfare, an unthinkable proposition to American politicians.

In 1999, two Chinese colonels, Qiao Liang and Wang Xiangsui, published *Unrestricted Warfare*, a theoretical examination of how the People's Republic of China might engage its most powerful rivals, using its key resources to best advantage. To Qiao and Wang, the Chinese government should refuse to follow the patterns of warfare established by Western powers. Having observed the American conventional dominance of Iraq in the Persian Gulf War, they correctly surmised that fighting a conventional military engagement against the United States would be an extremely costly undertaking, at best, and would court disaster. The Americans were simply too accomplished at seizing air dominance and using it to punish large ground forces with impunity. Instead, they reasoned, the best approach would be to attack the United States where it was inherently vulnerable, rather than attacking its strengths. This would entail fighting across the full spectrum of potential engagements, including a massive information warfare campaign that might affect civil society in the United States. The colonels correctly surmised that Western democracies struggle to engage in war, or to sustain war efforts, without the full support of the population, and that cyber attacks might allow a direct attack upon the civilians' will to continue the fight. To prepare for a massive cyber war, they argued that China should focus upon modernizing and expanding its cyber capabilities, through the methodical development of an enormous organization of skilled cyber warriors. This unit could then take advantage of the Americans' lax approach to computer security, and to the ongoing drive to network all sources of U.S. military information. Essentially, the American government, in its attempts to link its defense organizations, would bring together all of the information that the Chinese needed to make major strides in improving their military technology.

In effect, the Chinese government placed an enormous portion of its resources into a major cyber espionage campaign (Wu 2006, 178–79). Rather than domestically developing military technology that could compete with American advances in weaponry, they would simply steal as many technical plans as possible and then benefit from American research initiatives without paying the cost of entry. While this approach would inherently leave them behind, as they would have to wait for American developments before they could steal them, they could concentrate on other aspects of Chinese society that might contribute to the defense of the nation, including expanding the Chinese economy. Not only would they seek to steal military technical data, Chinese hackers soon began a systematic campaign to steal corporate secrets, allowing Chinese government–dominated companies to compete with Western firms in the production of industrial goods. The cheaper cost of Chinese labor and the looser standards regarding worker safety, human rights, and environmental issues would in turn allow Chinese companies to outcompete their peers, expanding their own economy and undermining the West (Blane 2002, 14–15).

One of the earliest major cyber espionage campaigns that appears to have originated from China and attacked dozens of defense companies in the United States was code-named Titan Rain. The attack began no later than 2003 and managed to infiltrate the networks of Lockheed Martin, the National Aeronautics and Space Administration (NASA), Redstone Arsenal, and Sandia National Laboratories, among others. There is no way to determine how successful the attacks actually were, but from the available cyber forensic evidence, the hackers were able to steal data and documents measured in terabytes (Carr 2009, 4; Rosenzweig 2013, 38). One of the most telling aspects of the lack of cyber security at these targets was the fact that the entities removing the data encrypted it before sending it to control servers, a fact that demonstrated that it was not already encrypted by the host institutions. Once the attackers managed to gain unauthorized access to the computer networks they targeted, they were able to roam largely unimpeded and copy any files of interest. Their approach seems to have been essentially to grab as many files as possible, encrypt them, and send them out of the system as quickly as they could, out of fear of detection. However, when the initial thefts went unreported, and their means of entry remained open, the attackers became more brazen, sending increasingly large chunks of data with less effort to cover their tracks (Marvel 2010, 15–24).

Chinese cyber campaigns have not been limited to stealing technology-related materials. They have also used the cyber domain as a key way to keep tabs upon potential dissidents within the Chinese empire. In 1950, the Chinese People's Liberation Army invaded and quickly conquered Tibet, initially establishing an autonomous zone but eventually driving the Dalai Lama, spiritual leader of the Tibetan people, into exile in 1959. The notion of a free Tibet has never disappeared, much to the frustration of the Chinese occupation forces, and the advent of the Internet made it much easier for activists calling for a Chinese withdrawal to communicate with one another. The Dalai Lama has been a particular source of irritation and frustration to the Chinese government, particularly when his supporters set up Tibetan exile centers in major democratic cities around the world.

The Chinese government's paranoia about maintaining internal order and preventing any form of external threat to coalesce around an insurrection has consumed government resources for decades. In 1950, fear of a UN invasion during the Korean War triggered a Chinese invasion of the Korean Peninsula and nearly three years of grueling attritional warfare. Suspicions that Soviet and Indian agents were inciting Chinese dissidents in the western provinces led to a series of border skirmishes with China's two largest neighbors in the 1960s and 1970s, and almost certainly pushed India into creating a nuclear weapons program. Despite the fact that the Tibetan government in exile has no possibility of successfully overthrowing Chinese control of Tibet without a massive international support base, the Chinese government remains obsessed with the behavior of the Dalai Lama's officials.

In 2009, cyber security researchers working for the Infowar Monitor, tracking the actions of a Chinese-based advanced persistent threat, contacted the Dalai Lama's staff and notified them of a possible cyber intrusion on their computers. The Tibetan exiles then requested assistance in analyzing their networks and tracking down any unauthorized access attempts. Further research into the situation turned up compromised systems in Tibetan embassies throughout the world, with more than 1,300 infected machines in 103 different countries. The researchers dubbed the campaign "GhostNet" and found that the controlling servers for the botnet were all located inside of China, the only state actor likely to have such a thorough interest in the activities of the Dalai Lama's leadership network. Systems infected with the GhostNet program could potentially be completely controlled by the external server, to include activating the computers' cameras and microphones, and turning the infected systems into excellent surveillance platforms (Carr 2009, 183; Rosenzweig 2013, 78; Stiennon 2010, 43).

Not surprisingly, the Chinese ambassador to Great Britain adamantly denied any involvement in the establishment or control of the GhostNet system. Despite the overwhelming evidence, the Chinese government claims that the entire network is an elaborate attempt to frame China, possibly constructed by the United States, Russia, or Tibetan operatives. The brazen official Chinese denial, even when confronted with proof of the involvement of Chinese computers, demonstrates one of the great frustrations of attempting to assign blame in the cyber environment. There is almost no way to prove beyond a doubt that the

Chinese government is involved, due to the interconnected nature of the cyber domain. Even with the identification of a specific man trained by the Chinese government to engage in cyber activities as one of the principal actors of the campaign, the Chinese stonewall remains unchanged (Ventre 2011, 377–79).

In January 2010, Google revealed that it had been hacked by a Chinese state organization and that it had evidence of similar attacks upon at least two dozen more companies. After Google's announcement, several other technology firms, including Adobe Systems, Symantec, and Yahoo, reportedly confirmed that they had been hit by similar intrusions with the same goal. The attackers, who appear to have been members of PLA Unit 61398, the most advanced cyber attackers under the direct control of the Chinese government, attempted to penetrate the internal networks of high-technology firms like Google to plunder their source code for software development. By stealing this information, not only would the attackers facilitate return attempted intrusions; they might also transmit the information to Chinese competitors, who could then copy the products derived from the source code and engage in a trade war to dominate global information markets. They might also be able to actually modify the source code, which could ruin the underlying software upon which many of these corporations were based (Brenner 2011, 45–52).

The attack was first detected by Dmitri Alperovitch, the chief threat researcher at McAfee Labs. He dubbed the campaign "Operation Aurora," using what appeared to be the attacker's own reference code for their activities. According to some media reports, a source within the Chinese government leaked that the campaign had been ordered by the Politburo. Like the intrusions upon Tibetan networks, the primary objective of Operation Aurora appears to have been an attempt to monitor dissidents. Specifically, the attackers attempted to use the Google source code to enable monitoring of Gmail users who have been linked to antigovernment rebels, primarily located in the western provinces (Wortzel 2010, 90–91).

Some investigators, including the cyber security firm HBGary, have tracked the intrusions back to Shanghai Jiao Tong University and Lanxiang Vocational School, two schools directly tied to Baidu, a Chinese search engine that competes domestically with Google. As is their standard response in these matters, the Chinese government not only denied any involvement, but also immediately accused the United States of orchestrating the entire scenario. In response to the discoveries, Google announced in 2010 that it would no longer comply with the Chinese government's censorship demands in China, and that it was considering pulling out of its Chinese headquarters. Google's first mechanism to remove censorship from its search engine was simply to redirect all traffic from the mainland Chinese version of the site (google.cn) to the Hong Kong version (google.hk), which did not have the same level of government control. Shortly after this shift, all Google programs stopped functioning in China, a clear signal from the Chinese government that it would not tolerate a complete removal of the censorship. After a one-day outage, Google users regained access to the website, but many of the most provocative filtering controls quietly returned to the site.

The Current State of Cyber War

Cyber war is currently one means by which states might choose to attack one another, possibly without provoking a greater confrontation in the physical world. Thousands of attacks are launched each day, which suggests that many of the most technologically advanced states are currently willing to tolerate the status quo, as there has not been a major international push to restrict or prohibit such activities. The nature of the cyber realm makes determining the source and intent of cyber attacks a very difficult proposition. Should kinetic conflicts erupt, cyber attacks will almost certainly be a part of the physical warfare between states, just as they have accompanied smaller diplomatic provocations.

The cyber domain, if it should even be considered a separate domain, is currently simply a new area for struggle, an entirely manmade environment where networks come into conflict in an attempt to dominate the possession and processing of information. The changing nature of the environment, which shifts as new devices are attached, new software is created, and the fundamental architecture underpinning the system is altered, does not have the predictability of the physical world, despite the obvious "machine logic" aspects of the domain. Information in cyberspace is not quite as trustworthy as physical observation, due to the ease with which it might be deleted, changed, or hidden. Cyber conflicts, like their counterparts in the physical world, are largely a battle of adaptation and technological advancement. The cyber domain is a realm that blends intelligence collection and military activities in a way that has seldom been seen in previous conflicts. Unlike previous forms of conflict, the more connected to the domain a nation happens to be, the more vulnerable it is, with no corresponding inherent gains in offensive capabilities (Ventre 2011, 4). There is not a long history of previous conflicts and examples to draw upon, leaving cyberspace as almost a tabula rasa upon which states will attempt to impose their vision of conflict. The United States must consider not only its own approaches and predilections in cyberspace should it choose to engage in cyber warfare; it must also examine and evaluate the background and decision-making of potential enemies (Thomas 2009, 487–88). If the future of warfare will be dominated by the possession and control of information, the cyber domain will change how societies fight (Arquilla and Ronfeldt 1997, 4–5; Bousquet 2009, 34–35; Stocker and Schöpf 1998, 26–32).

References

Arquilla, John, and David Ronfeldt. 1992. *Cyberwar Is Coming!* Santa Monica, CA: RAND Corporation.

Arquilla, John, and David Ronfeldt, eds. 1997. *In Athena's Camp.* Santa Monica, CA: RAND Corporation.

Blane, John V., ed. 2002. *Cyberwarfare: Terror at a Click.* New York: Novinka Books.

Bousquet, Antoine. 2009. *The Scientific Way of Warfare: Order and Chaos on the Battlefields of Modernity.* New York: Columbia University Press.

Bowden, Mark. 2011. *Worm: The First Digital World War.* New York: Atlantic Monthly Press.

Brenner, Joel. 2011. *America the Vulnerable: Inside the New Threat Matrix of Digital Espionage, Crime, and Warfare.* New York: Penguin Press.

Brenner, Susan W. 2009. *Cyberthreats: The Emerging Fault Lines of the Nation State.* New York: Oxford University Press.

Carr, Jeffrey. 2009. *Inside Cyber Warfare: Mapping the Cyber Underworld.* Sebastopol, CA: O'Reilly Media.

Clarke, Richard A., and Robert K. Knake. 2010. *Cyber War: The Next Great Threat to National Security and What to Do about It.* New York: HarperCollins.

Kramer, Franklin D., Stuart H. Starr, and Larry K. Wentz, eds. 2009. *Cyberpower and National Security.* Dulles, VA: Potomac Books.

Leyden, John. 2012. "Hack on Saudi Aramco Hit 30,000 Workstations, Oil Firm Admits." *The Register*, August 29.

Marvel, Elisabette M., ed. 2010. *China's Cyberwarfare Capability.* New York: Nova Science Publishers.

Poroshyn, Roman. 2013. *Stuxnet: The True Story of Hunt and Evolution.* Denver, CO: Outskirts Press.

Reveron, Derek S., ed. 2012. *Cyberspace and National Security: Threats, Opportunities, and Power in a Virtual World.* Washington, DC: Georgetown University Press.

Rid, Thomas. 2013. *Cyber War Will Not Take Place*. New York: Oxford University Press.

Rosenzweig, Paul. 2013. *Cyber Warfare: How Conflicts in Cyberspace Are Challenging America and Changing the World*. Santa Barbara, CA: Praeger Security International.

Siroli, Gian Peiro. 2006. "Strategic Information Warfare: An Introduction." In *Cyberwar, Netwar, and the Revolution in Military Affairs*, edited by Edward Halpin, Philippa Trevorrow, David Webb, and Steve Wright. New York: Palgrave Macmillan.

Singer, P. W., and Allan Friedman. 2014. *Cybersecurity and Cyberwar*. New York: Oxford University Press.

"Solar Sunrise." 2011. GlobalSecurity.org. Retrieved from http://www.globalsecurity.org/military/ops/solar-sunrise.htm.

Stiennon, Richard. 2010. *Surviving Cyber War*. Lanham, MD: Government Institutes.

Stocker, Gerfried, and Christine Schöpf. 1998. *Info War*. New York: Springer-Verlag.

Thomas, Timothy L. 2009. "Nation-State Cyber Strategies: Examples from China and Russia." In *Cyberpower and National Security*, edited by Franklin D. Kramer, Stuart H. Starr, and Larry K. Wentz. Dulles, VA: Potomac Books.

Ventre, Daniel, ed. 2011. *Cyberwar and Information Warfare*. Hoboken, NJ: John Wiley & Sons.

Wortzel, Larry M. "China's Approach to Cyber Operations: Implications for the United States." In *China's Cyberwarfare Capability*, edited by Elisabette M. Marvel. New York: Nova Science Publishers, 2010.

Wu, Chris. 2006. "An Overview of the Research and Development of Information Warfare in China." In *Cyberwar, Netwar, and the Revolution in Military Affairs*, edited by Edward Halpin, Philippa Trevorrow, David Webb, and Steve Wright. New York: Palgrave Macmillan.

Cyber warfare is such a new concept that it offers many more questions than it does solutions. The role of cyber assets in national defense, the question of whether a cyber strategy is feasible, and even the issue of whether the term "warfare" should be applied to cyber operations are all issues that trigger substantial debate. Many cyber activities, such as crime, espionage, and terrorism, resemble aspects of warfare, while not fitting within its traditional definitions. Clear delineations between these types of activities may hold less value in the cyber domain than in the physical one. Ultimately, two key issues emerge regarding cyber warfare. The ability to clearly attribute attacks to certain actors, and the role of people in the cyber domain, will continue to create problems for cyber warriors for the foreseeable future.

Is a Cyber War Possible?

Just as beauty is in the eye of the beholder, acts of war are in the eyes of the recipient. Not every attack is treated as an act of war, but the decision to make an attack essentially cedes the decision to the victim. Traditionally, the term warfare has encapsulated

---

A VeriSign Inc. booth at the RSA Conference in San Francisco on February 7, 2007. VeriSign manages the .com and .net domain names registries, and supplies verification of secure websites as a means of deterring cyber attacks. (AP Photo/Paul Sakuma)

armed attacks by one nation upon the property or people of another nation. Such attacks are carried out in a direct and open fashion—fomenting an insurrection is not engaging in warfare per se, although it will almost certainly be considered a hostile act by the victim. Wars might be fought for complete conquest, creating a conflict over national survival; or they might be fought for much more limited objectives, such as the right to use a disputed resource or the form of government that will be practiced in a nation. The United Nations Charter specifically forbids member states from engaging in warfare against other members except in a defensive fashion, and it theoretically requires all members to come to the assistance of an aggrieved party. This has probably prevented or at least mitigated some disputes from growing into armed conflicts, but it has also served to push some wars into less traditional forms of conflict. These irregular wars often involve an unconventional aspect and include insurgencies and civil wars. The cyber warfare of the future is far more likely to resemble the small wars of irregular conflict than the major engagements of open warfare (Van Creveld 1999, 416–20).

International law has developed over centuries to establish who can legally carry out acts of warfare and who must remain apart from engaging in conflict. To be considered a lawful combatant, a belligerent must bear arms openly; wear a uniform or recognizable device; belong to an organization with a clear hierarchy of leaders responsible for the actions of subordinates, and obey all of the laws of armed conflict (LOAC). To fail on any of these points is to relinquish legal standing as a lawful combatant and, by extension, to lose any of the protections extended by the LOAC. These protections include a prohibition upon inflicting unnecessary suffering and a requirement that an offer of surrender will be accepted (Darnton 2006, 148–49).

Civilians, at least in theory, are largely protected from the direct violence of conflict. In exchange for that protection, they are expected to refrain from direct engagement in combat and to consent to peaceful occupation should their uniformed defenders vacate their area. Thus, civilians are not allowed to launch guerrilla attacks and then return to their everyday lives; they must remain aloof from combat at all times. Those working in direct support of a war effort are in a bit of a legal gray area—for example, civilians working at a factory producing military equipment may be considered a legitimate target, and thus placed in danger of enemy attacks.

It is an important question, particularly to this work, to decide whether it is even possible to engage in warfare through cyberspace. Cyber attacks do not typically include a physical effect, although there have been a handful of notable exceptions to that rule. They might not discern between legitimate warfare targets, such as government and military entities, and illegitimate targets, such as civilians not directly related to the war effort, due to the uncontrolled nature of some cyber attacks. They are rarely conducted in the open, and have thus far never been limited to uniformed members of a nation's military. The term "cyber weapon" is often bandied about, but it hardly fits the traditional notion of weaponry, given that it is an electronic construct, a program designed to alter or disrupt the function of a target network or computer. Thus, for some, even the term "cyber war" is a facetious and silly concept, as any such conflict is completely alien to the traditional construct of human conflict (Darnton 2006, 139–53; Reveron 2012, 15; Ventre 2011, 11).

Yet, there is a growing body of evidence that nations—and, for that matter, nonstate actors—are looking to cyber assets as a mechanism for inflicting damage upon opponents (Carr 2009, 37–43). Certainly, the most advanced militaries in the world have become incredibly dependent upon their cyber systems, and while they may be capable of functioning without them, they will do so at a greatly reduced level of both effectiveness and efficiency. Potential enemies cannot overlook the value of cyber operations as a means to erode the enemy's fighting capabilities, and hence cyber operations are certainly a part of the conflicts of both the present and the future.

The improving capabilities of cyber attacks, coupled with the increasing reliance of nations upon cyber infrastructure, mean that a well-designed cyber attack might be more devastating and useful than a physical attack against the same structure. Kinetic attacks to destroy electrical generation systems, for example, tend to require an enormous expenditure of combat power, and often cannot be counted upon to completely shut down the power grid. A well-crafted computer worm or logic bomb, on the other hand, implanted into the Internet-connected computer systems that run the grid, might do a more thorough job of shutting down the entire grid. A further attraction of such an attack is the likelihood that it can be stopped, or even reversed, should the attacker wish to call off the use of force. Coalition forces devoted years to rebuilding the devastated electrical infrastructure of Iraq, and still have not returned the Iraqi power grid to the level of generating capacity prior to the 1991 Persian Gulf War. Had the same destruction been created by a cyber attack, it might have been repaired in a matter of days, rather than decades.

The prevailing habit in Western civilization of using the term "warfare" to describe any quest or crusade has had the unfortunate effect of eroding the stability of the term. When President Lyndon Johnson declared a "War on Poverty," he wished to convey the seriousness of his goals and the level of effort that would be required to achieve victory. The same can be said of his successor's "War on Drugs," an effort that has sent millions of Americans to prison without showing any signs of stopping the flow of illegal substances into the nation. When President George W. Bush declared a "War on Terror," many military intellectuals cringed, knowing the futility of declaring war on a concept, an ideology, or a specific behavior. The fact that there is no agreed-upon definition of terrorism, either in international circles or in use by the U.S. government, further clouds the issue. It may not be possible to ever declare victory against poverty, drugs, or terrorism, and thus should the terminology remain unchanged, the United States and other Western nations may be on a perpetual pseudo-war footing.

The question of whether or not a state of warfare can exist without a physical component is largely a red herring. Cyber capabilities are a powerful tool in the hands of national actors and certain subnational organizations, and they are a part of conflict in the world of the twenty-first century. Just as military commanders of the Cold War could not imagine engaging in a major ground offensive without at least some modicum of air support, modern military leaders cannot ignore the role of cyber attacks in modern conflicts. Nations simply cannot consider engaging in conflict without taking steps to secure their own networks, and will not attack an enemy with physical forces without also seeking to disrupt that enemy's cyber systems. Further, if the effects created by cyber war are essentially the same as those caused by physical attacks, the debate is largely moot—to the victims of attacks, the method of inflicting punishment will be largely irrelevant. Cyber war is thus a part of the modern notion of war, whether it can stand alone or not. Perhaps most importantly, Secretary of Defense Leon Panetta announced in 2012 that the United States reserved the right to classify cyber attacks as acts of war and to retaliate by any appropriate means. Panetta remained deliberately ambiguous about what type of attacks might provoke a retaliation, and whether retaliation would be confined to the cyber realm (Panetta 2012).

Cyber as a Military Domain

Most military operations are largely defined in terms of the domains in which they occur. In turn, most national military forces are divided by the domain in which they operate, with the two oldest domains being land and sea power. In the early twentieth century, with the advent of powered heavier-than-air flight, air forces began to develop around the world and, in time, became recognized as independent branches of their respective national militaries, signifying an acceptance that the air domain was a separate war-fighting environment. For some of the most technologically advanced nations, nuclear-armed military forces constitute a completely separate domain of warfare, with different rules of engagement, expectations, and strategic options from those of the conventional forces. In the twenty-first century, two domains of potential conflict, space and cyber, are sources of controversy regarding the separation of military forces by domains.

The oldest organized human military forces were naturally formed on land. Fragmentary references still exist of armies of conquest operating in Mesopotamia nearly 5,000 years ago. The name Sargon of Akkad has managed to survive to the present day largely due to his successful leadership in land campaigns. The earliest organized navies came much later in human social development, and first existed primarily to convey land forces from one point of the coast to another. However, as sailing techniques improved, and ship construction allowed for true oceangoing vessels, naval commanders began to leverage the unique aspects of their domain, leading to the general independence of naval forces from their land counterparts. In the classical antiquity period, commanders of fleets might have been chosen from land generals, but by the fifteenth century, naval specialists demonstrated the importance of understanding the fundamentals of sea power. Thus, a clear delineation of land and sea forces as well as the development of a substantial amount of military theory applying to each domain, but not to both, began to develop.

For some nations, the inherently independent nature of far-flung naval commands produced a substantial amount of consternation. Particularly insular societies, such as China during the Ming dynasty, feared the potential pernicious influence of outside contacts and did not trust naval commanders to remain loyal to the leadership of the empire. Their most common form of recourse was simply to eliminate naval support and the potential trading relationships that might accompany being a naval power, out of a need to retain control over society. Even in the twenty-first century, the Chinese navy is still regarded as a relatively small and insignificant branch of the People's Liberation Army, in part because naval forces played little role in bringing the current government into power during the Chinese Civil War. For most modern nations, though, the navy remains separate and equal to the army, allowing the necessary specialization to produce a professional class of military officers functioning in one domain. The exceptions tend to be nations with extremely small military forces who find the costs of specialization to be unacceptably high, or nations with little or no coastline who maintain small naval forces, if they choose to form them at all.

For most nations, the rise of aerial forces began under the army. This is primarily due to the inherent challenges associated with early airpower, including the need to build and protect airfields for aircraft to operate near an active military theater. Further, the primary function of early air forces operating in World War I was to fly over enemy territory and gather useful information for ground commanders. Although aircraft made enormous advances in size, capabilities, and range during the war, they did not conduct strategically significant operations during the conflict. However, the potential striking power of the airplane, which might simply bypass an enemy's defenses and strike at the heart of an opponent's society, was not lost upon military leaders. In particular, the British government seized upon the concept, formally creating the Royal Air Force (RAF) as an independent branch of military service in 1918. The RAF leadership emphasized the notion of strategic bombardment as a unique capability of their component. Air Marshal Hugh Trenchard envisioned fleets of heavy bombers attacking an enemy city using incendiaries and poison gas, not only destroying structures on the ground, but also sowing panic among the civilian population. In his estimation, the effect of such bombardment upon enemy morale would trigger a revolt by the civilian population against their leadership, forcing their capitulation as the only means of ending the terrifying attacks.

Other nations, most notably France, Germany, and the Soviet Union, perceived airplanes not as instruments of strategic attack, but instead as extremely powerful infantry-support weapons for traditional land campaigns. Thus, they worked to develop the technology necessary to allow for accurate attacks upon ground forces by dive-bombing aircraft, while also refining their military doctrine to use aircraft as a form of flying artillery. The Germans in particular devised ways of using their airpower as a shock force that might blast holes in an enemy's defenses, allowing a massive land attack to pour through the resulting gaps. Unlike the grinding stalemate of World War I, they believed their new "Blitzkrieg" concept would restore mobility to the battlefront and prevent another ruinous war of attrition such as they had faced in that war.

In the United States, the political Progressive movement included the notion that if warfare must occur, it could still be made a more humane undertaking. Airpower might allow rapid strikes against the key centers of an enemy's entire defense network, thus eliminating the need for an expensive and bloody conquest of fielded forces. Because modern military forces relied upon an entire industrial network to sustain them in the field, American planners believed that precision attacks against key nodes of that industrial network might bring it to a grinding halt. If so, the enemy military would be incapable of offering further resistance due to a shortage of necessary equipment, and would have no choice but to surrender without even being defeated in the field. To that end, American theorists began to design aerial campaigns that might target critical industrial infrastructure upon which a nation's entire production rested. While the United States was one of the slowest nations to create an independent air force, and in fact retained its strategic bombardment forces under army control until after World War II, in some ways, the American concept of airpower far outreached that of the other nations and foreshadowed the modern utility of strategic airpower.

In each of these domains, military leaders have repeatedly argued that specialization within a domain is the only means by which a commander can possibly function in the modern war environment. That said, few military leaders are pushing to separate their national space assets into a separate military force. Outer space is officially demilitarized by international treaties, although there have been a number of tests in the past decade of weapons designed to destroy space assets from the ground. Currently, satellites offer a substantial advantage to military forces by providing communications bandwidth, reconnaissance, and global positioning data. However, because of the inherent physical difficulties of operations within the space domain, there has been little push to actually create true space military forces, although there have been theoretical discussions regarding the feasibility of beam weapons or kinetic-strike platforms in space. In reality, there is no way to hide, or even protect, assets in space from terrestrial attack, and efforts to do so would be ruinously expensive due to the costs associated with boosting anything into orbit (Johnson-Freese 2009, 8–20). A few nuclear devices detonated in the most common orbital pathways would probably serve to render virtually every satellite completely useless, although space detonations of nuclear weapons would create a host of secondary problems. For most nations, space forces associated with the military remain under the control of the respective air force, although some armies retain the responsibility, and some nations have simply made no effort at incorporating space specialists into their military forces.

Cyberspace is considered by many individuals to have developed to the point that it should be considered a separate military domain. Unlike the other domains, which are defined largely in terms of their natural physical properties, the cyber domain is entirely manmade, and its most significant features are its nonphysical aspects, rather than the hardware that gives rise to its existence. Unlike the other realms, where physical principles remain immutable, in the cyber realm, the principles under which the domain operates can theoretically be changed through shifts in either the physical architecture or the software operating in cyberspace. There are no unchanging laws in cyberspace; in practice, there is no equivalent force to gravity, for example. The only limits that currently apply to cyberspace that are the same as the physical world are the importance of the electromagnetic spectrum, upon which it is completely dependent in its current configuration, and the speed of light, which places an upper limit on the speed of cyber communications.

The cyber realm influences and interacts with all of the other domains and can play a major role in successful military operations conducted within each. Cyber communications are often the only means to interact with space satellites; they enable control over terrestrial and naval assets in the field; and they can be used to reroute aerial forces, whether flown by human pilots or by machines. In the past several decades, American military forces have made enormous strides in putting aside their traditional service-based rivalries to work together in joint operations. The result has been an enormous increase in U.S. conventional military power, as the specialties of each service have been leveraged into campaigns across the domains. In 1986, a formal requirement for such cooperation was created through the Goldwater-Nichols Act; its effects could be seen in the Persian Gulf War, Operation Enduring Freedom, and Operation Iraqi Freedom.

The real question is not about the utility of cyber power; it is about the domain's ability to independently influence the outcome of conflicts between nations. Has cyber power developed to such a sufficient degree that it might be possible to fight a war entirely within the cyber realm? In many nations, there is a movement to create independent cyber forces, not bounded by the traditional roles of other domains. For the United States, the closest example of such a creation is U.S. Cyber Command, which unifies the cyber units of each of the military services into a single joint agency. While under the control of the Department of Defense in the form of a four-star flag officer, U.S. Cyber Command includes the National Security

Agency (NSA), an intelligence service tasked since its creation in 1952 to oversee the signals security of the United States. The NSA is a highly secretive agency that has developed a reputation as the foremost cyber agency in the nation, capable of offering significant assistance in securing military and government networks while also potentially launching offensive cyber operations.

A further question centers around the nature of military forces in general—are they the best mechanism for harnessing a nation's ability to influence events in cyberspace? The public's notion of a "cyber warrior" often does not match its idea of a soldier, sailor, or flyer in uniform. Performing cyber feats does not require a major dedication to physical fitness, for example, and some of the most creative and effective cyber operators have demonstrated an unwillingness to follow the strict discipline expected by professional military forces. Further, the legal rules governing military operations, enshrined in Title 10 of the U.S. Code, might not allow for the most effective utilization of cyber assets, a fact that is reflected in the different expectations for intelligence agencies, covered by Title 50 of the U.S. Code. The everyday lives of military personnel might turn away some of the most desirable cyber warrior recruits, a fact that has yet to change the military's approach to the issue.

The general trend of the early twenty-first century has been to gradually accept cyberspace as a separate warfighting domain, but to keep warfighting as the exclusive province of military forces. While this might be temporarily necessary due to the legal issues surrounding the laws of international conflict, it might also simply reflect the fact that the legal system has a difficult time keeping up with revolutionary changes in the nature of warfare. If the cyber domain is officially recognized as a separate realm of conflict by the legal system, as it largely is by society, it is likely to be policed and contested by official agents of national governments, but not necessarily by those wearing uniforms of the military organizations.

Cyber Strategy

Strategy is commonly defined as planning to achieve a major or overall aim. The term is most often associated with military operations, although it is not inherently a military activity. Most strategic theorists recognize that there are at least a few immutable principles of strategy, although they occasionally differ on precisely how to define those principles. Such debates are often highly academic, although in practice, national military strategies that violate the general theories of strategy tend to be doomed for failure before they are even acted upon by military forces.

National military strategies exist as a means to pursue political objectives set by a nation's leadership. They are merely one component of national strategies writ large, meaning that all of the elements of a nation's power can and should be harnessed as a means of pursuing a nation's goals. That said, national military strategies are the mechanism by which military forces pursue their responsibilities to a nation. At their most fundamental level, a nation's military services exist to protect the nation and its citizenry. This defensive function is their primary goal but may require expeditionary activity as a means to achieving homeland security. For the United States, in particular, modern military strategy has relied upon the notion that conflicts should be kept as far from the nation's borders as possible. If military conflict must occur, it should be fought on the enemy's soil or, at the very least, at a distance great enough to prevent direct attacks upon the American homeland. For the most part, the United States has been remarkably effective in pursuing this objective. No major enemy incursions have threatened American soil since the War of 1812, although there have been minor skirmishes on the periphery of American territory since that time. In the twenty-first century, the greatest American traditional defensive asset, geographic location, has been rendered far less useful than it proved in the first two centuries of the nation's independence. While the U.S. Navy remains the largest and most capable sea power in world history, it cannot guard against every potential attack that might be launched via air power, from space, or by using intercontinental ballistic missiles.

Cyber power is not remotely constrained by physical geography. There are no rivers to be crossed and no mountains to be climbed within the cyber realm. As such, cyber attacks have an inherent capability to bypass the traditional symbols of national defense and potentially wreak havoc upon civilian institutions within the homeland. At the same time, the attribution of responsibility for cyber attacks can be exceedingly difficult, particularly if attackers take pains to hide their identities. Any strategy devised for the cyber realm must account for the inherent ambiguity associated with attacking and defending within a computer network (Libicki 2012, 46–47).

Modern military theorists often point to the pioneering work of Prussian major general Carl von Clausewitz as the most important published volume on the theory of military strategy. His *On War* is an examination of the fundamental nature of human conflict. In it, Clausewitz posits that war is composed of the interactions of three forces, specifically the trinity of violence, chance, and reason. He argued that the belligerent most emotionally invested in the conflict would be most likely to win, all other factors being equal. In this, he essentially pointed out that a nation fighting a war of survival would be far more likely to take the necessary risks in order to emerge victorious, while a nation attempting to win only limited goals would not feel sufficiently invested in a conflict to overcome the determination of the enemy. Clausewitz discussed the need for military strategy to support the achievement of political goals, and suggested that it could do so in one of two fashions. Either military strategy could serve to eliminate an enemy's ability to resist, thus leaving that nation prostrate and open to conquest and occupation; or military strategy could serve to support the acquisition of limited goals, a far more realistic objective in modern warfare. Clausewitz seemed to favor the former, perhaps in part due to his eyewitness experiences during the Napoleonic Wars.

While many military theorists have been writing since the publication of *On War* in 1832, none has achieved the same level of cachet with professional army officers. Unfortunately, much of what Clausewitz offers has little utility in the event of a cyber conflict. Most computer conflicts involve little or no violence, and the digital domain has few of the external stimuli to offer significant uncertainty and chance. Cyber warfare by itself is almost by definition a conflict for limited objectives, although it might stand in support of larger objectives being carried out in the physical world. Finally, in cyber warfare, the defensive is rarely the stronger form of war, regardless of how pressing the conflict might seem to the participants involved (Arquilla and Ronfeldt 1996, 93).

Of course, the theory of military strategy has not been limited to land concepts. Two naval theorists, both writing near the turn of the twentieth century, have emerged as dominant thinkers regarding maritime strategy. The first, U.S. Navy captain Alfred Thayer Mahan, advocated the construction of a large surface navy centered on all-big-gun battleships that could batter their way through any opposing vessels. Mahan argued that the fleet must be wielded as a single unit, rather than being broken piecemeal into squadrons. Upon the commencement of conflict, it should be brought together and flung toward the enemy in pursuit of a decisive battle at sea. Once the enemy's fleet had been smashed, their homeland would lay open to invasion and conquest. After annihilating enemy opposition, the surviving fleet could establish a blockade and target merchant shipping, bringing a powerful economic pressure to bear upon the enemy.

Mahan's concepts were largely based upon the behavior of the Royal Navy in the eighteenth and nineteenth centuries. In virtually every conflict that Britain entered, the Royal Navy's first priority was the destruction of enemy warships, followed immediately by a complete blockade of enemy ports and, if possible, even the enemy coastline. While this strategy might require a long period of time to have a significant effect, it also allowed Britain to fight wars with minimal risks, so long as it maintained the most powerful navy in the world. While an enemy's economy slowly collapsed, the British could continue to access the commerce of the world. Properly employed, this approach would even allow the British to establish new trading relationships, supplanting their enemies in foreign ports and capturing a larger share of international commerce. Such a strategy failed during the American Revolution, in part because the British did not have a large enough fleet to impose a blockade while also fighting the French navy. However, it served admirably in the eventual downfall of the Napoleonic Empire, as the British managed to essentially blockade the entire European continent while maintaining enough ships to attack French colonial possessions at will. Mahan believed that the United States possessed the unique characteristics of geography, population, and resources to become the largest and most powerful maritime force in the world, a prediction that came true in the three decades after his death and remains accurate today.

Mahan's primary competition in the field of maritime strategy comes from a British armchair historian, Sir Julian Corbett, who argued almost the total opposite of Mahan's emphasis upon maintaining the fleet as a single unit. While he agreed that the destruction of the enemy fleet was an important goal, he argued that no sane enemy would agree to do battle with a much larger and more powerful fleet. By concentrating forces in a single location, a commander would deter the enemy from ever engaging in a decisive battle, and at the same time would expose his lines of communication to the dispersed attack of an aggressive opponent. Corbett believed that the lines of communication across the seas were by far the most important objective of naval strategy, and that maritime commanders should remain on the strategic defensive, employing offensive tactical operations when it was possible to lure an enemy into a battle under favorable conditions. Like Clausewitz, Corbett saw warfare as an activity practiced in support of national objectives, and he believed that a nation's economic strength was its most important characteristic for victory in war.

In the cyber realm, it is almost impossible to mass forces in the manner suggested by Mahan, although it is true that a computer center operating multiple powerful machines in unison will have a much greater capacity for brute force attacks than a dispersed collection of machines that are only loosely linked. Of course, it is not necessary for the computers to be physically in close proximity to one another; they need only to be capable of acting in unison. Corbett's notion of dispersed attacks against an enemy's lines of communication translate more easily into computer warfare, through attacks upon the connections between computers within a network. However, Corbett's ideas about maintaining the strategic defensive offer the initiative to the enemy in a cyber conflict, and might leave a defender vulnerable to being overwhelmed in the early stages of a cyber war.

Airpower theory has many early proponents, but the one who has garnered the most recognition remains Giulio Douhet of the Italian Air Force. Writing in the aftermath of World War I, Douhet argued that airpower offered a unique capability to political leaders and military commanders, in that it could directly threaten the civilian population of the enemy without first requiring the destruction of the opponent's fielded forces. In Douhet's mind, airplanes could launch surprise attacks of devastating force, overwhelming the enemy in a matter of a few hours and forcing a nation's surrender before it could even muster the units necessary for resistance. Douhet did not envision any means by which attacking airplanes might be stopped; thus he considered defensive measures to be wasteful and unnecessary. Instead, he recommended using a nation's entire military budget to create a massive aerial fleet that could conquer the airspace over an enemy and rain destruction down upon its cities, conveniently ignoring the existence of interceptor aircraft and missing the significance of experiments in radar technology.

Douhet massively overestimated the destructive power of aerial bombardment, which requires either a substantial amount of precision to inflict catastrophic damage upon the enemy industrial network, or a willingness to create massive casualties among the enemy population through the use of incendiaries and chemical weapons. Not until the advent of laser- and GPS-guided weapons could Douhet's theories truly be put to the test, unless one was willing to employ nuclear weapons in every conflict after 1945. The bomber aircraft of World War II simply did not have the ability to target with anything approaching precision; only area incendiary attacks against cities showed any level of success during the war, and it came at a horrific cost to the enemy civilian population.

In 1988, U.S. Air Force colonel John Warden published *The Air Campaign*, a treatise arguing that aerial technology had finally reached the necessary point to achieve many of Douhet's concepts of strategic attack. Warden argued that an enemy society could be paralyzed if significant pressure could be brought to bear against five different types of targets. Unfortunately, he illustrated his concept as a series of concentric rings, leading many readers to incorrectly assume that the central ring was the only important target set. Instead, Warden intended to illustrate that concentrating upon a single aspect of the social framework, as American bombers had done in World War II when they attacked German and Japanese industrial targets, would be insufficient to devastate an enemy and force its surrender. What was needed was a series of parallel attacks upon leadership, key infrastructure, means of production, the population, and fielded enemy forces. By hitting all five targets simultaneously, it would be impossible for the target society to adapt and overcome the effects of the campaign. In 1991, coalition forces operating under American leadership in the Persian Gulf War only partially followed Warden's plans, and they diverted a disproportionate number of aerial sorties to attacking Iraqi fielded forces. In the 2003 invasion of Iraq, Warden's theory was more closely followed, with the result that the Iraqi government essentially lost control and even communication with its military and civilian population in a matter of days.

The idea of an overwhelming cyber attack is a popular aspect of the public's conception of cyber war. It may be possible to launch a major cyber offensive against a wide array of targets that are connected to the Internet, particularly in an open Western society. Such an attack might create aspects of chaos and paralysis and serve to essentially paralyze an opposing nation's cyber capabilities. By attacking an enormous number of servers and nodes, particularly in a number of different types of targets such as military, industry, government, and private networks, a well-orchestrated cyber campaign could have a lot of unintended, yet ultimately beneficial effects, particularly as the victim attempted to shift assets to prevent further damages. However, without an accompanying physical attack, the cyber assault would likely result in only temporary problems and frustrations, and might provoke a massive retaliation in both the cyber and the physical domains.

Since the first usage of nuclear weapons in 1945, a number of theorists have emerged who have argued for decades about whether it is even possible to create a strategy for nuclear war, particularly in an era when potential enemies have enough weapons to inflict a devastating response even after absorbing a massive attack. The first significant discussion of the issue was offered by Bernard Brodie, who argued that the primary task of nuclear-armed powers had changed from winning wars to preventing them, as the consequences of nuclear war would be unthinkable (Brodie 1959). Thus, deterrence became the order of the day, and to ensure that an enemy would not launch a nuclear first strike, nuclear nations needed to develop enough nuclear weapons to ensure a credible retaliation capability. For the United States, this led to the development of the nuclear triad, a combination of manned nuclear-capable bomber aircraft, submarine-launched nuclear missiles, and intercontinental ballistic missiles. Given the massive destructive power of even a single nuclear warhead, it quickly became impossible for a potential enemy to contemplate attacking the United States because it would be impossible to destroy the entire nuclear arsenal and prevent a second strike.

While Brodie concentrated upon the political strategy associated with nuclear deterrence, other theorists, most notably his colleague at the RAND Corporation, Herman Kahn, contemplated the actual mechanics of fighting a nuclear war. He theorized that even a nuclear war might be confined to limited objectives, and thus it would not necessarily escalate to a total war. He also argued that a nuclear war could be winnable, and would not inevitably result in the demise of humanity even if it escalated out of control. Rather, the survivors of the conflict would simply be forced to adapt to the changed conditions of the world that remained, in much the same manner of survivors of previous calamities in world history (Kahn 1962). Not surprisingly, many of Kahn's conclusions horrified his contemporaries, even though he never actually advocated nuclear war. Rather, he recommended that political and military leaders be made fully aware of the consequences associated with nuclear rhetoric, and prepared to accept them. Otherwise, they should not engage in provocative behavior that might offer incentives to the Soviet Union to start a nuclear conflict, as deterrence would only function as long as the Soviets believed the United States was prepared to engage in nuclear war.

The all-or-nothing elements of nuclear warfare bear little resemblance to the potential devastation to be felt in a cyber conflict. Even in an all-out cyber war, the number of casualties from immediate cyber effects would likely be low, although disruptions in supply chains and emergency services would undoubtedly cause a significant number of losses over time. The primary lesson from discussions of nuclear strategy for the would-be cyber strategist comes from the notion of doomsday predictions associated with the unknown. Such predictions are extremely common within the cyber arena, but very unhelpful for the practical aspects of determining national goals and methods to achieve them. A full-scale cyber attack is less a weapon of mass destruction, in the manner of a nuclear explosion, and more a weapon of mass disruption, forcing the victim to devise less efficient means to accomplish the same everyday tasks. The other similarity between nuclear and cyber strategies revolves around the lack of much quantifiable data or case studies to confirm the theories in question. There have only been two nuclear explosions in warfare to date, and both were in August 1945. There have been limited cyber conflicts, but nothing approaching full-scale cyber warfare between global powers. Thus, in both cases, theorists seeking to determine the overarching principles of conflict must rely upon supposition and inference, making their arguments inherently more open to criticism.

Thus far, no cyber theorist has achieved the same level of notoriety and general acceptance of their ideas as any of the prominent military theorists within other domains. In part, this is because most military theorists require examples to build their concepts. It is probably also due to the recent emergence of the concept of cyber war, although the nuclear strategists began publishing significant works within a few years of the first atomic explosions. Of the active writers on cyber warfare, the most influential theorists thus far have largely come from the realm of think tanks, particularly the RAND Corporation, which has employed John Arquilla, Martin Libicki, and David Ronfeldt; and the Brookings Institution, home to Allan Friedman and Peter Singer. Government officials such as Joel Brenner and Richard Clarke have proven influential in policy discussions of cyber activities, but have done little to offer a general theory of cyber conflict. Founders of private companies associated with cyber security, such as Jeffrey Carr and Paul Rosenzweig, have offered their own unique perspectives, based upon their experiences within the field. Recent events have offered sufficient examples of the potential of cyber warfare that a true cyber theorist may emerge in the near future to at least create a starting point for discussion of the overarching principles of cyber warfare.

The lack of a unified cyber strategy has not stopped nations from applying the term strategy to public pronouncements regarding cyber operations. Such positional papers are often more akin to a cyber doctrine, or a list of future hopes regarding cyber capabilities, than to a coherent strategy of how cyber power might be utilized to achieve national goals. In the near future, cyber strategy will almost certainly remain largely a supporting activity to facilitate the function of kinetic aspects of military power, with a secondary function as an intelligence-gathering and economic tool. However, the establishment of a true cyber theory might also clarify the most successful usage of cyber assets for a nation-state and make a certain degree of cyber stability more likely.

Instruments of National Power

International relations specialists often define the instruments of national power with the acronym DIME; specifically referring to diplomatic, informational, military, and economic assets. Each of these instruments might be effective in attempts to influence another nation. In most cases, several are brought to bear at the same time, in different ways, to suit the needs of the nation employing them. In theory, only the use of military instruments might constitute an act of war, although all of the instruments certainly play a role in international conflict. Also, all four of the instruments of power are heavily influenced by the presence of cyber capabilities, which can enhance both their effect and their efficiency, but which can also create new vulnerabilities.

Some argue that war erupts when diplomacy fails, but this conception fails to account for both the role that diplomacy plays during a conflict and the fact that certain fundamental disagreements between nations cannot be resolved via diplomatic solutions.

Even when wars are underway, diplomatic efforts might serve to bring the violence to an acceptable conclusion. Diplomatic overtures to neutral third parties can serve to create the conditions necessary for peace negotiations, or at least to influence the boundaries of the fight, both geographically and in the means employed. Maintaining alliances always requires a certain degree of diplomatic effort, lest coalition members begin to pursue narrow national goals to the exclusion of any overarching coalition objectives.

The cyber realm offers intriguing new possibilities for diplomacy during a conflict. It enables sub rosa communications between warring nations, which offer a less public means for developing an accommodation (Libicki 2009, 128–29). Cyber communications might offer less ambiguity, as a written message transmitted through cyberspace does not have the same translation issues as a verbal negotiation; it is a solid artifact that can be consulted and reexamined in ways that a verbal conversation cannot. On the other hand, cyberspace communications tend to lose many of the nonverbal cues of personal diplomacy. Further, they are theoretically vulnerable to interception, disruption, and even covert modification in ways that other forms of communication do not face. A clever cyber warrior might manage to drive wedges into enemy alliances by using the cyber realm for false messages between cooperating forces, sowing confusion and discord under the guise of collaboration.

Intercepted diplomatic communications have a long history of influencing international conflicts, and are certainly not a new problem unique to cyberspace. For millennia, military forces have sought to intercept diplomatic messages sent by enemies. That might include overtures of new alliances or calls for coalition partners to maneuver their forces in a certain fashion. At times, intercepted diplomatic communications have served as a triggering mechanism for conflicts. In 1898, Cuban revolutionaries stole a personal letter from the residence of the Spanish governor in Havana, Don José Canelejas. Written by Spanish minister to the United States Enrique

Depuy de Lôme, the letter made a series of disparaging remarks about the intentions of President William McKinley. De Lôme counseled his friend not to worry about American intervention in Cuba, as the American president did not have the courage to attack Spanish forces. The rebels delivered the letter to the *New York Journal*, which translated and published the inflammatory note on February 9 ("Worst Insult" 1898). Coupled with the mysterious destruction of the USS *Maine* in Havana Harbor, the de Lôme letter, which the ambassador did not deny, provided the necessary stimulus to push the United States to declare war upon Spain.

By the twentieth century, electronic communications had greatly sped up the ability to relay messages but had also created new vulnerabilities. In 1917, while World War I raged across Europe, the United States appeared to be on the verge of entering the conflict. Germany, already on the edge of collapse, feared that American intervention might prove the decisive element in ending the stalemate on the Western Front. To preempt such an event, German foreign secretary Arthur Zimmermann sent a telegram to Heinrich von Eckhardt, the ambassador to Mexico. In the message, Zimmermann instructed Eckhardt to coordinate with the Mexican government for a surprise attack against the United States. In return, Germany promised to provide assistance in regaining much of the territory taken from Mexico in 1848, presumably after completing the war in Europe. In reality, Germany had little possibility of influencing any war on the North American continent, but its government was desperate to prevent American entry and willing to make any promises necessary to achieve that end. What the Germans apparently ignored was the fact that the trans-Atlantic cable used to transmit their message ran through England, where intelligence operatives quickly decrypted the encoded transmission and passed it on to the American government. The United States had already severed diplomatic ties with Germany over the use of unrestricted submarine warfare, but the cable certainly provided impetus for President Woodrow Wilson to request a declaration of war.

For its part, the Mexican government quietly ignored the offer and remained neutral in the conflict, having discerned the obvious dangers of launching an attack on its northern neighbor.

By World War II, efforts to intercept communications between members of the enemy coalition had reached new heights. German intelligence operatives attempted to tap into trans-Atlantic cables, both on land in London and by using submarines to try to locate the underwater cable. Radio transmissions, even when encrypted, were a key target for counter-intelligence operatives, who established massive antenna networks in the hopes of gaining key information about how the enemies cooperated and planned operations. Germany had direct lines of communication to its European ally, Italy, but coordinating any type of war effort with Japan required very complicated communication efforts over vast distances that were extremely vulnerable to interception by the Allies. Shortly after the start of the war, Germany and Japan essentially stopped engaging in diplomacy with one another except through the occasional exchange of envoys. Rather than coordinating their efforts, they each fought their own wars, making their defeat even more likely.

Cyber networks have made coordinated diplomatic efforts far easier for nations, as it is possible for political leaders to offer almost instantaneous guidance to their representatives in embassies around the world. As such, the Internet has facilitated diplomatic initiatives, sped up negotiations, and reduced the number of misunderstandings in international communication efforts. However, those same networks have proven extremely vulnerable to cyber exploitation, as it is almost impossible to completely control how packets of cyber data travel across the Internet's infrastructure. Former NSA contractor Edward Snowden demonstrated the danger of conducting diplomatic efforts via cyberspace when he released thousands of U.S. diplomatic messages to and from the Department of State. Many of the messages, intended only for U.S. operatives in the field or in the centralized bureaucracy, included disparaging assessments of foreign leaders, which proved extremely embarrassing when they were released to the public. Some analysts have credited the Snowden leaks with setting back American diplomatic efforts by decades. Had the traditional forms of diplomatic communication been retained and used, it is highly unlikely that Snowden, or even a major nation-state's intelligence service, could have compiled even a fraction of the diplomatic cables released in a single data dump in 2013.

The second instrument of national power, informational, includes traditional information-gathering efforts by covert means (espionage), public sources of data such as media broadcasts, and internal communications that might provide insights into a nation's strategic objectives and operational planning process. Given that cyberspace assets are inherently associated with the transmission of information, and that the Internet has proven to be the most efficient and effective means of information transmission ever devised, it is unsurprising that cyber war would be intimately associated with information operations at the national level.

Nations have always sought to collect as much information as possible about other nations, even those considered close allies. Particularly desirable types of information include technological advances, economic information, and political leaders' priorities for future activities. All of these types of data might be readily available through the cyber realm, and hence vulnerable to hostile powers capable of discovering and extracting the information from cyber networks. Regardless of the risks, though, the cyber realm simply makes it much easier to store and transmit such information, and thus it is highly unlikely that these desirable pieces of data will be cordoned off from computer networks. Technologically advanced nations are devoting an ever-increasing share of their budgets to cyber security, but they still remain the continual victims of information theft (Putrich 2014).

When an enemy is known to be attempting to collect information, that fact might be turned against them. Thus, during the U.S. Civil War, Confederate forces emplaced logs painted to resemble cannon in their fortifications defending Richmond in 1862. Union cavalry scouts could not approach close enough to discover the ruse, and reported back to Major General George McClellan that the enemy possessed a far larger supply of artillery than previously assumed. In response, McClellan slowed his advance upon the enemy capital, allowing vital time for Confederate reinforcements to arrive and drive the invaders back. In 1944, as American and British forces mustered in England for an attack upon the European mainland, German defenders sought to build robust defenses to prevent them from gaining a foothold. German spies sought without success to discover where the amphibious invasion would be launched. To take advantage of this fact, American and British agents began a massive disinformation campaign, designed to convince the German High Command that the attack would occur at Pas de Calais, rather than along the Normandy coastline. In support of this effort, the Allies created a fake army that transmitted radio signals simulating the assembly and training of a massive army. Lieutenant General George Patton, one of the most successful and feared American ground commanders, was a direct participant in the effort, a sure way to rivet the Germans' attention upon the wrong location. A final touch was provided by handcuffing a briefcase to an unidentified body that was allowed to wash ashore in France. Inside the case were counterfeit documents, ostensibly for the French Resistance, calling for disruption behind the lines near Calais. The German intelligence operation swallowed the bait, and even after American, British, and Canadian troops began wading ashore in Normandy, the Germans held back reserves from the front on the assumption that the attacks were just a feint designed to draw them away from the real invasion site (Barbier 2009).

Of course, cyber networks have made both the transmission and the interception of information far more easily performed. Many cyber criminals specialize in the trade of illicitly gained information, including the necessary data to steal identities, clone credit cards, and counterfeit identification documents. Malicious cyber actors working on behalf of nations tend to have a much larger and more ambitious goal than mere financial crimes. They may instead seek to gain access to information regarding military capabilities, data used in the governance of rival nations, and other metadata that might help a country to set its national goals. This type of information is stored on cyber networks around the world, and thus available for exploitation if the cyber attacker is skilled enough to penetrate computer defenses established to guard it.

The third instrument of national power in the DIME model is the nation's military. The United States has by far the most powerful military force in the world, with the largest navy and air force and the most technologically sophisticated army. America is more reliant upon space assets than any other nation, which serve as a major enabling force for all of its armed services. The United States is also more dependent upon the cyber realm than any other country, and without a functioning computer system, the American military becomes a far less efficient and effective machine. While it is possible for American military forces to operate without cyber systems, a training scenario that is routinely practiced in defense exercises, they lose many of their most important advantages if an enemy can render their cyber networks nonfunctional (Siroli 2006, 33–39).

Military organizations around the world rely upon cyber systems for command and control of subordinate forces as well as the collection of intelligence, surveillance, and reconnaissance data. Although military forces often serve as the most overt element of national coercion, sometimes their most important function is simply to exist as a persistent threat, which serves as a deterrent against potential aggression by other national and nonstate actors. When military cyber systems are compromised, the unique capabilities of military organizations, and their potential vulnerabilities, become exposed to the hostile cyber attacker. For this reason, military forces in many nations also serve as the lead organizations for both cyber attack and cyber defense. The United States is a prime example of this phenomenon. The U.S. Department of Defense provides oversight for both the National Security Administration (NSA) and U.S. Cyber Command, two key elements of American military cyber power. Defense spending serves as a key enabler for the development and deployment of cyber weapons and cyber defenses (Putrich 2014). Thus, as is true for the diplomatic and informational aspects of national power, cyber is a key component of the military forces of a nation.

The final element of national power within this construct is the economic power of a nation. The United States has possessed the largest economy in the world for more than a century, and has leveraged its economic power not only to support the world's largest defense organization, but also as a key method of influencing other nations. American technological innovations have had a transformative effect upon the world for more than two centuries, a fact that has contributed enormously to the development of the U.S. economy. American industrial production in the nineteenth and twentieth centuries led to the development of global markets, with the important interdependencies created by economic relationships between partner nations. By the late twentieth century, much of the American economy had transitioned to the production of services rather than tangible goods, including financial instruments, scientific and medical innovations, and entertainment media. In this regard, elements of the American economy have had an enormous influence over the development of a global culture. Communications via the Internet have only sped up the effect, helping to make English the most-spoken second language in the world, effectively the language of commerce used around the globe.

The development of the Internet opened up entirely new avenues of economic opportunities, and it also enabled the exchange of resources. Global banking structures have become almost completely dependent upon computers not only for tallying accounts but also for financial transfers. While this has facilitated greater globalization within the economy, it has also created a system from which billions of dollars are extracted every year by malicious actors. Further, it has created a new vulnerability, as cyber attackers will almost certainly attempt to disrupt the cyber networks used by financial institutions in the event of a major war. Such disruptions and their potential effects were amply demonstrated in the 2008 hacking attacks upon Estonia, which included a massive distributed denial of service attack upon the largest Estonian banks. Citizens found themselves unable to use any kind of electronic credit device, but also could not withdraw money from bank accounts due to the computer networks crashing. Economic chaos followed, as did pressure upon the Estonian government to take any necessary measures to restore the banking network (Brenner 2011, 128–31; Singer and Friedman 2014, 98–124).

The instruments of national power are not the only means to conceive of how nations interact with one another, but it is a useful model. For the purposes of a discussion of cyber power, particularly in the context of cyber warfare, this model demonstrates how important cyber communications have become to virtually every aspect of modern state functions. A generalized effort to shut down the computer networks of a hostile nation, if successful, is likely to create massive secondary problems for the victim, which will spend enormous amounts of time, resources, and effort trying to fulfill the everyday functions of a modern society. Unfortunately, even understanding how interrelated cyber networks are with the fundamental elements of national power does little to increase the security of modern states in the cyber realm.

Cyber Crime, Cyber Espionage, Cyberterrorism

Crime, espionage, and terrorism are all unfortunate, and undeniable, aspects of modern society. None of these activities constitutes an act of war, no matter how annoying and expensive each of them individually may be (Arquilla and Ronfeldt 1996, 5). The use or nonuse of cyber resources for crime, espionage, and terrorism has no effect either upon their definitions, or upon their applicability to warfare. However, in the cyber domain, it is far easier to misinterpret one act for another, and a cyber criminal, cyber spy, or cyberterrorist bears a very close resemblance to a cyber warrior. Further, each of these types of activities might lend itself to a nation's service during a cyber war and constitute a key national resource for such a conflict.

Cyber criminals use computers and networks for the same motivations that criminals in the physical world pursue. At its core, crime tends to be about the illicit gain of resources, usually financial in nature. Cyber criminals may attempt to hack into a bank's computer network and transfer money from one account to another, as opposed to a robber waving a gun around and demanding money from the teller. Quite frankly, a successful bank robbery is likely to result in relatively modest gains—so little cash is actually secured in most such robberies that banks instruct their employees to comply with the criminals' demands, and trust in law enforcement methods to catch the perpetrators. While banks create both active and passive defense mechanisms against physical threats, such as keeping most of the cash in locked vaults, placing cameras throughout the lobby and on the exterior of the building, having physical barriers between customers and employees, and possibly employing armed guards, they accept the possibility of armed robberies and take measures to minimize the losses. Banks have centuries of experience in this regard, and the most successful bank robberies in American history have only netted sums in the tens of millions on a handful of occasions. Not only is it difficult to obtain the money, it is even harder to actually get away with it. Ten million dollars, even in the largest U.S. denomination, the $100 bill, weighs over 200 pounds and requires a fairly large bag—a briefcase will not come close to holding it.

In comparison, the most lucrative cyber intrusions, which have only been possible for a relatively modest two decades, have collected billions of dollars per year. In part, this is because the electronic transfer of funds is a much simpler problem than actually carrying off cash. In part, it is because physical security is a much better-understood problem than cyber security, and flaws in physical security are much easier to spot. Often, the first clue that there is a cyber security flaw is when it has already been exploited by an attacker, and the only hope is to prevent further intrusions using the same manner. Such thefts might involve the direct transfer of funds, but they might also include stealing the data for millions of credit cards, which can be used for fraudulent purchases or sold on the black market, passing the risk of arrest on to lower-level criminals.

Of course, cyber criminals do not limit their attacks to financial institutions, which tend to take cyber security very seriously. Instead, many cyber criminals imagine far more novel schemes. Rather than attempting to transfer millions of dollars out of a single bank account, it might be far easier to obtain a few dollars from millions of victims. Because consumers have become very dependent upon electronic forms of payment, including credit card processors, there are literally billions of potentially vulnerable transactions each day. This problem is increased by the archaic technology being used by the U.S. credit card industry, which for its own reasons adamantly opposes any measures to beef up security within its system. When a large merchant chooses to store the information from consumer credit cards in an insecure way, or does not protect that data during transit from the store to the processing center, it becomes vulnerable to hackers. Two massive attacks illustrate the problem, and the potential costs to corporations that are careless about protecting consumer data.

In 2007, the TJX Corporation, owners of TJ Maxx and Marshalls, among other commercial enterprises, admitted that they had been the victims of a two-year cyber attack that managed to steal the credit card information for more than 45 million shoppers. Later, they actually revised the estimate up to more than 100 million compromised credit cards.

The attack demonstrated how little the retailer had done to secure customers' personal information, and how poor general practices were for storing credit card data. After years of investigation and remuneration, the final cost of the attack was more than $250 million, and no individuals were arrested or prosecuted for the crime (Stiennon 2010, 109). The money had effectively evaporated, but the trickle-down effects for consumers whose information had been stolen continued for years. While American law does not hold credit card users liable for security breaches of their information, credit card companies cannot simply accept the loss of such an enormous amount of revenue. Instead, the result is rising interest charges, increased fees upon cardholders, and efforts to find and legally prosecute the criminals. Unfortunately, the incident did not lead to improved security measures across the industry, such as the inclusion of a microchip inside credit cards that would make cloning cards a far more difficult proposition. In 2009, TJX settled a lawsuit, launched by state attorneys general, for less than $10 million, a pittance when compared with the losses faced by the credit card companies due to the TJX negligence.

Even with the TJX example, Target Corporation failed to improve its own internal cyber security. Over a period of only three weeks in 2013, Target managed to lose control over the credit card information of more than 50 million shoppers, including the security codes on the back of cards designed to prevent online fraud. Although industry best practices standards strictly prohibited companies from retaining the security code data, Target's registers still collected and filed it for each transaction, essentially handing cyber thieves a list of valid credit card numbers with all of the information necessary to exploit them. Security companies investigating the data thefts eventually tracked the cyber penetration to a fairly unsophisticated program written by a Russian teenager, which reached the Target corporate servers through the company's heating and air conditioning subcontractor.

The Target case demonstrates a number of important points for any discussion of cyber conflict. First, the constant push to create an interconnected computer network often results in decisions that fail the common sense test. There was no pressing need for an environmental subcontractor to have direct access to the corporate network, and certainly no reason to allow any programs to be loaded from the contractor to the much larger system. Second, while the financial industry might offer guidance on the best practices regarding efforts to safeguard customers' personal information, there is no means of compelling corporations to follow those practices. Third, corporate decision-makers who have control over the technical aspects of a company's cyber security often have little, if any, knowledge of cyberspace, and are far more likely to be graduates of a business program than programmers or security experts. Fourth, there is little effort to hold companies responsible for security breaches, beyond what normal market forces might trigger. Although both TJX and Target saw short-term declines in stock prices, both companies managed to rebound and rebuild their customer bases, largely on the basis of offering small discounts for return business. Once consumers returned to their earlier shopping patterns, neither company saw any significant repercussions for the poor decision-making that had allowed the breaches.

Like cyber crime, cyber espionage is merely an age-old practice that has adapted to a new technology. Unfortunately, the computer revolution has made the exfiltration and analysis of enormous volumes of data a much more practical activity. Whereas high-level espionage activities might have required months or even years to obtain a few key files in the twentieth century, in the twenty-first century, such information might be acquired in a matter of minutes if it is not properly secured. Complicating the problem, such data can be easily copied and stored in multiple locations, which reduces vulnerabilities to hardware failures but also creates a number of opportunities for interception and appropriation by hostile cyber entities.

Nations have always engaged in espionage against other states, and even their allies have been potential targets. Espionage activities have included attempts to determine a political leader's likely future decisions and obtaining embarrassing information about such leaders that might be used to influence those decisions. They have also included attempts to steal technical data about weapons systems, information about national defenses and the location of military assets, and at times even to obtain examples of military hardware that might be taken out of the country and copied. Sometimes, these copies have been extremely overt, such as the case of American B-29 bombers forced to land in the Soviet Union during World War II. Because the Soviets did not join the war against Japan until August 1945, any American aircraft or aircrews that landed in the neutral Soviet nation were immediately interned. Soviet engineers disassembled the aircraft in the hope of making replicas, which soon entered the Red Air Force as the Tupolev Tu-4 and remained in service for two decades. Soviet agents did everything possible to penetrate the Manhattan Project, the joint American-British effort to construct an atomic bomb, and the materials they were able to obtain greatly sped the Soviet effort to build its own bomb.

Espionage can be a double-edged sword. Enemy counterintelligence operatives constantly seek not just to control the exfiltration of classified information, but also to insert misinformation into a spy's collected materials. Acting upon stolen information can be a very dangerous practice, as there is little recourse when a nation is tricked by stealing inaccurate information. In the 1970s, the Federal Bureau of Investigation (FBI) discovered a widespread effort by Soviet agents to steal industrial secrets. KGB spies were tasked with capturing as much corporate data as possible, in virtually every type of company, in the hopes of raising the Soviet economic system up to the level of the United States. Rather than simply arresting the perpetrators, the FBI worked in conjunction with Central Intelligence Agency assets to plant flawed technical plans in a number of locations, hoping that the KGB would capture the documents and not possess the expertise to tell the difference between accurate and inaccurate information. Sure enough, KGB agents penetrated a Canadian pipeline company and stole plans for natural gas pipelines, valves, and controlling equipment. They did not realize that the CIA had planted the material and deliberately included a fatal flaw in the system, one that would be noticed only in a thorough examination by a very skilled civil engineer. In 1982, a Siberian pipeline constructed in accordance with the stolen plans erupted in a massive explosion with the force of 3,000 tons of TNT, one of the largest nonnuclear explosions in the history of the planet. The pressure wave of the explosion shattered windows more than 100 miles from the site, and trees were flattened for miles around the explosion. The resulting Soviet investigation revealed the flaw in the stolen plans, but the Soviet government could hardly protest at the United Nations that its agents had been tricked while stealing files from private corporations. The message was clear, and the incident caused the KGB to question all of the other materials it had appropriated in the program, wondering when the next catastrophe might occur (Stiennon 2010, 126–27).

Prior to the creation of the Internet, it was impossible to fathom that a nation's secrets might be theoretically directly available to enemy agents. Instead, the key information was likely to be protected by formidable physical defenses, or to be locked inside the minds of only a few individuals. With the networking movement of the 1990s, though, there was a much greater push to create efficient systems, particularly in the aftermath of the Cold War, than there was to maintain cyber security. In the same time period, the U.S. government, in particular, began to outsource an enormous amount of military research that had previously been conducted at government facilities. Thus, contractors obtained the necessary access to sensitive information, and yet did not have the best track record for protecting classified data. Every private contractor became a potential access point for obtaining secret information, if only they could be exploited by enemy cyber experts (Clarke and Knake 2010, 9–11).

The 1990s were also noteworthy because in that decade, the United States demonstrated its utter superiority in conventional forms of warfare. American technology had simply outstripped its competitors, and U.S. strategists had devised highly effective doctrine and organizations to take advantage of this prowess. American dominance seemed unchallengeable, so long as every other nation would agree to fight in the manner preferred by the United States. Other nations studied the American experience in Iraq and the Balkans and drew different conclusions from those held by the U.S. military and political leaders. While the United States did indeed possess a massive advantage in both the quality and the quantity of its military equipment, it also betrayed a certain arrogance that all future wars would resemble those of the recent past. In many ways, the United States became a victim of its own success, as it forced other nations to seek creative means to create asymmetrical advantages that might be exploited to defeat the American military machine. In particular, China, which saw itself as both the hegemon of Asia and the logical successor to the Soviet Union, began to consider alternative means of pressing a conflict. Rather than engaging in a conventional fight pitting front-line forces against the United States, even on the Asian mainland, Chinese theorists considered the possibility of extending warlike activities into other domains. At the same time, they recognized the need to close the gap, both economically and technologically, between their nation and their potential enemy. Thus, they embarked on a massive cyber espionage campaign against American government and corporate networks, seeking to take advantage of the enormous security flaws in these systems before the American leadership even knew it was under attack (Carr 2009, 171–75).

In a series of major cyber espionage campaigns, Chinese government–supported cyber attackers have managed to steal unprecedented volumes of data from American and allied military organizations, financial institutions, and technology companies. These thefts, coupled with a refusal to abide by Western copyright regulations, have allowed the Chinese command economy to flood the international market with copies of Western-technology products, often sold at a net loss as a means to eliminate competition and secure larger sectors of the global marketplace. Stolen military technological research has enabled a massive modernization program to quickly improve the resources of the People's Liberation Army, making a conventional war with China a much more dangerous prospect. Attempts to hold China accountable for its cyber intrusions have been met with both denials and veiled threats, and China's position as the largest foreign holder of American debt weakens any American complaints about cyber espionage. After all, if the Chinese government decided to sell its holdings of U.S. debt, even at a loss, the effect upon the U.S. economy could be devastating.

Espionage has never been cited as a justification to engage in a war, even if that espionage is designed in part to facilitate a future conflict. That said, there has never been an espionage campaign in history that has come close to the amount of information stolen by the Chinese government in just the past decade, and there is little sign that their efforts will be slowed in the future, unless sufficient cyber security measures can be devised and adopted to prevent their success. The Chinese government does not seem to fear retaliation, perhaps in part because it maintains a much tighter control over its national access to the Internet. Unlike the United States, China could theoretically sever its national connections to the Internet in relatively short order, and without inflicting catastrophic damage upon its own governance and economic activities.

Cyberterrorism has been one of the most overhyped threats of the twenty-first century, in part because the groups that might wish to employ cyber assets for terror attacks are extremely skilled at manipulating media outlets, and in part because most potential terror targets do not understand the cyber domain sufficiently well to evaluate the prospects for success in a cyberterror campaign. Like crime and espionage, terrorism is a problem that is thousands of years old and that has vexed humanity almost constantly from the dawn of civilization. Despite the long experience with the phenomenon of terrorism, international bodies have thus far failed to even agree upon a single definition of the concept. Most agree that terrorism involves the threat or use of violence to coerce or deter a target population in support of a political goal. Almost every nation considers terrorism to be an illegitimate use of violence, although individual states often refer to terrorists as guerrillas, insurgents, or freedom fighters, all of whom are presumably allowed to engage in acts of violence against oppressive regimes.

Cyber capabilities certainly offer the prospect of spreading fear to an extremely large target population, although in this regard, computers might be more a means of communication than an actual tool for inflicting violence. Terrorists have seized the opportunities presented by social media sites to freely convey their messages, naturally in the most positive light that they can muster, both to recruit more members and to influence their targets (Libicki 2007, 45–48). Because shutting down websites can be extremely difficult, this medium has allowed a certain globalization to terror organizations that would have been unthinkable prior to the invention of the Internet. Yet, the Internet also offers the opportunity for interested parties to investigate the less savory aspects of terrorism, and it is a method that can be used, and in some cases controlled, by governments with at least as much ease as the terror organizations. For every video that purports to show a righteous attack against a tyrannical government, there is another that shows atrocities being committed by the terror organizations.

Just as computer assets have become an absolute requirement for military operations in the modern age, so too they have become a necessity for any efforts at influencing global audiences and sharing propaganda with the world. In theory, a terror organization can access the Internet from almost anywhere in the world; but in practice, any exposure to the Internet creates an avenue of attack for antiterror cyber warriors, who are likely to have far more experience, skill, and resources than their nonstate foes. Therefore, it is unsurprising that there have not been a huge number of terror attacks against potentially devastating targets—while a nation might have enough cyber resources to coordinate an attack upon a nuclear power facility, for example, most terror organizations can do little more than spread propaganda or occasionally deface websites. Terrorists might have the motive and willingness to launch destructive attacks, but they just do not have the technological capability (Stiennon 2010, 77).

Unfortunately, the three elements of crime, espionage, and terrorism in cyberspace have the potential to coordinate with one another and create synergistic effects that might actually threaten even major cyber nations. Cyber criminals have shown some aversion to working with terrorists, in part because such a cooperative effort will likely bring a much greater level of scrutiny upon them. However, if the payoff is high enough, there are probably cyber criminals that are willing to sell their services to a terror organization (Bucci 2012, 65). Very few terrorist groups have enormous funds, in part because of the challenges of raising such sums, and in part because of the cost of launching attacks and remaining out of the hands of law enforcement or military opposition. Al Qaeda once had a seemingly limitless supply of money, in part because it short-sold airline stocks on the American market just before the September 11 attacks. What Al Qaeda failed to realize, though, is that it would not be able to hide its bank accounts from the determined cyber sleuths that began to relentlessly pursue the organization in the aftermath of the largest terror attack in history. Not only did American cyber investigators find and seize many of the largest Al Qaeda bank accounts, but they also took major steps to halt the flow of fresh money to the terror organization. Al Qaeda was soon forced to engage in many contraband industries, including narcotics smuggling, which drew resources away from the group's central mission. As of this writing, the best-funded terror organization in the world is the Islamic State of Iraq and Syria (ISIS), which captured portions of Iraq and Syria in the spring of 2014. They did not fund themselves through cyber attacks, though, so much as through the seizure of the central bank of Mosul, where an estimated $450 million in American cash was being held.

ISIS has used the Internet very effectively to recruit new members from outside of their immediate region. This has included thousands of citizens from Western nations, most of whom hold legal passports and can thus return to their home countries after being radicalized by ISIS propaganda. ISIS has also used the Internet to sow fear and discord among potential enemies. In the summer of 2014, ISIS leaders repeatedly vowed to make war upon all enemies of Islam, a threat backed up by a photoshopped picture of the White House with an ISIS flag flying overhead. On August 19, a masked ISIS member beheaded American media correspondent James Foley and posted video of the incident to a number of public websites. Not only did the act incite revulsion among Western viewers, but it also triggered a wave of attempts to ransom other Western citizens held by the radical group.

Espionage and terrorism have also interacted on a number of occasions, and will continue to do so in the foreseeable future. A number of major terror organizations in the world are directly or indirectly supported and controlled by state intelligence organizations. For example, Hizbollah, the largest terror organization in Lebanon, derives an enormous amount of funding from Iranian and Syrian intelligence agencies. Those same state organizations also supply most of the weapons that Hizbollah uses against Israel and non-Shiite Lebanese citizens. The governments of Iran and Syria can deny direct responsibility for triggering attacks, while at the same time working to undermine the stability of the Lebanese government and maintaining terrorist pressure against northern Israel. Cyber networks have enabled easier communication between these types of groups, and have also allowed intelligence agencies to supply specific data gathered by state assets, such as satellite photography, to their terrorist proxies.

At times, state intelligence agencies have shown an interest in cooperating with cyber criminals. In this regard, the Russian examples are by far the most prominent. When Russian hackers launched devastating DDoS attacks against Georgian government and media websites, they largely attacked a list of targets that was almost certainly provided by Russian intelligence operatives. This type of cooperation is inherently destabilizing, as it blurs the line between military and civilian operations (Libicki 2012, 22–23). The actual attacks did not come directly from state hacking organizations; the first wave of activity was actually launched by the Russian Business Network (RBN), one of the largest cyber crime organizations in the world. The intelligence agencies gained a major cyber asset in the form of botnets with millions of zombie computers that could combine to shut down Georgian Internet traffic while maintaining official deniability for any responsibility (Bowden 2011, 89–90; Schiller et al. 2007, 98). Unfortunately, that official deniability did little to alter the public perception that the attacks were ordered by the Russian government.

Although crime, espionage, and terrorism are not warfare in the classical sense, to their victims, that may be a difference without a distinction. In the cyber domain, each of these activities more closely resembles the mechanics of warfare than in the physical realm, in that they are less distinguishable from true acts of war. For that reason, they are inextricably linked with warfare and may wind up modifying the definition of warfare as a result. Given that these activities are more likely to attack civil rather than military targets, they also demonstrate the blending of victims that often occurs in the cyber realm (Brenner 2009, 10).

The Problem of Attribution

One of the most challenging aspects of cyber war is the concept of attribution. Specifically, this refers to the difficulty of ascertaining who was responsible for a particular cyber action, and thus might be the logical target for any retaliatory action that a victim might wish to undertake, whether in the cyber or physical domains. Cyber attribution includes determining the originating network address of a cyber attack, which is theoretically a relatively straightforward process, at least from a technical standpoint. Unfortunately, backtracking a cyber action becomes far more difficult when it involves an international border, which most attacks do. Attackers will almost always route their attacks through servers in several countries, and prefer to use nations that are hostile to cyber investigation efforts, including countries that have not seen fit to criminalize cyber attacks. Further complicating the issue, individual Internet service providers (ISPs) often refuse to disclose the identities and locations of individual network users, in part because there is very little incentive to do so, and currently few negative consequences for an intransigent stance (Brenner 2009, 80–94).

On the rare occasion that a cyber attack can be traced to a specific Internet protocol (IP) address, that still does not guarantee that the actual originator of the attack has actually been located, so much as it narrows the attack down to a specific piece of hardware in a certain position at one point in time. Determining to whom that hardware belongs, and who was using it at the time of the attack, is a completely separate and equally thorny problem. Proving such attribution is often impossible, although attackers often leave clues as to their identity. Some will brag about their exploits in digital forums, others might announce their presence by defacing a website and proudly taking credit for their actions. The most dangerous cyber actors, though, will do everything they can to prevent detection of an intrusion, and to cover their tracks sufficiently enough to prevent any counterattack, either in the cyber domain or in the physical world (Rid 2013, 144–46).

The traditional methods of determining responsibility for a crime or a military attack do not translate well to the cyber domain. For example, motivations in cyberspace do not necessarily correlate to motivations elsewhere. Because a military attack is usually an overt action, it does not tend to be very difficult to ascertain who was responsible, and motivation for the attack usually becomes a secondary consideration, if it is considered at all (Brenner 2009, 10). In the cyber realm, though, motives for activity might be a much more clouded issue. Close allies have no motivation to attack one another in the physical world, and yet, time and again they are accused, or at least suspected, of spying upon one another. For example, Israeli hackers have been caught engaging in massive cyber campaigns of espionage in the United States, despite the extremely close relationship between the two governments (Blane 2002, 67). Likewise, the United States has been conclusively proven to be a repeat offender guilty of substantial cyber espionage against its closest allies in the North Atlantic Treaty Organization, often for no apparent reason (Greenwald 2014; Gurnow 2014).

In cyberspace, it is much more difficult to tell friend from foe, and much easier to pretend to be something that you are not. Thus, a cyber attack might be launched in an overt manner, ensuring the attackers will be quickly discovered. This type of attack might be an example of spoofing, an electronic frame-job that has a twofold purpose. First, the aggressor launches the original attack and derives whatever benefit might be gained from it against an adversary. Second, the target might be fooled as to the identity of the attacker and take a retaliatory action against the wrong target. In a best-case scenario for the originator of the attack, the target and the framed nonactor will then engage in a series of escalatory, retaliatory actions against each other, while the original miscreant continues to feign innocence.

Unlike most military actions, cyber attacks are typically launched in an indirect fashion. While military theorists might laud the notion of indirect strategy and launching attacks from unexpected directions, or pursuing operations in a creative and unconventional manner, at the tactical level, most attacks are fairly direct. A soldier raises a weapon, aims, and shoots at the target, rather than trying to bounce a bullet off of three surfaces before it strikes the enemy. In the cyber domain, the more "ricochets" an attacker can use, the harder it will be to determine where the attack came from, and thus the most successful attacks are often the most indirect in nature. One particularly effective method of attack in the cyber realm is to use the enemy's resources against them, by seizing control over computers in the target nation and launching the attack from within the victim's borders. This is extremely effective in the case of a DDoS attack, where the basic mechanics are simple brute force. These types of cyber actions are not very sophisticated, but they are annoyingly effective and, in at least one prominent case, managed to bring the entire Internet to a halt for a period of several hours (Bowden 2011, 78–79). Attacks in cyberspace may rely upon programs implanted in a target computer months or years in advance. These computerized time bombs might lie in wait until activated by a seemingly innocuous message, or they might go off at a predetermined time. In either case, their eruption might catch the target completely off guard, and hit at a time when no perceived enemy can even be blamed for the attack (Brenner 2011, 99–113; Singer and Friedman 2014, 167–68).

It is always important to remember that in the modern cyber war environment, the most obvious attacker may not be the actual culprit, with the exception of small-scale, nuisance attacks. Even if the victim manages to correctly figure out who was responsible for the attack, it will probably not have enough proof to bring about any form of legal action against the attacker. Thus, the victim of the attack will then have to decide whether to retaliate on the basis of incomplete information, and if so, how to launch such a retaliation, either through cyberspace or in a separate fashion.

Any act of war has the possibility of provoking a counterattack, and such a retaliation may be out of proportion to the initial attack, depending upon the actors involved. In kinetic warfare, the international laws of armed conflict require that a counterattack be proportional. Thus, if one country bombs an enemy's radar station, the original victim would not be justified in launching a poison gas attack against the aggressor's largest city. However, the original victim is not required to launch a replica of the first attack—a proportionate response in this scenario might instead be a salvo of artillery rounds against a military outpost. In cyberspace, though, determining proportionality is often a very difficult proposition. One major reason for the difficulty is because the norms have not been defined by the international community. While there are thousands of years of history to examine for precedents in physical conflicts and, within that time period, tens of thousands of military engagements, there have been relatively few cyber attacks that might constitute an act of cyber war. Also, the recipient of a retaliatory attack, even if the correct attribution has been made by the original victim, may perceive an escalation where one was not intended, and decide to escalate in their next response.

A major complicating factor in maintaining proportionality in cyber attacks is the simple fact that in a cyber conflict, the aggressor has a substantial advantage over the defender. A nation that undertakes a first-strike cyber attack has the luxury of preparing for such a strike and choosing the exact means for launching it. The victim, on the other hand, may feel a certain pressure to respond in kind, as quickly as possible. Unless the victim has spent substantial time and resources to prepare a strike, though, it will be unlikely to launch an equally unpleasant counterstroke against the aggressor. A weak cyber counterattack might prove completely ineffective, particularly against an enemy that expected just such a retaliation, and thus might provoke even more cyber aggression. Thus, the temptation for the counterattack will be to launch an escalatory attack, one guaranteed to inflict pain upon the enemy, possibly through the use of a brute-force cyber method, such as a DDoS, rather than as a custom-designed attack program. Or, the retaliator might choose to launch a cobbled-together attack, one that might have unexpected consequences. Controlling a DDoS is relatively easy, as the attacking network can simply halt the attack at any point. Controlling a virus or worm, on the other hand, can sometimes prove impossible—if it is written without an "off switch," it can potentially grow out of control and spread far beyond the intended target, possibly triggering nasty responses from every other nation that is accidentally hit by its unintended effects.

At any time, any of the participants in a cyber conflict might decide to shift domains for a response. Thus, a country that is very strong at cyber activity but has little in the way of physical defenses might hope, and fail, to confine a conflict to cyberspace. Likewise, a country that is weak in the cyber domain might quickly resort to a physical response. Keeping proportionality in a shift to or from the cyber domain might be an impossible prospect, as there is little way to compare the quality of a cyber asset and a physical asset. While no nation has overtly responded to a cyber attack via a kinetic response to date, such a retaliation is almost guaranteed to happen in the relatively near future. Making it all the more likely, no major world power has sworn off a physical retaliation for cyber attacks, and in fact, most have explicitly reserved the right to respond in any fashion they see fit to a cyber intrusion (Panetta 2012). In comparison, most nuclear nations have agreed not to escalate any war with a nonnuclear power to the point of using nuclear weapons, although an exception would undoubtedly be made if the nuclear power was on the verge of losing a conventional war and saw its atomic arsenal as its last hope. Such a scenario is not as far-flung as diplomats might hope, particularly with the recent nuclear proliferation efforts of North Korea and Iran. Both nations are engaged in low-level conflicts with rivals who possess nuclear weapons and greater conventional capabilities, and both seem determined to use the threat of nuclear war as a balancing mechanism. Not surprisingly, both nations are also very active in launching attacks in the cyber realm (Stiennon 2010, 55–59).

Actors in the cyber domain have not created any system of agreed-upon levels of activity, although there are certainly some lines that might be inferred based upon previous interstate conflicts. In this regard, the Cold War might serve as the best historical guide to cyber conflicts. During that five-decade rivalry, the United States and the Soviet Union struggled constantly for global dominance and to establish regional hegemony throughout the world. Yet, there were certain understood limits, behaviors that were beyond the pale of the rivalry. Espionage was perfectly acceptable, although any captured spies faced imprisonment or possible execution, depending upon the circumstances of their capture. Support for insurgent groups or small nations that threatened allies of the rival was also considered the norm. In this regard, the Soviets openly supplied both the Viet Cong and the North Vietnamese in their fight against the United States. In turn, the Soviet invasion of Afghanistan ran into serious difficulties when the Afghan mujahedin began to field weapons supplied by the United States. Despite all of these activities though, the United States and the Soviet Union never engaged in direct conflict with one another, even though both sides war-gamed the possibility on a constant basis. Further, the only time there was a true threat of nuclear war, during the Cuban Missile Crisis, cooler heads prevailed in both nations, and steps were taken to ensure that no accidental escalation could spin out of control in the future.

In the cyber realm, it is conceivable that measures could be taken to prevent a terrible series of escalations. Currently, though, there are few mechanisms to formally prohibit such a sequence of events. Instead, there are almost constant cyber intrusions by hundreds of state and nonstate actors, blending the concepts of cyber crime, espionage, and warfare into a single information struggle. Before any international under-standing can be created regarding cyber warfare, or any proto-cols can be enacted to prevent such a conflict, nations will need to come to an understanding of the acceptable behaviors in cyberspace, and which types of activities should be consid-ered completely off limits.

People and Paranoia

At its heart, every computer network is operated by people, and those people often represent the greatest security risk. The vast majority of computer users in the world have no real concep-tion of how a computer actually functions, and no capability to determine whether a line of software code is malicious, benign, or beneficial, in large part because very few computer users have even the slightest programming skill. Further, com-puter users tend to be somewhat intimidated by the aspects of the technology that they cannot understand, making them sus-ceptible to anyone who claims to have a greater understanding of computer function. Users want the convenience of com-puters, but require no knowledge of precisely how they function.

The U.S. Department of Defense provides an excellent recent example of the problem created by convenience and security. DoD cyber experts realized in 2008 that USB flash drives, often called "thumb drives," represented a major secu-rity flaw in their network. When plugged into a USB connec-tion, these drives are capable of automatically running executable programs, making them an excellent vector for the distribution of computer viruses. At the same time, they are an extremely convenient way to quickly move information from one computer to another, and their small size and afford-ability makes them even more attractive. Many computer users assume that these drives are perfectly safe because they are in the users' possession at all times, while they assume that infor-mation transmitted over a computer network or through the

Internet is inherently vulnerable to interception and theft. Thus, they deceived themselves into thinking their USB drives were more secure ways to store and transfer information, adding to the allure of the ubiquitous drives.

Unfortunately, this simply shows the ignorance of the users, who did not realize that their favorite transmission method could quickly get infected with malware without their knowledge, and then spread it into other networks. Even computers supposedly protected from intrusions by air-gapping proved susceptible to worms transmitted via USB drives, as too many individuals made the mistake of using the drives to transfer information, and at the same time malware, from one network to another. Thumb drives became an additional security risk because they proved very easy to conceal, and hence to steal from classified areas. Military investigators found hundreds of USB drives containing classified information for sale in the bazaars surrounding U.S. military bases in Iraq and Afghanistan. It was soon determined that most were probably stolen by local laborers providing contracted support on the bases, including janitorial crews who could more than double their income through simple pilferage.

In 2008, the DoD banned the use of all USB drives from military computers, in the mistaken belief that such a ban would stop their usage. While the ban undoubtedly slowed down the use of USB drives, the devices were simply so useful and convenient that they continued to be a common sight at military installations around the world. Not until the military's cyber experts redesigned the entire network operating systems, reprogramming them to look for USB connections, check them against approved devices, and report any unauthorized connections did the number of uses begin to drop. Soon, DoD computers became programmed to automatically disconnect from the NIPRNet if an unauthorized device was connected, essentially creating a computer quarantine that could not be undone by the user. While this created both a deterrent and a punitive effect for computer users who still ignored the DoD directives, it made for a fairly impractical approach to the security problem.

In any computer system, the need for security will always be countered by the desire for access and utility. If a computer network has a particularly onerous security system that makes its use difficult for the computer operators, it is almost guaranteed that those operators will discover a way to defeat even the most complex security processes for their own convenience. Further, a network that relies upon users to continually update their software to eliminate vulnerabilities will always have opportunities for exploitation. Humans simply are not reliable enough to be the first line of defense in a computer system, even if they are operating a computer equipped with automatic updates. For this reason, many cyber security experts have essentially called for taking humans out of the loop when it comes to cyber security.

Ironically, even though people are the source of most security breaches in the cyber realm, they are also one of the greatest problems due to the paranoia of decision-makers. The cyber domain is one characterized by extreme efforts to maintain high classification levels in government organizations, refusal to share information among private entities, and a focus upon perception rather than reality in victims breached by cyber attacks. This emphasis upon secrecy often makes identifying threats more difficult, and containing them once discovered a much more onerous task. While some cyber security companies have started to publicly share every threat that they identify, they do so under a variety of nomenclatures, and they have no means to compel victims to admit to their failures in security operations. Many targeted companies refuse to share the full details of their breaches, making further intrusions against other institutions, possibly using the same methods and even the same software, far more likely. For its part, the U.S. government has a tendency to place the highest level of secret classification upon virtually every aspect of cyber operations, meaning that organizations tasked with cyber security often cannot communicate effectively with one another about their operations. This emphasis upon secrecy does little to keep the cyber opponent out of classified systems, but it certainly contributes to slowing down effective cyber responses.

Cyber Ethics

Interestingly, in some ways, cyber warfare may have the potential to be the most ethical form of warfare devised by humanity (Brenner 2009, 45–55). The basis of ethics in military activity essentially comes down to two factors, proportionality and discrimination, both proposed by Dutch jurist Hugo de Grotius in his seventeenth-century works, *Jus Ad Bello* and *Jus In Bello*. The principle of proportionality states that for any enemy action, the ethical response should be at approximately the same level of violence and destruction. Thus, a small border incursion, even by an armed party, is not sufficient to provoke an invasion and occupation of an enemy state, as the response would be completely out of proportion to the original offense. Discrimination is the idea that there are legitimate and illegitimate targets in warfare, most easily conceived as combatants and noncombatants, and warring states have an obligation to target only combatants and to minimize the risk to noncombatants as much as possible. Even if a key enemy leader is known to be hiding within a village, it would be indiscriminate to level the village and kill all of its inhabitants in order to eliminate the leader.

Of course, both proportionality and discrimination can present significant problems in practice. For example, a state may not have the ability to respond in kind to every enemy provocation. Weaker states may not be able to dish out the same level of punishment that they receive, but that does not give them a free pass to start wars with stronger powers, content that the enemy will limit its activities to keep the conflict fair. Determining what can be considered proportionate can also be problematic. In a limited conflict, both sides may agree, explicitly or implicitly, to restrict their actions and their objectives. In a war of national survival, however, the limits on behaviors tend to be quickly discarded, as no state is under an obligation to lose a war solely to maintain the principle of proportionality. In World War II, the Imperial Japanese Navy managed to launch a highly successful surprise attack at Pearl Harbor, killing approximately 3,000 American citizens in the process, most of them sailors in the U.S. Navy. Less than four years later, the U.S. Army Air Force dropped two atomic bombs on Hiroshima and Nagasaki, killing over 100,000 Japanese civilians in the process. These attacks culminated an aerial firebombing campaign that leveled virtually every Japanese city, killing hundreds of thousands and leaving millions more homeless. The American bombardment campaigns have often been criticized in the intervening 70 years, but rarely on the grounds of proportionality.

Discrimination has also always presented significant problems. In war, belligerents rarely agree to fight all of their battles in open fields far away from any civilian population centers. Rather, armies go where they will, and take shelter in virtually any potential location, including in heavily populated urban centers. Attackers usually do not call off their advances solely on the basis that enemy civilians might be in the vicinity. Likewise, all weapons have a limit to their precision, and preventing all civilian casualties is an impossible, and arguably inadvisable, goal. While it sounds nice in theory, in practice, were a belligerent to announce that it would not risk killing enemy civilians, every opponent would potentially choose to use its own civilian population as human shields, or worse, would simply dress its entire army in civilian garb, gaining a tremendous military advantage in the process.

Cyber attacks, unlike any other form of wartime activity, theoretically can be programmed to be as precise as a software creator can envision. Any form of command might be included in malware code to ensure that the notions of proportionality and discrimination were both followed. The Stuxnet attack upon the Iranian nuclear facilities at Natanz demonstrates these principles. Compared with the potential damage that might be created by a kinetic attack, either by bombs dropped from aircraft or by cruise missiles, the Stuxnet worm managed to inflict the same level of damage without killing or injuring any humans, and without damaging the actual structure of the facility (Poroshyn 2013, 48–50). Thus, it was a far more proportionate and rational response to the Iranian nuclear ambitions than a preemptive military strike. At the same time, it had a much greater psychological effect upon its victims, who would certainly have noticed if bombs and missiles began exploding at their research laboratory, but who did not realize they were under cyber attack. Instead, they began to consider themselves incompetent at relatively basic scientific and engineering tasks, given that they did not seem to be able to install and operate even the most basic of industrial equipment without continual failures.

Stuxnet was an extremely discriminate and, one could argue, considerate piece of malware (Rosenzweig 2013, 10–12). While the worm was found on hundreds of thousands of machines outside of the targeted facilities, the only thing that it could do on those machines was to propagate itself in the hope of reaching the correct target. Stuxnet's creators even programmed a specific limit into the number of times that the program could copy itself, thus preventing a massive, uncontrollable expansion that might have created an inadvertent risk to networks as a whole, even if each machine was completely safe. Further, the program included a self-destruction order, whereby it erased itself at a prearranged date, July 24, 2012, further minimizing the chance of causing any accidental damage (Gross 2011). Of course, both of these measures also served to help the virus remain undetected, and thus it could be argued that they were added for the benefit of Stuxnet's creators, not to protect cyber noncombatants from harm.

References

Arquilla, John, and David Ronfeldt. 1996. *The Advent of Netwar*. Santa Monica, CA: RAND Corporation.

Barbier, Mary Kathryn. 2009. *D-Day Deception: Operation Fortitude and the Normandy Invasion*. Mechanicsburg, PA: Stackpole Books.

Blane, John V., ed. 2002. *Cyberwarfare: Terror at a Click*. New York: Novinka Books.

Bowden, Mark. 2011. *Worm: The First Digital World War*. New York: Atlantic Monthly Press.

Brenner, Joel. 2011. *America the Vulnerable: Inside the New Threat Matrix of Digital Espionage, Crime, and Warfare*. New York: Penguin Press.

Brenner, Susan W. 2009. *Cyberthreats: The Emerging Fault Lines of the Nation State*. New York: Oxford University Press.

Brodie, Bernard. 1959. *Strategy in the Missile Age*. Princeton, NJ: Princeton University Press.

Bucci, Steven. 2012. "Joining Cybercrime and Cyberterrorism: A Likely Scenario." In *Cyberspace and National Security: Threats, Opportunities, and Power in a Virtual World*, edited by Derek S. Reveron. Washington, DC: Georgetown University Press.

Carr, Jeffrey. 2009. *Inside Cyber Warfare: Mapping the Cyber Underworld*. Sebastopol, CA: O'Reilly Media.

Clarke, Richard A., and Robert K. Knake. 2010. *Cyber War: The Next Great Threat to National Security and What to Do about It*. New York: HarperCollins.

Darnton, Geoffrey. 2006. "Information Warfare and the Laws of War." In *Cyberwar, Netwar and the Revolution in Military Affairs*, edited by Edward Halpin, Philippa Trevorrow, David Webb, and Steve Wright. New York: Palgrave Macmillan.

Greenwald, Glen. 2014. *No Place to Hide: Edward Snowden, the NSA, and the U.S. Surveillance State.* New York: Metropolitan Books.

Gross, Michael Joseph. 2011. "A Declaration of Cyber-War." *Vanity Fair*, April 2011. Retrieved from http://www.vanityfair.com/culture/features/2011/04/Stuxnet-201104.

Gurnow, Michael. 2014. *The Edward Snowden Affair: Exposing the Politics and Media behind the NSA Scandal.* Indianapolis, IN: Blue River Press.

Johnson-Freese, Joan. 2009. *Heavenly Ambitions: America's Quest to Dominate Space.* Philadelphia: University of Pennsylvania Press.

Kahn, Herman. 1962. *Thinking about the Unthinkable.* New York: Horizon Press.

Libicki, Martin C. 2007. *Conquest in Cyberspace: National Security and Information Warfare.* New York: Cambridge University Press.

Libicki, Martin C. 2009. *Cyberdeterrence and Cyberwar.* Santa Monica, CA: RAND Corporation.

Libicki, Martin C. 2012. *Crisis and Escalation in Cyberspace.* Santa Monica, CA: RAND Corporation.

Panetta, Leon. 2012. "Remarks on Cybersecurity." October 11, 2012. Retrieved from http://www.defense.gov/transcripts/transcript.aspx?transcriptid=5136.

Poroshyn, Roman. 2013. *Stuxnet: The True Story of Hunt and Evolution.* Denver, CO: Outskirts Press.

Putrich, Gayle. 2014. "Defense Budget Zeroes in on Cyber Spending." *FCW*, March 4, 2014. Retrieved from http://fcw.com/Articles/2014/03/04/budget-defense.aspx?p=1.

Reveron, Derek S., ed. 2012. *Cyberspace and National Security: Threats, Opportunities, and Power in a Virtual World.* Washington, DC: Georgetown University Press.

Rid, Thomas. 2013. *Cyber War Will Not Take Place.*
New York: Oxford University Press.

Rosenzweig, Paul. 2013. *Cyber Warfare: How Conflicts in Cyberspace Are Challenging America and Changing the World.* Santa Barbara, CA: Praeger Security International.

Schiller, Craig A., Jim Binkley, David Harley, Gadi Evron, Tony Bradley, Carsten Willems, and Michael Cross, eds. 2007. *Botnets: The Killer Web App.* Canada: Syngness Publishing.

Singer, P. W., and Allan Friedman. 2014. *Cybersecurity and Cyberwar.* New York: Oxford University Press.

Siroli, Gian Piero. 2006. "Strategic Information Warfare: An Introduction." In *Cyberwar, Netwar, and the Revolution in Military Affairs,* edited by Edward Halpin, Philippa Trevorrow, David Webb, and Steve Wright. New York: Palgrave Macmillan.

Stiennon, Richard. 2010. *Surviving Cyber War.* Lanham, MD: Government Institutes.

Van Creveld, Martin. 1999. *The Rise and Decline of the State.* New York: Cambridge University Press.

Ventre, Daniel, ed. 2011. *Cyberwar and Information Warfare.* Hoboken, NJ: John Wiley & Sons.

"Worst Insult to the United States in Its History." 1898. *New York Journal,* February 9, 1898.

KEEP
CALM
AND
CYBER
ON

CDX

Proxy Server

3   Perspectives

These selections offer five viewpoints on pressing issues regarding cyberspace. Dr. Martin Libicki, a senior research analyst for the RAND Corporation, is widely regarded as one of the foremost cyber theorists in the world. He has examined the issues of attribution, signaling, and cyber deterrence in his works on cyber conflict. Here, he offers perspectives on the unique challenges presented by escalation of a crisis in cyberspace. Dr. Nicholas Sambaluk teaches at the United States Military Academy in West Point, New York. In this essay, he examines efforts by the U.S. Department of Defense to develop cyber-minded officers for the U.S. Army, beginning with their undergraduate education. Dr. S. Michael Pavelec of the Joint Advanced Warfighting School in Norfolk, Virginia, continues on Sambaluk's theme by investigating whether the military does an adequate job of creating cyber warriors through the Professional Military Education system, the process of higher education for mid-career and senior-level officers. Major Heidi Dexter of the U.S. Air Force, a product of PME education, demonstrates the type of analysis that military officers make regarding emerging threats as she examines the ways that terror organizations have made use of cyber resources to facilitate their activities. Major Brian Tannehill, also of the U.S. Air Force, has spent most of his

U.S. Military Academy cadets participate in the 2014 Cyber Defense Exercise. These cadets helped create a computer network that is under attack by experts from the National Security Agency and the Department of Defense. (AP Photo/Mel Evans) *career working with space platforms, and demonstrates the unique relationship between those assets and the cyber domain.*

Escalation in Cyberspace[*]

Martin Libicki

The need to manage conflict escalation in cyberspace arises if one party attacks another in cyberspace and the latter wants to respond, or when two parties are in conflict in the physical world and one side wishes to alarm or cripple another by an attack on its systems and infrastructure.

The primary motives for escalation in cyberspace are similar to those in the physical world: to gain an advantage in conflict, to signal seriousness, to demonstrate power and capability, or to test the temper of opponents. Similarly, the basic reason for managing—basically, limiting—escalation is to avoid suffering the consequences of uncontrolled conflict. That noted, there is little agreement on how damaging unlimited cyber attacks may be. The Defense Science Board, for instance, believes they can be bad enough to warrant a nuclear response (there are comparably apocalyptic Chinese and Russian sources). Yet, so far, no one has died from a cyber attack, and Stuxnet remains unique as the only cyber attack to have broken something. However, what starts in cyberspace may not, after sufficient escalation, end in cyberspace.

Escalation risks look different in crisis as opposed to conflict. In a crisis, some cyber operations, if done properly and hence discretely, ought not to excite reaction: e.g., increasing defenses, accelerating cyber espionage, or inserting implants to prepare the target for further instructions. Other activities, such as demonstrating offensive capabilities or stifling contentious

---

[*]This essay is adapted from Martin Libicki, *Crisis and Escalation in Cyberspace* (Santa Monica, CA: RAND Corporation, 2013).

communications channels, are inevitably or deliberately public, and hence present some escalation risks.

In a conflict, the operational use of cyber attacks to cripple a capability (e.g., an air defense radar) that otherwise would merit kinetic attack should not, by rights, present escalation risks. Whether it does so depends on what the other side thinks. If others deem cyber attacks somehow illegitimate, they may feel themselves justified in reacting to the manner of the attack rather than its effects. Yet, because networks are not necessarily confined to within combat zones, the effects of a cyber attack on military systems may breach the bounds that both sides have observed in order to localize the conflict. Other escalation risks may be associated with deliberate attacks on systems with civilian uses. Attacks that persuade the other side that its command and control over regime-critical systems (e.g., instruments of police repression) or strategic systems (e.g., nuclear) is at risk may be warranted, but the other side could react disproportionately. Likewise, attacks on what may be deemed strategic targets may lead to inferences about what the attacker's real goals in the conflict are; this alone may lead to escalation by the other if convinced that the rules have changed.

Once in a conflict, the natural (and in important ways, validated) approach to managing escalation is tit-for-tat (often called "intrawar deterrence"): one side's escalation is met by the others so that the side that crossed the line is reminded why the line was there in the first place. Yet, the extension of such a strategy to cyberspace is problematic.

One reason why is that the environment of cyberspace is so noisy that there may be a mismatch between what they think they did and how they think you responded. Their perceptions of damage to you may not equal your perception. Your notion of equivalence may not match theirs. The effects of your response may match what you intended to do, and their perception of the effect may be different from the actual damage. A response could therefore be perceived as underwhelming or overwhelming vis-à-vis the initial trigger because of these many serial uncertainties.

A second reason is that cyber attacks, particularly against hard targets, require considerable scoping. If the other side hits a set of previously off-limits targets, unless one has scoped targets of theirs that you had considered off limits, the ability to strike them *effectively* may be diminished perhaps to where the former's escalation will be perceived as unanswered.

A third reason, common to all escalation but probably exaggerated in cyber war, is that the effective communication of limits via retaliation require some agreement on what the red lines are. If we attack their afloat naval supply capability and they respond by attacking, say, Guam's port systems, we may perceive that they escalated to an attack on our homeland, but they may think that both of them were attacks on military support systems. If we respond by going after one of their ports, we may think that we responded in kind, but they may consider this an escalation from attacks on military support to attacks on their civilian infrastructure. And so on.

The fourth reason, again common to kinetic warfare but probably worse in cyber war, is inadvertent escalation; perhaps our attack on the military side of their port-management software resulted in shutting down their civilian side as well.

A fifth reason to be cautious about using tit-for-tat with any precision is the possibility that either side's civilian vigilantes will take it upon themselves to touch hitherto sacrosanct targets: something difficult to imagine in a high-intensity military conflict, but not so hard to imagine in cyberspace.

One conclusion is that the process of two-side escalation will look nothing like Herman Kahn's hypothesized series of incremental steps. It is likely to be sudden, jerky, and could easily get out of hand faster than either side intends. How much that matters is another question, though.

If a tit-for-tat policy would do more good than harm, each or both sides need to hold their fire until they have the opportunity for a clean shot. The side that needs to be persuaded not to escalate matters (lest it find itself being hit back with worse) must believe that:

- it will be blamed for the cyber attack;
- the target of its attack has the means to retaliate;
- the target has the will to retaliate;
- if it does *not* cross a boundary, it will *neither* face escalation *nor* lose face;
- retaliatory escalation has no compelling rationale; and
- the red lines in question are well defined, and fair (and thus do not favor the other side).

This is a nontrivial list.

Those who would retaliate must pay some mind to how *others*, including third parties, will make inferences about the retaliator. Here are some:

- The retaliating country detected and attributed the attack correctly.
- It *can* escalate.
- It *would* escalate.
- It was sufficiently hurt or embarrassed by the instigating attack.
- It does not like risking casualties by responding kinetically.

If the instigating attack was of doubtful origin or the retaliation was disproportionate, the retaliator might look like a bully. Conversely, a state that failed to respond may allow the reverse inferences to be made.

Third-party involvement can also plague the management of escalation, or more broadly, the management of any serious conflict in cyberspace. Third parties can create crises in wartime in ways unavailable in peacetime. If good escalation management requires controlling third parties, the prospect may become hopeless.

Attribution remains nontrivial, even if in a conflict. One would think that if two countries and two countries alone were at war, knowing who raised the *ante* would be easy (i.e., the other guy). But would it? Take, say, a confrontation between the United States and Iran following the failure of current nuclear negotiations. At first one can imagine a simple contest among the two, with the United States adding cyber attacks to the many ways that it can economically pressure Iran, and Iran countering with annoying attacks on the United States to make the point that acting against Iran is not costless. But would Iran stop there? It might decide to harass the UK, a country Iran keeps thinking is conspiring against it. Israel's involvement would have sufficient cause and ample precedent. The Gulf States may also want to keep Iran off balance for sectarian reasons of their own. Russia and China could easily sit out this conflict, but if they think they can test how the U.S. military responds to a cyber attack while believing that they can escape blame because the United States would likely assume that Iran did it, what is to lose? Incidentally, if U.S. intelligence sources divined that an attack thought to be of Iranian origin actually came from a superpower, the path of prudence for the United States may be to pretend it did not, particularly if no one else suspects as much. In such a mess, would either the United States or Iran inhibit itself on the theory that the cyber battlefield would lay bare who did what, and thus who would be punished?

A parallel set of problems arises when a superpower decides to use cyber attacks to help one side in a conflict—and even more so when the other side in a conflict also has superpower friends. If the targets of such cyber attacks are the local systems of the local adversary, the potential for escalation may be modest. But if the local systems have privileged access to the systems of its superpower friend—or if these local systems are actually part of the superpower's systems—then such attacks suddenly become attacks between superpowers. The latter carries considerable escalation potential. Hence the problem of how to ensure that each superpower can carefully delineate what is local to the conflict (and hence a target) and what is global (and hence not a target without serious thought).

Finally, the prospect of escalation calls into question the current command-and-control arrangements in which cyber warriors report to CYBERCOM/STRATCOM and not to the regional commanders. Understandable reasons underlie the reluctance to hand over one-time-use-only exploits to regional commanders. But a regional COCOM responsible for both prevailing and managing escalation in distant conflicts has to be able to regulate the use of cyber weapons whose effects may lead to unwanted escalation.

Conclusions

The potential for escalation in cyberspace may not be the most consequential risk in war but it may be one of the trickier ones. Countries should also take the time to consider escalation carefully and abjure the use of tit-for-tat techniques unless and until the other side's reaction to escalation in cyberspace is well understood.

Martin Libicki (PhD, University of California, Berkeley, 1978) has been a senior management scientist at RAND since 1998, focusing on the impacts of information technology on domestic and national security. He wrote two commercially published books, Conquest in Cyberspace: National Security and Information Warfare, *and* Information Technology Standards: Quest for the Common Byte *and numerous monographs, notably* Crisis and Escalation in Cyberspace, Global Demographic Change and its Implications for Military Power, Cyber-deterrence and Cyberwar, How Insurgencies End *(with Ben Connable),* How Terrorist Groups End *(with Seth Jones), and (as editor)* New Challenges New Tools for Defense Decision-making. *His prior employment includes 12 years at the National Defense University, three years on the Navy staff as program sponsor for industrial preparedness, and three years for the GAO.*

He has also received a master's degree in city planning from UC-Berkeley (1974).

Training Tomorrow's Cyber Warriors

Nicholas Michael Sambaluk

Energy and vigor characterizes the way that the Army, like the other branches of the armed forces, is approaching the education of tomorrow's cyber warriors. To be effective, education and training must be promoted by field grade officers and officer instructors, its organization must be facilitated and nurtured by top-ranking leaders, and it must be pursued by future officers themselves. Some officers are voicing analysis of cyber issues, and institutionally the Army has established its research node where it can have the most concentrated impact on the future officer corps. These developing leaders are engaged with the issues, questions, and realities of cyber security. The effort is a collaborative one, and it is an important first step, vital for a dynamic and potent realm.

Cyber security questions are beginning to receive growing attention in the service journals such as *Strategic Studies Quarterly* and *Parameters*. This encourages greater awareness and dialogue amongst some field grade officers. It also reflects interest by people who include uniformed and civilian faculty at the service academies. For example, the Spring 2014 issue of *Strategic Studies Quarterly* ran three articles on cyber topics, one authored by a visiting professor at the United States Naval Academy questioning the applicability of "grand strategy" to cyber warfare. In another article, retired Air Force lieutenant colonel Martin Stytz (now at Georgetown University) and computer engineer Sheila Banks outlined their vision for improving cyber security. Technologically, this involves a shift from a perimeter concept to a "dynamic layered cyber defense" and is in keeping with other recommendations and insights in this field (Stytz and Banks 2014, 56).

Stytz and Banks also commented on effective training of cyber defenders, who should "expect their tactical defenses to be breached." Defenders will need to be able to cope successfully with psychological stress, know that incomplete or inaccurate information is a part of the Clausewitzian friction inherent in warfare, and overcome factors like expectation biases or loss/risk aversions that could otherwise hinder U.S. efforts to maintain cyber dominance (Stytz and Banks, 2014, 58). In short, practice through realistic simulations will be an integral part of training capable cyber defenders, whether these people wear uniforms or are civilian. The line dividing the military (U.S. Code, Title 10) from the intelligence and covert entities (U.S. Code, Title 50) engaging in cyber security efforts is itself a point of discussion. Authors in the Winter 2013–2014 issue of *Parameters* argued for the separation of the military Cyber Command from the National Security Agency (NSA). Asserting that cyber tools and methods are "not an instrument of the weak or the strong," but instead "an instrument—period," they stressed the need to build a robust ability to wage cyber operations (Cilluffo and Clark, 2014, 113).

Interest in normalizing the military's role, participation, and authority in the defensive and offensive applications of cyber is logical. To help pioneer its cyber efforts, the U.S. Army established a multidisciplinary entity to research the arena and develop both ideas and Army talent. Envisioned to include over 120 specialists from an array of fields applicable to different aspects of the cyber challenge, Army planners knew that this office would need to be located in a unique environment leveraging diverse experience, perspectives, and skills. The idea, propounded by U.S. Army chief of staff General Ray Odierno, was to establish military, industrial, and civilian government partners to study war to "provid[e] cyber security and cyber operations advice and consultation, research, and education." The Army Cyber Institute (ACI), was established at the United States Military Academy, West Point, in 2013.

Cyber is not a new topic for U.S. armed forces academies. Since 2000, the NSA has sponsored a Cyber Defense Exercise, with participants including the Army, Navy, Air Force, Coast Guard, and Merchant Marine academies as well as the Air Force Institute of Technology, the Naval Postgraduate School, and the Royal Military College of Canada; participants seek to secure cyber communications from simulated hacking attacks. But West Point's ACI is going a step further for Army cyber education.

Placing ACI at West Point marked a significant decision with two distinct and valuable dividends. First, starting in the relatively immediate term, the personnel who constitute ACI work beside a veritable phalanx of energetic and thought-provoking peers who are committed full-time to teaching cadets. The connection between ACI cadre and peers strengthens both groups. Second, in an even more enduring sense, siting ACI at West Point means that four thousand future Army officers are in close proximity to the Army's leading hub for cyber research.

ACI's location at West Point lets its personnel teach some sections of cadet classes—in electrical engineering, in social science, in law, in history, and other respective fields. The Air Force Academy and the Naval Academy have each established centers for cyber research to promote cadet education, but ACI leads the Army's cyber research, and cadets can participate in that process. Interested and capable West Point cadets have an opportunity to be part of major research projects. Cadets, through their senior thesis projects, frequently support larger objectives of interest to the Army. Cadets learn while further developing the country's cyber capability.

Already, some cadet senior theses are turning ambitiously toward sophisticated studies of cyber security issues. In the spring of 2014, several cadets presented research into technical, organizational, and policy applications and techniques. One group of cadets presented research titled "The Army Cyber Officer: Defining the Role." Dovetailing with current expert opinion, they advocated clarification of Title 10 and Title 50 responsibilities and they commented favorably on the likely long-term impact of establishing a 16th Army branch, devoted to cyber activity. The cadets asserted that the best long-term approach for gaining cyber defenders involved identifying young people interested in service who also showed an aptitude in STEM (science, technology, engineering, and mathematics) study and in electronics during middle and high school.

As Cadet Matthew Welch emphasized, cyber officers need to be "innovative, disciplined, and ethical" (Dixon, St. Pierre, Washington, and Welch, 2014). This is a particularly important issue, identified in the wake of deliberate leaks by individuals such as Edward Snowden. The need for trustworthy defenders is not as unprecedented as it is sometimes presumed to be (Andress and Winterfeld 2014, 100). One advantage of multidisciplinary teams such as ACI is the ability to benefit from historical insight, technical familiarity, and legal expertise to know what is new, what is possible, and what is practicable. Cadets, who are routinely vetted for security clearances, have a ringside seat in this process—and they have a chance to have a seat at the table.

The path forward is a complex one. As cyber historian Jason Healey has observed, "historical lessons [about cyber security] derived from past cases are still relevant today" (Healey 2013, 85). Martin Libicki of RAND suggests that "by its very nature, cyber war has to continually morph to retain its relevance" (Libicki 2014, 37). While that is undoubtedly correct, it is axiomatic in a sense that transcends more than cyber activity. Warfare is dynamic, because it is an interaction of opponents who know that acting predictably can be a roadmap to defeat. Chris Demchak observed that resilience in the face of cyber threats requires trial and error and an "endorsement of long-run, slow, steady results" and the capacity to innovate (Demchak 2011, 173). By combining the value of the multidisciplinary approach to cyber with an institutional tie to the Army's service academy and its cadets, ACI is pioneering a new model for building cyber-savvy defenders. In preparing tomorrow's cyber warriors, the tenets of innovation continue to be valuable, as the academies and the services that they support move to advance into new cyber territory.

Nicholas Sambaluk is a professor of practice in military science and technology, under a dual appointment between Purdue University and the Army Cyber Institute at West Point. His first book is The Other Space Race: Eisenhower and Space Security *(Naval Institute Press, 2015).*

Cyber Warfare in the Professional Military Education System

S. Michael Pavelec

Cyber technology is a new capability that has been implemented across the globe. Within the United States, cyber networks monitor, maintain, and manage our daily lives from money transactions to traffic control to information transfer. But as with any new technology, it has taken the military time to develop doctrine and written strategy to comprehend and employ cyber effectively and efficiently. Furthermore, as compared to military hardware systems, the danger and benefit of cyber is that it has permeated daily life of the entire American society—government, military, and civilian alike. In an effort to increase data transfer and information access, the U.S. military relies heavily on cyber technology daily. Thus, it is important for the military to be able to protect its cyber capabilities so that it can continue to function. In 2014, few can envision society or a military that does not have access to functioning cyber capabilities.

In 2006, the U.S. Air Force formalized the importance of the cyber domain and attempted to create a "cyber command" to unify the management of high-technology information systems for the military. Based on its familiarity with high-technology systems, the Air Force was convinced that it was the correct branch for oversight. However, the secretary of defense thought otherwise, realizing that cyber was important to all the branches, and in 2008 established USCYBERCOM under U.S. Strategic Command. USCYBERCOM has direct oversight over all .mil networks, both unclassified (NIPRNet) and classified (SIPRNet). The Department of Homeland Security was given jurisdiction over all .gov accounts.

USCYBERCOM is in charge of protecting all military computers and the information pathways that communicate vast amounts of data that move throughout the military's cyber domain. USCYBERCOM's procedures are mostly defensive and reactive; they concentrate on keeping the information flowing between authorized users and denying unauthorized attackers. It is estimated that there are as many as 10 million cyber attacks on the Department of Defense daily (Center for Strategic and International Studies 2010). In response, the DoD has increased the budget for USCYBERCOM to $4.7 billion for FY 2014. In addition, DoD employees have seen increased levels of security and layers of protection including personalized access cards and complicated password protection, multiple layers of firewalls and blocking mechanisms, and heavy network monitoring. These measures slow the rate of information transfer, but ostensibly keep the network safe from prying information thieves. In the past few years, USCYBERCOM has started to go on the offensive, counterattacking cyber pirates.

But the question remains: Is the U.S. military dealing effectively with threats in the cyber domain, and are they using the technology to its best advantage? As to the threats, there is an undercurrent of dissent within the military about how to best use cyber to counter threats. As with most technology, the older generations of leaders at the highest levels do not have a real grasp of the potential abilities and limitations of the technology. Many mid-level officers have opined that the cyber domain is important enough for its own branch, equal to the Army, Navy, and Air Force. Colonel Robert Costa, USAF, argued in a 2002 Air Command and Staff College thesis that

"[Information] has proven to be the most vulnerable, even as US society becomes more dependent on it in peace, conflict, and war. To attack these centers of gravity, an adversary will use the weakest decisive point, ... the Information IOP (Instruments of Power)." He continues, "The Information IOP however, is rudderless, lacking both Unity of Action and Unity of Command" (Costa 2002). He argued that for the best results for both offensive and defensive capabilities, there should be a separate branch of the military dedicated to the cyber domain. A dedicated U.S. military presence in cyberspace may make the entire network more resilient and safe, but brings up issues of privacy and censorship; the American public would likely be resistant to overwhelming military presence on the Internet.

To exploit the benefits and overcome the limitations of the cyber domain, it may be in American national security interests for the military to take a more active role. But this may also mean that traditional qualifications for manpower may be dated. Most cyber warriors are young, independent, and highly intelligent, but few will pass the existing physical qualifications currently required by the U.S. military. In short, they will not fit the mold of modern American warriors. Further, they will likely be resistant to existing hierarchical military structure, and may have financial incentives to seek employment outside of the military.

One key way to enhance the U.S. military's abilities in the cyber domain is through education. At every level in Joint Professional Military Education (JPME), there is increasing emphasis on understanding the technology and educating personnel on the threats. From Computer Based Training for computer security to lectures and lessons on the cyber domain, instructors have focused on basic information regarding cyber capabilities. Unfortunately, there is not a great deal of scholarship on the topic, and there are very few experts who possess the security clearances to access all of the current data. It is a growing field, but there is little crossover from traditional academia to the high-technology field. Most of the officers who deal with the cyber domain in their daily lives are required to learn on the job and maintain strict secrecy about U.S. capabilities and efforts. It is ironic that a technology that is supposed to offer swift transfer of information and transparency is shrouded in so much secrecy.

In my opinion, as a faculty member who has taught at a number of different JPME institutions, there is a wide variety of instruction on the topic within the military. At the School of Advanced Air and Space Studies (SAASS), the Air Force's top strategy school, 45 officers are given a three-week course on the theory of cyber dominance and control. At the other end of the spectrum are the rest of the JPME institutions, who offer only a few days on theory and practice. Most of the schools within the DoD system adhere to regulations by at least talking about the topic, but few provide more than a cursory examination of the theory, practice, or capabilities of cyber. In all cases, actual capabilities and DoD operations are held in strict confidence, known only to those in USCYBERCOM and trusted colleagues in the Pentagon. Security requirements hide the reality of cyberspace, while theorists and academics can only guess at capabilities and operations. Invariably, it is only with time that people find out what events are happening in the cyber domain, when revelations of cyber attacks are exposed. One example is the Stuxnet computer virus, sent to Iran to cripple their nuclear centrifuges in summer 2010. Six months after it damaged Iranian equipment, the public found out about the cyber attack; four years later, there is still only speculation in the general public as to who wrote the code and introduced the virus to the Iranian systems.

U.S. military commanders must understand that the cyber domain is an all-pervasive technology that is integrated into every aspect of both civilian and military life. Cyber technology is a Kuhnian paradigm shift, from which information-age societies will never revert, barring massive existential warfare. Military commanders will have to understand the benefits and drawbacks of the technology, and what it can do. Their staffs will have to include officers who know how cyber works, to secure systems and ensure redundancy to maintain system security and stability. At the highest levels, whether USCYBERCOM is subordinate or independent, the U.S. military needs intelligent people who understand cyber power and can manipulate the domain for American strategic advantage. We are not yet there; more effort is needed now.

Cyber power and the cyber domain will continue to be an increasingly pervasive technology for U.S. domestic and military capabilities. The military relies on the cyber domain for the transfer of information, command, and control. From e-mails and presentations to flying unmanned aerial vehicles on the other side of the world, the U.S. military must strive to protect the transfer of information throughout its networks. It will require education on the importance of the domain, passive defenses for protection, and active measures to counter cyber attacks. Maintaining the capability and freedom of action in the cyber domain are important today and will be increasingly important into the future. The U.S. military has begun to perceive the importance of the cyber domain and has taken the first steps to safeguard capabilities, but there will have to be dedicated effort and money allocated to secure the cyber domain against all threats, foreign and domestic. American reliance on the technology will only increase; it will be the job of the U.S. military to ensure the safety of DoD networks and the cyber domain.

Dr. S. Mike Pavelec was recruited to JAWS after teaching at the Naval War College, Air Command and Staff College, and the School of Advanced Air and Space Studies (SAASS). He received his PhD from Ohio State University in 2004 and teaches graduate-level courses in military and diplomatic history, international relations, and security studies. As of this writing, he had three books in print and three under contract and was writing a survey of American military history for publication in 2015. His follow-on project is on airpower in World War I, with a focus on the Gallipoli campaign. His passion is motorcycles.

Waging e-Jihad

Heidi L. Dexter

On October 11, 2012, Defense Secretary Leon Panetta warned of the possibility of a "cyber Pearl Harbor" should an aggressor nation or extremist group gain control of critical switches or infrastructure (Panetta 2012). Panetta described an attack as more destructive than 9/11, one that could cause devastation across the country with derailed trains, spilled chemicals, contaminated water, and widespread power outages; but is an extremist group capable of conducting an attack critical infrastructure through cyberterrorism? (Panetta 2012) Cyberterrorism, defined as using "technology to bring about political, religious, or ideological aims, actions that result in disabling or deleting critical infrastructure data or information," is a growing concern for the United States, but the extremist groups are not yet sophisticated enough to manipulate critical data (Tafoya 2011). Rather, they use the cyberspace to solicit funds, communicate, recruit and indoctrinate new members, reconnoiter for future attacks, and brag about successes. A catastrophic cyber attack requires advanced technological knowledge to hack into and manipulate a well-protected system. This scenario would currently require a partnership between a terrorist group and a rogue hacking group, or well-funded and well-equipped nation-state.

One of the primary ways terrorists exploit the Internet is to raise funds to conduct operations. This is done by directly soliciting funds, or through credit card fraud, often referred to as carding. "Cybercrime has now surpassed international drug trafficking as a terrorist financing enterprise" (Theohary and Rollins 2011). Imam Samudra, an Indonesian terrorist executed in 2008 for his role in the 2003 Bali nightclub bombing, used carding as a means to fund his attacks (Sipress 2004). In his autobiography, "Samudra urges fellow Muslim radicals to take the holy war into cyberspace by attacking U.S. computers, with the particular aim of committing credit card fraud"

(Sipress 2004). He was reported to be extremely technologically savvy and adept at programming in several languages. However, though he had grandiose ideas about penetrating vulnerable American networks, he was only successful in causing relatively minor damage to the U.S. public, and did not impact critical infrastructure at all.

Terrorists are aware that their correspondence and activities are being closely monitored. Osama bin Laden was extremely paranoid and lived mostly off the grid in an effort to evade U.S. forces, but relied on e-mail to communicate with his top leaders. To keep his e-mails from identifying his location, he did not have Internet access at his compound, and communicated though e-mails saved to thumb drives and sent by couriers in Internet cafés (Stanglin 2011). Even when messages were intercepted, U.S. forces were able only to trace the links to the café. E-mail is not the only method of communicating across the Internet, and terrorists have evolved to become more adept at covert communication. Web chat through multiplayer online video games allows terrorists the ability to communicate in real time with a relative amount of anonymity. These chat sessions take place in real time, and voice data are not recorded, making detection and monitoring incredibly difficult. "Extremists choose realistic 'first person' conflict games because they can disguise their discussions as harmless web chat. In the games, players work through a complex simulation of war scenarios, carrying out missions and battling enemy fighters" (Willetts and Wells 2012). Differentiating between planning a simulated attack for the game and an actual attack could be incredibly difficult.

Another way terrorist organizations evade messages from being monitored is through a technique known as electronic dead dropping. Spies have been using dead dropping for many years; exchanging information at a prearranged location, which prevents the parties from having to meet face to face. Electronic dead dropping puts a modern twist on this age-old technique. Using this method, geographically separated people can communicate with a smaller chance of being monitored by drafting a message on an e-mail account known to both parties. The message is then left in the draft folder or placed in the deleted folder for the second person to access. Electronically sending the information to another address through multiple mail servers would allow the possibility for a third party to intercept it, but dead dropping allows the information to be stored on only the server where it was originally drafted. This method can also be used to electronically store information a terrorist does not wish to carry for fear it will incriminate him or divulge information if captured (*Daily News and Analysis* 2009). Dead dropping can be used through mail servers, or cloud computing through applications that allow a user to access documents from anywhere in the world with the correct login information.

Terrorists also use social media websites, forums, and blogs to recruit and indoctrinate members to their cause. Social media sites have "been employed by terrorist organizations to radicalize new recruits, deliver operational training and resources for the radicalized, raise funds, highlight successes, and shape public perception regarding ongoing hostilities" (Soufan Group 2012). Al Qaeda in the Arabian Peninsula (AQAP) uses a widespread electronic magazine titled *Inspire* to recruit new members and promote its message to a wider audience (Access ADL 2012). By publishing in English, *Inspire* focuses its recruiting on Westerners and targets populations at war with Muslims, specifically the United States, Britain, and France. Recent editions request stories from members on their successes against the West, posting deliberately inflammatory information to lay the framework of recruiting, urge others to action, or deliver a psychological blow to the American public. Terrorists post violent footage of recent attacks to highlight successes and recruit new members through clips that extol the virtues of martyrdom. Social networks can also be used to indoctrinate new members such as Jihad Jane, an American woman who posted messages on jihadist websites and chat rooms to facilitate terrorist attacks (Soufan Group 2012).

Social media sites often forbid explicit material, but moderators struggle to quickly identify and remove inappropriate material.

Technology has become so integrated with daily lives, as well as small and unobtrusive, that modern societies seem to disregard the constant monitoring. "Analog surveillance systems were difficult to hack into by people who lacked the adequate knowledge, but IP [Internet protocol] cameras ... can be quite easily physically located and their stream watched in real-time by anyone who has a modicum of computer knowledge" (Slashdot.org 2011). The abundance and unobtrusive nature of this technology can easily be exploited to a terrorist's advantage. A quick online search can help a novice hacker find a live view of an area and enable detailed reconnaissance without raising suspicion. In some extreme cases, the webcams are unsecured, allowing the viewer to pan, tilt, and zoom. This allows a would-be attacker to easily gather months of sensitive information from the privacy of their own home, determining what type of security measures are in place, how many guards are employed, times of shift change, peak hours, or to monitor ingress and egress routes. Anything that would have previously aroused suspicion if someone was continuously monitoring and gathering notes can now be done without detection (Connor 2011).

Successful cyber attacks by terrorist organizations have been mostly primitive denial of service (DoS) attacks and website defacement. DoS attacks flood the victim with thousands of requests that overload the server and render it incapable of processing requests. Though there may be limited loss of revenue while the server is offline, there is no kinetic damage inflicted. There are websites that provide information on how to conduct a DoS attack, or outsource to an online application to launch a low-level cyber attack (Theohary and Rollins 2011). In 2005, Scotland Yard arrested Younis Tsouli, who went by the handle "Irhabi007," Arabic for terrorist007, for conspiracy to commit murder and raising funds for terrorism. Tsouli was reportedly skilled at hacking and programming and maintained a large online presence through password-protected websites associated with Al Qaeda. He posted a message titled "Seminar for Hacking Websites" in an attempt to create "a network of technology-savvy terrorist disciples" (Kaplan 2009). However, Tsouli mostly posted videos with messages from key leaders and reports about recent activity of Al Qaeda in Iraq. Even with his reportedly advanced knowledge of computer systems and vulnerabilities, Tsouli's efforts succeeded in distributing information, not in executing attacks.

Should a skilled hacker become disgruntled enough to conduct cyberterrorism, it is possible that he could become a hacker-for-hire and assist a terrorist organization in conducting a cyber attack. The recent recruiting efforts in English aimed at well-educated Western men show this could be a valid concern. Additionally, as computers become more common and computer literacy spreads, the technical ability of new recruits will improve as well (Lachow 2009, 442–45). Recent reports show that terrorists in the Middle East and South Asia may be increasingly collaborating with cybercriminals (Theohary and Rollins 2011). Since terrorists do not currently possess the ability to conduct a sophisticated cyber attack, collaboration with hackers, cybercriminals, or nation-state sponsorship may be a logical approach to conducting cyberterrorism. A partnership is advantageous for the terrorist group because it would not require that they have the technical knowledge to develop or implement an attack. Similarly, this may be advantageous to the hacker or criminal who would be well paid for their skills, or the nation who would like to covertly attack American interests without fear of reprisal. However, cyber criminals rely on network infrastructure to conduct operations for financial gain, and thus seek not to be detected or to destroy equipment (Lachow 2009, 451–52).

The common belief among the security experts is that "it would take a dedicated and well-financed team several years of effort to prepare a truly serious strategic attack on

U.S. infrastructures" (Lachow 2009, 448). The question then becomes, why would they go through the effort? An obvious reason is the actual damage that could be inflicted to the U.S. infrastructure, the second-order impact to the economy, and psychological fear that would be inflicted from this large-scale attack. Attackers have not been successful in an attack on American soil since the strike on September 11, 2001. A successful cyber attack would not only inflict kinetic damage, it would be a successful psychological win for the terrorist in telling the American people that they are vulnerable and that an attack can come at any time, from anywhere.

Though terrorists have had incredible success using the Internet to raise funds, recruit, plan, and communicate, the ability to launch and sustain an attack against critical infrastructure remains beyond their capability. Increased collaboration with cyber criminals and recruiting better-educated members improve their technological ability, but any damage from an attack in the near future will be "comparable to that which takes place daily from Web site defacements, viruses and worms, and denial of service attacks. While the impact of these attacks can be serious, they are generally not regarded as acts of terrorism" (Lachow 2009, 448). Though terrorist groups do not possess the skills or equipment to conduct a large-scale cyberterrorist attack that is capable of widespread destruction, the Unites States should still look toward securing critical infrastructure systems from known vulnerabilities. "The Internet has presented investigators with an extraordinary challenge. But our future security is going to depend increasingly on identifying and catching the shadowy figures who exist primarily in the elusive online world" (Sipress 2004).

Major Heidi Dexter joined the U.S. Air Force two months before the September 11, 2001, attacks. She currently serves in the Internal Affairs division of the Secretary of the Air Force's office. As a holder of a certification in information systems protection and a certification as an ethical hacker, Major Dexter is keenly aware of the potential threats that cyberterrorists might pose, and the ways in which they currently utilize the Internet.

The Relationship between Space and Cyber Assets

Brian Tannehill

On Saturday, April 27, 1986, at 12:32 a.m., a hacker calling himself "Captain Midnight" devised a mechanism to jam Home Box Office's (HBO) signal for four and a half minutes. Instead of the intended programming, viewers were treated to a surprising message on their screens, stating "Good Evening HBO from Captain Midnight. $12.95/Month? No way! (Showtime/Movie Channel Beware!)" John MacDougal, the self-styled Captain Midnight, was protesting higher fees and scrambling equipment that was wiping out his locally owned satellite TV dealership in Florida. Earlier in the year, Home Box Office became the first pay TV service to scramble its signal full time, and other channel owners began to follow suit. MacDougal's business was dwindling, and as he says, "I was watching the great American dream slip from my grasp." To help supplement his income, he worked evenings part time at Central Florida Teleport, a company that uplinks television services to satellites. On April 26, at the end of his shift, MacDougal slewed the antenna into a position aimed at the Galaxy 1 Satellite, which carried HBO's signal, and transmitted his message. "It was the act of a frustrated individual who was trying to get his point across to people who didn't seem to listen" (NirvanaNet n.d.).

Fast forward 30 years and envision a scenario in which a high-altitude electromagnetic pulse (EMP) is triggered when a nuclear weapon explodes 250 miles above Washington, D.C. The pulse knocks out street lamps 800 miles away, and is seen as far away as 1,400 miles. The initial blast knocks out the majority of the 400+ orbiting satellites in low Earth orbit (LEO). Half of the GPS satellites in medium Earth orbits

(MEO) are wiped out, with the rest slowly decaying over the next 24 to 72 hours due to destruction of their solar arrays and electrical subsystems. Communication satellites in the highest orbit, geosynchronous (GEO), 22,000 nautical miles above Earth, are degraded severely as well, but only 25 percent of those are damaged, as the rest reside out of line of sight from the initial blast. The intense blaze of light acts as a dazzler, blinding all the optical sensors in the line of sight. At the same time, all Earth-based electronics at ground zero are wiped out. Cell towers and phones stop working, traffic signals fail, satellite TV is disrupted, ATMs stop dispensing cash, and power grids collapse. Essentially, every unshielded electronic device within 300 miles of Washington, D.C., is damaged or destroyed, either due to its reliance on satellites or the original EMP burst. A huge region of the United States is essentially blind and deaf for the next 72–96 hours.

Why did the U.S. government not see this coming? Days earlier, a hacker planted a virus on the uplink channel to a military satellite. This satellite has the ability to crosslink with other satellites in its constellation. The virus then found its way through the satellite and onto the downlink back to the master control station. It infected ground-based computers responsible for the command and control of the satellite constellation. It not only attacks the master control station, but also any user that has access to the information from the satellite. Locations that conduct military operations, including missile warning and space control stations, were affected. End users that need the information to make real-time combat decisions are knocked off the network. Essentially, with a single, relatively low-yield nuclear weapon, an adversary of the United States could create enormous first- and second-order effects should it be detonated in space rather than being directed against a terrestrial target.

Cyberspace is a domain characterized by the use of electronics and the electromagnetic spectrum to store, modify, and exchange data via networked systems and associated physical infrastructures. In effect, cyberspace can be thought of as the interconnection of human beings through computers and telecommunication, without regard to physical geography. A simpler definition of cyberspace is a loosely defined term that encompasses the global patchwork collection of civilian, government, and military computer systems and networks. In today's world, we are connected almost 24 hours a day to the Internet. People have smartphones, computers, televisions, and even refrigerators connected to the Internet that can download caloric information about the food you eat. The U.S. military is a very technologically dependent fighting force. The same network they rely upon for integration into military platforms they also use for social media. Their use of satellite communications (SATCOM), the global positioning system (GPS), unmanned aerial vehicles (UAVs), and numerous other data collection centers to view real-time information anywhere in the world has increased tremendously since the first Gulf War, and the increasing demand has largely been supplied by civilian sources outside of direct military control. "Over 80 percent of SATCOM bandwidth used by the military to conduct OIF and Operation Enduring Freedom (OEF) has been commercial SATCOM," a global connection that was not available just 40 years ago (*AU-18 Space Primer* 2009, 183). Net-centric warfare (NCW) as it is called today "generates increased combat power by networking sensors, decision makers, and shooters to achieve shared awareness, increased speed of command, high tempo of operations, greater lethality, increased survivability, and a degree of self-synchronization" (Office of the Secretary of Defense 2005, 4). It is almost entirely dependent upon a functioning communications system, and thus cannot be conducted without vital space assets.

Every military operation is affected in some way by space and cyber platforms, from the airman manning the finance desk processing travel vouchers to the pilots dropping bombs on targets. Space and cyber provide advanced capabilities that have increased situational awareness and the speed of decision making for the warfighter. We are dangerously reliant upon space and cyber, and training exercises that include efforts to function without the space and cyber domains are often cancelled once the utility of the missing assets is demonstrated. Space is becoming more congested, contested, and competitive. With the advance of technology, what used to be high-dollar technical equipment can now be bought on the cheap by anyone with a credit card. The Captain Midnight scenario required expensive commercial satellite equipment not accessible to the public in 1986, but today, products are available commercially off the shelf for a couple thousand dollars that can perform the same functions. Cyber tools for hacking are free and published all over the Internet. All someone needs is a computer and an Internet connection to launch an attack and be almost untraceable.

In the event of a cyber war, space assets would bring to bear the same assets used in a terrestrial war. Intelligence, surveillance, and reconnaissance (ISR) satellites would monitor actions like missile launches, capture imagery, and monitor communications of authoritarian regimes. The one big difference is the vulnerability of these assets. On the most basic level, electronic transmissions are composed of ones and zeros. Once this information is decoded, the order and whether it is a one or a zero makes up the information. In the cyber domain, physical presence is not required, and space systems are no different from a home computer. Adversaries could launch a cyber attack on a satellite with very little risk and hardly any traceability or accountability (Kallberg 2012, 134–35). Several incidents occurred in 2007 and 2008, demonstrating how readily satellites can be hacked. One satellite command-and-control link was hijacked for two minutes, giving malicious users full control of the satellite and all of its capabilities. Another incident lasted nine minutes before defensive cyber teams could counter the threat. Unfortunately, those attacks were relatively unsophisticated, despite their evident success. The resources of a nation could undoubtedly provide a much greater threat to the integrity of the satellite system (Paganini 2013). One of the requirements for someone to attack a satellite is to be within the satellite's footprint, or within view of the satellite transmission. Since advances in technology have dropped the price of equipment, and with techniques readily demonstrated on the Internet, satellite jamming is on the rise. Satellite feeds are particularly targeted by despotic regimes desperate to keep outside influences away from their citizens, especially in the Middle East, North Africa, and Southeast Asia. At least two satellite companies, Arabsat and Nilesat, have complained about the jamming of their satellites. They both provide television feeds to the Middle East, Africa, and Europe as well as broadband, telephone, and very small aperture terminal (VSAT) services such as point of sale credit card services. "Jamming and rounding up satellite dishes has become a common practice for governments wishing to limit unfavorable coverage in their own (or sometimes other people's) countries" (Klingler 2012). Most of the complaints fall on deaf ears since there is no organization like the Federal Communications Commission (FCC) in the United States, which strictly prohibits jamming.

Disrupting a signal does not take much effort and could be very hard to identify if the originator makes even a slight effort to hide their location and identity. Jamming not only disrupts the signal, which costs the companies money; it can potentially destroy a satellite if enough power is applied to the transponders. Technology has enabled others to not only jam and disrupt signals, but to steal and decrypt signals as well. In many cases, the camera feeds from U.S. UAVs operating in the skies of Iraq and Afghanistan have been broadcast unencrypted. In 2008, Shi'ite militants in Iraq were able to intercept a Predator's datalink using a piece of $26 software (Shachtman and Axe 2012). While this signal stealing did not include the ability to actually control the aircraft in question, it did allow hostile forces to determine the location and visual coverage of the UAV. Signal encryption, which can prevent this type of electronic eavesdropping, requires additional bandwidth, and hence increases the cost to operate military systems. According to *Defense Industry Daily*, "In 2009, U.S. UAVs alone generated 24 years worth of video if watched continuously. New UAV models are expected to produce 30 times as much in 2011" (Shachtman and Axe 2012). When 80 percent of all communications are leased through commercial satellites, the cost adds up quickly. As the United States and other nations become increasingly dependent upon such systems, they create a need for additional communication satellites, each of which costs tens of millions of dollars to be placed into orbit.

So what is the military doing to combat all these space and cyber threats? Education and training are the key. Red Teams, also called Aggressor Units, are required to train U.S. military members to know how to react in the event of a cyber or space attack. Aggressor Units first appeared in U.S. Air Force training exercises in the form of pilots who simulated enemy attackers at Red Flag exercises, held at Nellis Air Force Base. There are now cyber Aggressor Units who launch controlled network attacks to test the vulnerability of military systems. For the first time in March 2011, cyber and space operators were fully integrated into the massive Red Flag exercises, providing realistic threat simulations designed to match potential real-world conflict scenarios. In the space domain, the 572th Space Aggressor Squadron and the 26th Space Aggressor Squadron provide threat emulation in GPS and satcom jamming. In the cyber domain, the 57th Information Aggressor Squadron along with their sister squadron, the 177th Information Aggressor Squadron from the Kansas Air National Guard, provide threat emulation and red teaming.

John MacDougal might have simply been an angry small business owner, lashing out at what he perceived to be the faceless machine responsible for his declining income. Nevertheless, his actions provided not only an early example of how to disrupt a satellite signal, but also a harbinger of the importance that space and cyber assets might play in the twenty-first-century global economy. His petty electronic vandalism pales in comparison to the potential damage and chaos that might be created by any disruption to the space and cyber domains.

Brian Tannehill is a retired space operator with over 15 years' experience in military space operations. He has provided secure communications via command and control of the MILSTAR satellite constellation as well as provided enemy threat replication through GPS and SATCOM jamming at the 527th Space Aggressors.

References

Access ADL. 2012. "Al Qaeda's Inspire Magazine Resurrected!" May 2. Retrieved July 15, 2014, from http://accessadl.blogspot.com/2012/05/al-qaedas-inspire-magazine-resurrected.html.

Andress, Jason, and Steve Winterfeld. 2014. *Cyber Warfare: Techniques, Tactics and Tools for Security Practitioners.* Boston: Syngress.

AU-18 Space Primer. 2009. Maxwell Air Force Base, AL: Air University Press. Retrieved July 1, 2014, from http://aupress.au.af.mil/digital/pdf/book/AU-18.pdf.

Center for Strategic and International Studies. 2010. "Cybersecurity Discussion with General Keith B. Alexander, Director of the NSA, Commander of U.S. Cyber Command." Retrieved February 15, 2014, from http://csis.org/event/cybersecurity-discussion-general-keith-b-alexander-director-national-security-agency.

Cilluffo, Frank J., and Joseph R. Clark. 2014. "Repurposing Cyber Command." *Parameters: The US Army War College Quarterly* 43.4 (Winter 2013–2014).

Connor, Tom. 2011. "Peep Show: Inside the World of Unsecured IP Security Cameras." January 11. Retrieved July 15, 2014, from http://arstechnica.com/gadgets/2011/01/one-mans-journey-through-the-world-of-unsecured-ip-surveillance-cams/2/.

Costa, Robert. 2002. "Supporting the Information-Centric 2001 Quadrennial Defense Review: The Case for an Information Service." Master's thesis, Air Command and Staff College, Maxwell Air Force Base, AL.

Daily News and Analysis. 2009. "Headley Used 'Electronic Dead Drop' Method for Communication." *Daily News and Analysis* (India), December 17. Retrieved July 15, 2014, from http://www.dnaindia.com/india/report_headley-used -electronic-dead-drop-method-for-communication _1324633.

Demchak, Chris C. 2011. *Wars of Disruption and Resilience: Cybered Conflict, Power, and National Security* Athens, GA: University of Georgia Press.

Dixon, Chelsea, John St. Pierre, Kelley Washington, and Matthew Welch. 2014. "The Army Cyber Officer: Defining the Role," USMA Senior Thesis Presentation, West Point, NY, May 1.

Healey, Jason. 2013. *A Fierce Domain: Conflict in Cyberspace, 1986–2012.* Vienna, VA: Cyber Conflict Studies Association.

Kallberg, Jan. 2012. "Designer Satellite Collisions from Covert Cyber War." *Strategic Studies Quarterly*, 124–36.

Kaplan, Eben. 2009. "Terrorists and the Internet." Council on Foreign Relations, January 8. Retrieved July 15, 2014, from http://www.cfr.org/terrorism-and-technology/terrorists -internet/p10005.

Klingler, Dave. 2012. "Satellite Jamming Becoming a Big Problem in the Middle East." *Ars Technica*, March 28. Retrieved July 1, 2014, from http://arstechnica.com/science/ 2012/03/satellite-jamming-becoming-a-big-problem-in-the -middle-east/.

Lachow, Irving. 2009. "Cyber Terrorism: Menace or Myth?" In *Cyberpower and National Security*, edited by Franklin D.

Kramer, Stuart H. Starr, and Larry K. Wentz, 437–64. Washington, DC: Potomac Books.

Libicki, Martin C. 2014. "Why Cyber War Will Not and Should Not Have Its Grand Strategist." *Strategic Studies Quarterly* 14.1 (Spring 2014).

NirvanaNet.com. N.d. Retrieved July 1, 2014, from http://www.textfiles.com/100/captmidn.txt.

Office of the Secretary of Defense, Force Transformation. 2005. "The Implementation of Network Centric Warfare." U.S. Department of Defense, Washington: DC, May 5.

Paganini, Pierluigi. 2013. "Hacking Satellites." *H+ Magazine*, April 4. Retrieved July 1, 2014, from http://hplusmagazine.com/2013/04/04/hacking-satellites/.

Panetta, Leon E. 2012. "Remarks by Secretary Panetta on Cybersecurity to the Business Executives for National Security, New York City." October 11. Retrieved July 15, 2014, from http://www.defense.gov/transcripts/transcript.aspx?transcriptid=5136.

Shachtman, Noah, and David Axe. 2012. "Most Drones Openly Broadcast Secret Video Feeds." *Wired*, October 29. Retrieved July 1, 2014, from http://www.wired.com/dangerroom/2012/10/hack-proof-drone/.

Sipress, Alan. 2004. "An Indonesian's Prison Memoir Takes Holy War into Cyberspace in Sign of New Threat, Militant Offers Tips on Credit Card Fraud." *Washington Post*, December 14. Retrieved July 15, 2014, from http://www.washingtonpost.com/wp-dyn/articles/A62095-2004Dec13.html.

Slashdot.org. 2011. "Unsecured IP Cameras Accessible to Everyone." January 18. Retrieved July 15, 2014, from http://hardware.slashdot.org/story/11/01/18/1829230/unsecured-ip-cameras-accessible-to-everyone.

Soufan Group. 2012. "TSG Intel Brief: Cyber Series: Terrorism and Social Media." April 26. Retrieved July 15,

2014, from http://soufangroup.com/tsg-intelbrief-cyber
-series-terrorism-and-social-media/.

Stanglin, Douglas. 2011. "Bin Laden Used Thumb Drives to
Send and Receive Email." *USA Today*, May 13. Retrieved
October 23, 2014, from http://content.usatoday.com/
communities/ondeadline/post/2011/05/bin-laden-used
-thumb-drives-to-send-and-receive-email/1.

Stytz, Martin R., and Sheila B. Banks. 2014. "Toward
Attaining Cyber Dominance." *Strategic Studies Quarterly* 8.1
(Spring 2014).

Tafoya, William L. 2011. "Cyber Terror." *FBI Law
Enforcement Bulletin* 80, no. 11 (November). Retrieved
July 15, 2014, from http://www.fbi.gov/stats-services/
publications/law-enforcement-bulletin/november-2011/
november-2011-leb.

Theohary, Catherine A., and John Rollins. 2011. "Terrorist
Use of the Internet: Information Operations in Cyberspace."
Washington, DC: Congressional Research Service, March 8.
Retrieved July 15, 2014, from http://www.carlisle.army.mil/
dime/documents/Terroist%20Use%20of%20Internet
%20IO.pdf.

Willetts, David, and Tom Wells. March 20, 2012. "Terrorists
Are Using Online War Games Like Call of Duty to Plot
Attacks, *The Sun* Can Reveal." *The Sun* (United Kingdom).
Retrieved July 15, 2014, from http://www.thesun.co.uk/sol/
homepage/news/4205896/Terrorists-play-online-games
-like-Call-of-Duty-to-plan-attacks.html#ixzz2E2lOCwjd.

Any discussion of cyber warfare is influenced by a wide variety of actors and organizations. This chapter offers an overview of many of the key individuals and groups that have been involved in cyber conflict. It ranges from theorists who have attempted to discern the guiding principles of the cyber domain of warfare, to the practitioners who have launched some of the most important cyber operations of recent history. The organizations profiled in this section range from government entities to criminal networks, all of whom have sought to use cyber operations to their own advantage.

Alexander, Keith B.

Keith B. Alexander is a retired U.S. Army general who served as the 16th director of the National Security Agency (NSA) and the first commander of the U.S. Cyber Command (CYBERCOM). Alexander is most known for facilitating the growth and integration of military and civilian intelligence agencies and their ability to function in the cyber domain. He retired in the wake of revelations that the NSA was engaged in a massive amount of domestic surveillance upon American

Eugene Kaspersky, founder and CEO of Kaspersky Lab, addresses the International Conference on Cyber Security at Tel Aviv University on June 6, 2012. (AP Photo/Dan Balilty)

citizens, primarily released to the public by former NSA contractor Edward Snowden.

Alexander grew up in Syracuse, New York, and attended the United States Military Academy, graduating in 1974. His classmates included Generals Martin Dempsey, David Petraeus, and Walter Sharp. Although Alexander was commissioned as an armor officer, he soon became closely involved in military intelligence, developing an expertise in signals intelligence collection. He obtained advanced degrees in systems technology, physics, and national security strategy, making him very well qualified to lead agencies devoted to the collection and analysis of electronic communications. In 2001, he was appointed the commanding general of the U.S. Army Intelligence and Security Command, making him the top military intelligence officer in the Army. After a stint as the deputy chief of staff for the Army, he was nominated by President George W. Bush to direct the NSA, succeeding Michael Hayden.

While directing the NSA, Alexander pioneered a new approach to signals collection and analysis. Rather than attempting to track and trace individuals, the NSA began an attempt to collect every electronic communication in a region, beginning in Iraq. Once the entire sum of communications had been collected and stored, it became possible to conduct highly automated searches through the massive volumes of data, which could then identify targeted communicators for further investigation and tracking. This proved incredibly successful against Iraqi insurgents who had proven far too elusive for previous methods of intelligence collection. It may have also proven extremely alluring to expand the notion to other regions, as proposals soon circulated to conduct a similar program on a global scale, including within the domestic United States.

CYBERCOM, formally opened in 2010, includes the NSA in its list of subordinate organizations. On May 21, 2010, Alexander assumed command of CYBERCOM and was promoted to four-star rank at the same time. The new organization, which has an enormous budget and combines military and civilian cyber activities, offered the possibility of conducting a global intelligence collection effort of unprecedented size. On a number of occasions in 2012 and 2013, Alexander publicly denied that the NSA or CYBERCOM had collected data on American citizens. However, on June 5, 2013, former NSA contractor Edward Snowden released classified documents demonstrating that the NSA and CYBERCOM had been engaged in such activities on an unprecedented scale. Although there is no evidence that the NSA has been able to monitor and record every electronic communication in the United States, there is ample evidence of domestic surveillance as well as the ability to target any individual in the nation's communications, regardless of encryption measures. Alexander announced his retirement a few months after the Snowden revelations and, in March 2014, was relieved by Admiral Michael S. Rogers as both the commander of CYBERCOM and the director of the NSA.

Alperovitch, Dmitri

Dmitri Alperovitch is a computer security expert who has helped to pioneer the active defense strategy for cyber security. He has held a variety of key positions within the cyber industry, including his current roles as the chief technology officer of CrowdStrike, a company he cofounded, and as vice president of threat research for McAfee. Alperovitch was integral to the investigations of Operation Aurora and Operation Shady RAT, two major cyber espionage campaigns traced to Chinese state-sponsored hackers.

Alperovitch began his career at a series of small computer security firms before pursuing bachelor's and master's degrees in computer science and information security from the Georgia Institute of Technology. His natural skill at ferreting out clues for attack attribution made him a natural leader for the research team at Secure Computing, a role he assumed in 2006. Two years later, McAfee purchased Secure Computing and named him the vice president of threat research. In that role, he led the team investigating Operation Aurora, a series of Chinese attacks upon Google and other major Western companies, shutting down the campaign after a series of successful, high-level intrusions. He also served as the lead investigator into Night Dragon, a Chinese cyber espionage campaign targeting Western energy companies, presumably with the intention of plundering their data of known oil fields and using the information to launch competing bids for the development of the fields.

In 2011, Alperovitch cofounded CrowdStrike, a company that specializes in preventing and deterring cyber espionage attacks against corporations and government entities. The core of the business is in its concept of active defense, by which it raises the cost of cyber attacks for potential enemies by launching immediate counterattacks against attempted intrusions. The knowledge that an attack can no longer be launched with impunity, and is likely to be met with an equal or overwhelming response, probably has a much greater deterrent effect than simply raising increasing numbers of passive defenses, but not punishing attempted intrusions. Alperovitch has been hailed with a number of recent awards, including *MIT Technology Review*'s "Top 35 Innovators under 35" and *Foreign Policy*'s "Top 100 Leading Global Thinkers," both achieved in 2013. His new model of cyber security has shown promising results so far and is likely to revolutionize the nature of protecting cyber networks.

Anonymous

Anonymous is an international consortium of hackers and hacktivists that is deliberately decentralized but united by a common ideology. It has risen to prominence for a series of DDoS attacks and website defacements, often in response to perceived efforts by governments to engage in cyber censorship or surveillance of citizens. Public appearances by members of

Anonymous are often characterized by wearing Guy Fawkes masks, a reference to the protagonist of the popular 2005 film *V for Vendetta*, who rebelled against government censorship in a dystopian future Britain.

The group first appeared in 2003, when a group of users of 4chan discussed the idea of a global consciousness that had arisen through the Internet. The first hacking activities of members tended to be oriented toward entertainment and pranks, rather than political activities; but once the potential of the concept had been demonstrated, more hackers began to rally to the group, including radicals pushing for more extreme activities. In 2008, the group essentially declared a cyber war on the Church of Scientology and launched a series of coordinated attacks against Scientology websites. The group has had a varied track record of success in proclaiming its messages, in part because of the wide variety of targets. Members of Anonymous have called for attacks upon government agencies, child pornography websites, and financial organizations. In each case, because there is no central-ized control for the organization, any members of the group might decide to join in an attack, creating a certain momentum for cyber incidents.

The group has very few formal rules, although they expect all members to remain anonymous, to maintain the secrecy of the group, and to avoid attacking media outlets. In the final rule, they demonstrate a sophisticated understanding of the likely effects of a direct attack upon media outlets, even against the media companies who criticize their activities. The group has repeatedly used a popular tagline: "We are Anonymous. We are Legion. We do not forgive. We do not forget. Expect us" (Morris 2013). Members of the group took an active inter-est in antiauthoritarian protests that rocked North Africa and the Middle East in 2011, dubbed the Arab Spring. They attacked government websites in Tunisia, Libya, and Egypt and provided computer assistance to dissidents seeking to share their messages with the outside world. Later in 2011, Anonymous members provided support to the Occupy Wall

Street protest movement, helping to spread it to cities across America.

When in 2010, WikiLeaks began to publish secret communications that had been illegally obtained from classified networks, it provoked a massive backlash from a number of governments and financial institutions. PayPal, MasterCard, and Visa all refused to process donations to the group, an activity that Anonymous members perceived as a form of censorship. The group commenced a series of attacks against the financial corporations, which managed to disrupt the sites for all three companies for a few hours. PayPal managed to track the IP addresses of over 1,000 of the attackers in a DDoS attack and supplied them to the Federal Bureau of Investigation, which then moved to arrest the ringleaders of the attacks. While Anonymous had engaged in harassment and entertainment attacks, it had not drawn much law enforcement attention. However, the financial damages from the WikiLeaks support attacks, plus a series of direct attacks against the personal information of police officers, provoked a rapid response. Dozens of Anonymous members have been arrested around the world for coordinating destructive cyber activities. The arrests have provoked further Anonymous attacks, but have also had a chilling effect upon the more casual members of the group, particularly after several prominent members were convicted of fraud and conspiracy to commit computer crimes and sentenced to more than a year in prison.

Carpenter, Shawn

Shawn Carpenter is a computer security expert credited with discovering and investigating the Titan Rain cyber espionage campaign while working at Sandia National Laboratories. When he attempted to alert his superiors to the problems that he had found, he was ordered to stop investigating and concentrate only on the security of Sandia, even though he had developed evidence that the Titan Rain breach had penetrated numerous defense contractors and stolen enormous volumes of classified data. Carpenter approached the Federal Bureau of Investigation (FBI) with his information, and when his involvement with the federal law enforcement agency was discovered, he was summarily terminated from his position with Sandia.

Carpenter's investigations showed that Titan Rain hackers had managed to access classified materials held by Sandia, Lockheed Martin Corporation, Redstone Arsenal, the National Aeronautics and Space Administration, and dozens of other sensitive agencies associated with the federal government. He immediately informed his superiors of his discoveries and, on his own initiative, investigated the source of the cyber intrusions. Carpenter's inadvertent discovery showed that the attackers seemed to be a single group in China that was very efficient at finding and exfiltrating enormous volumes of data, much of which was stored unencrypted on Sandia's servers. Interestingly, the attackers actually chose to encrypt the material after removing it from the classified networks, demonstrating a much greater respect for basic computer security than the locations they were targeting.

When Sandia's management ordered Carpenter to stop his investigations and not share his information with other targeted agencies, he used his military contacts to open a communication channel to both the U.S. Army and the FBI. Carpenter worked as a confidential informant for six months before his continued cyber activities and relationship with law enforcement were revealed to Sandia's leaders. Upon this revelation, the company began immediate termination hearings, at which Sandia's chief of counterintelligence allegedly threatened to kill Carpenter for his activities.

Carpenter sued Sandia for wrongful termination and defamation of his character after the laboratory's officials made a number of public aspersions upon his person. After a jury trial in a New Mexico court, Carpenter was awarded over $5 million in compensatory and punitive damages and attorneys' fees, more than twice what his lawsuit had requested. In addition, the trial judge ordered that Sandia should pay 15 percent interest upon the award during any appeals it chose to make, reducing the incentive for the company to file countless appellate motions. Sandia still filed a number of post-trial motions, including a demand to throw out the jury's verdict, a request to reduce or eliminate the punitive damages, and a request for a new trial. Each of the motions failed, forcing Sandia to pay nearly $6 million into an escrow account during its appeals, without which Carpenter would have been entitled to seize corporate assets. In October 2007, the company, sensing that it had little chance of winning the case on appeals and that it would pay an enormous additional sum of money in the meantime due to the interest requirement, dropped its appeals of the case. Carpenter remains in the field of cyber security, working for NetWitness Corporation.

Carr, Jeffrey

Jeffrey Carr is a cyber security analyst who has written extensively about the concept of cyber warfare, and who has also organized a series of massive open-source investigations into many of the events that have been characterized as acts of war in the cyber realm. Carr is the founder and CEO of Taiba Global and a principal at GreyLogic, two world-renowned cyber security and investigation organizations.

Carr's cyber investigations, entitled Project Grey Goose, have brought together hundreds of volunteers to comb through publicly available records to attempt attribution of major cyber offensive campaigns, beginning with the attacks on Georgian infrastructure in 2008. Project Grey Goose periodically solicits volunteers to contribute to its activities, but is not open to every would-be cyber sleuth. Rather, volunteers are asked to submit their qualifications, and if selected, will be allowed to join the organization and participate. This methodology is designed to eliminate participants with no useful expertise, journalists, and, hopefully, infiltration by the very actors it is designed to investigate.

Carr's writings on cyber warfare include his 2009 work *Inside Cyber Warfare: Mapping the Cyber Underworld* and a long-running blog on the subject, IntelFusion.net. *Inside Cyber Warfare* is one of the best single-volume examinations of the practical status quo of cyber conflicts. It investigates not only the means by which cyber capabilities might be utilized to attack an enemy, but also the current legal controls, or lack thereof, on the use of computer networks as weapons. It describes cyber warfare as largely the province of nonstate actors, including cyber criminals and hacktivists. Carr argues that while nations use cyber for intelligence collection, they do not tend to use direct cyber attacks on a regular basis, in part because they have alternate means of power projection. They do, however, encourage nonstate groups to engage in malicious and irritating cyber activities, which maintains deniability while creating a certain degree of chaos for the target. He also notes that many states tolerate cyber crime, so long as it targets international victims, because cyber criminals can provide a laboratory to test new methodology for cyber attacks.

Clarke, Richard Alan

Richard Alan Clarke is the former national coordinator for security, infrastructure protection, and counterterrorism for the U.S. government. He was appointed to the position in 1998, by President Bill Clinton, after serving in a variety of government positions dating back to the administration of President Richard Nixon. Clarke has retired from government service, but continues to raise awareness of American vulnerabilities to cyber attacks and terrorism through his written works and speaking appearances.

Clarke was born in Boston in 1950, and attended the University of Pennsylvania, graduating in 1972. In 1973, Clarke accepted a management internship with the U.S. Department of Defense, a move that set him on the path to become a career bureaucrat. By the mid-1980s, Clarke had risen to the level of deputy assistant secretary of state for intelligence, a position he held during the Iran-Contra scandal. Despite his position, his career did not suffer from the incident, and as an assistant secretary of state in 1990, he worked to coordinate among coalition partners who participated in the Persian Gulf War. Like many career civil servants, Clarke successfully transitioned from one administration to the next, regardless of political affiliation, and was admitted to the National Security Council under Clinton, where he specialized in counterterrorism. He remained in this role during the transition to the administration of President George W. Bush and strongly advised the incoming president that Al Qaeda represented a major threat to national security.

Clarke's final year of government security was spent as the special advisor to the president on cybersecurity. He repeatedly expressed frustration in this role that neither the government nor private companies were taking the issue of cyber security seriously, and that lax standards were making the classified data of the nation vulnerable to enemy attack and theft. Despite his important roles as a cyber security czar for two presidential administrations, Clarke failed to get institutional momentum to build a truly secure cyber network. Since retiring from government service, he accepted the chairmanship of Good Harbor Consulting, a strategic planning and corporate risk management firm. He has also published in a wide variety of venues, including his 2010 book *Cyber War: The Next Great Threat to National Security and What to Do about It*. In that work, Clarke pushed for a series of straightforward, but potentially expensive, changes to the physical structure of the Internet to allow examination of virtually every packet of information passing along the so-called Internet Backbone. Such a system would presumably pay for itself by essentially ending Internet fraud and other forms of cyber crime, but privacy advocates fear that it would be a small step to go from machine-based inspection for malware to human interception of confidential information for government exploitation. Clarke continues to advocate for greater awareness of cyber security threats. In 2013, he joined a presidential advisory group for reforming the National Security Agency following the classified document leaks of Edward Snowden.

Defense Advanced Research Projects Agency (DARPA)

The Advanced Research Projects Agency (ARPA) was created in 1958 by President Dwight D. Eisenhower. It was founded immediately after the Soviet launch of the world's first artificial satellite, *Sputnik*, caught the U.S. government completely by surprise. American researchers had assumed that the Soviets were years, if not decades, behind American scientific development in rocketry. The strategic surprise of the Soviet satellite led to a determination on Eisenhower's part that the United States would never fall behind their rival in the technological realm, in part because American national defense policies rested upon the assumption that the United States and its allies would offset Soviet manpower advantages with superior equipment. ARPA was created expressly for the purpose of preventing technological surprises, which the organization has interpreted as a demand for developing revolutionary advances unforeseen by potential enemies.

In 1972, ARPA was renamed the Defense Advanced Research Projects Agency (DARPA) to more accurately reflect its relationship with the government. Although DARPA is a Department of Defense agency, it is not incorporated into any of the service branches and instead reports directly to the Office of the Secretary of Defense. This creates an important direct line to the secretary, who can then help to determine the priorities for DARPA's research efforts. DARPA commands an annual budget of approximately $3 billion, giving it the enormous resources necessary to recruit the very best minds in any field of study that it chooses to pursue.

Both ARPA and DARPA have played a major role in the development of information and communications technology since the time of their founding. The research agency contributed to the development of early time-sharing computer systems, which was followed by the creation of a wide-area packet switching network, ARPANet, that many historians of technology consider to be the forerunner to the Internet. DARPA's Strategic Computing Program helped with the development of advanced computer processing systems and modern high-speed networking technologies. There are seven program offices in DARPA; one, the Information Innovation Office, is dedicated to radically improving U.S. information technologies. Another, the Microsystems Technology Office, examines the microchip-scale integration of electronics, micro-electromechanical systems, and photonics, which may provide superior protection against the cyber attacks of the future.

The DARPA organizational structure stresses the maintenance of a small, flexible staff and a lack of hierarchy. There are fewer than 300 permanent DARPA employees, most of whom serve to coordinate large projects by bringing in experts on an as-needed basis for specific program requirements. This is done primarily through research grants to academic institutions and partnerships with private corporations. Most projects are largely conceptual and last for only a few years, at most, before being handed off to either the military services or private companies for further development, procurement, and fielding. This approach allows DARPA to remain most active at the strategic level, rather than become bogged down in the technical engineering details necessary to bring new technologies to full maturity. With their role as the creators of revolutionary technological changes, they are effectively specialists in changing the landscape of future technology at the earliest stages of development.

Defense Information Systems Agency (U.S.)

The Defense Information Systems Agency (DISA) is a major combat support agency of the U.S. Department of Defense (DoD). It is responsible for the information technology that supplies communications to the entire military service as well as the national command authority. While the U.S. Cyber Command and National Security Agency both draw substantial public attention for their roles in cyber warfare, DISA actually owns and operates the entire communications network needed to conduct military operations, and it is DISA systems that are subjected to constant intrusion campaigns by cyber attackers from around the world. DISA is responsible for the protection of the DoD e-mail system, the NIPRNet, SIPRNet, and JWICS networks, and all messaging and teleconferencing services for the U.S. military.

DISA was established in 1960 as the Defense Communications Agency and tasked to run the Defense Communications System. This was a major step toward standardizing and integrating U.S. defense communications. At the time, the military branches each had unique equipment that could not interface with the other services, making joint operations a very difficult venture. Further, the new organization needed to link a series of internal telephone networks into a single system that would promote better communications within the DoD. As satellites became a key proponent of global communications, DISA was given responsibility for developing secure satellite communication technology. When the Cuban Missile Crisis erupted in 1962, President John F. Kennedy had no way to directly contact his peer, Premier Nikita Khrushchev of the Soviet Union, making the crisis far more dangerous as each side had to rely upon indirect communication and signaling of intents. Less than a year after the crisis, DISA had cooperated with a Soviet agency to establish a dual-line direct connection between Washington and Moscow, often called the "Red Telephone."

The Vietnam War was the first major operation for the U.S. military after the creation of DISA, and the new organization established an integrated communication system throughout Southeast Asia to facilitate military commands. Soon, satellite communications were added to the network, ensuring that field commanders could reach any higher headquarters in an instant. DISA also created the Minimum Essential Emergency Communications Network (MEECN) in 1971. This emergency network served to keep U.S. nuclear forces in communication with the Pentagon and the president, even in the event of a nuclear attack by the Soviet Union. The network had to be secure, survivable, and functional at all times, triggering a renewed interest in the expansion of satellite communications technology.

More than two decades after its founding, DISA still could not force interoperability upon the military services' communications equipment. Not until the Goldwater-Nichols Act of 1986 was signed into law, mandating greater efforts at joint functioning, did DISA receive the necessary political clout to force the services into compliance. Just five years later, the United States led a coalition of military forces in a push to oust Iraqi military forces from Kuwait in Operation Desert Storm. In preparation for the campaign, DISA created a massive new telecommunications system in the region, using cutting-edge fiber-optic links, dedicated satellites, and microwave transmission relays. The system created an unprecedented amount of bandwidth for theater commanders and allowed a substantial use of real-time imagery in controlling the campaign.

The development of computer networks in the 1990s increased the need for a coordinated military system, lest each of the services develop its own cyber network that could not communicate with the others. DISA became the sole provider of DoD Internet services, creating an integrated network that could support the operational needs of more than two million uniformed service members along with the entire supporting force of civilians providing vital support to the Pentagon. In the aftermath of the September 11, 2001, attacks, DISA underwent a major series of security upgrades, creating a much-needed increase in bandwidth capacity to facilitate the use of dedicated video feeds from surveillance platforms. Total bandwidth requirements in the Iraqi theater of operations were 30 times higher in 2003 than in 1991, despite the fielding of a U.S. force less than half the size of the earlier deployment. DISA continues to expand its bandwidth capacity both in the United States and in support of deployed forces in the field, reflecting the constantly expanding amount of data generated by modern military forces.

DISA's Global Information Grid infrastructure faces constant attack from the cyber domain and has been penetrated on a number of occasions. Because DISA's primary responsibility is to keep communication systems functional, with security as a secondary priority, the DoD has created U.S. Cyber Command to undertake many of the network security and counterattack functions. Nevertheless, DISA remains a vital aspect of protecting the very networks that would be used for any form of cyber war, and has proved its value time and again by allowing field commanders to remain in constant contact with their subordinates in the theater of operations and their military and civilian leaders in Washington, D.C.

FireEye, Inc.

FireEye is a network security company based in Milpitas, California, founded in 2004 by Ashar Aziz, formerly of Sun Microsystems. Aziz personally invented the primary technologies upon which the company was based and used his expertise to obtain investors to expand his venture. FireEye specializes in offering malware protection to major corporations and has developed a niche market for its abilities to detect and defend against advanced persistent threats. The company is best known for its Malware Protection System, a line of software that engages in automatic threat detection and provides forensic analysis of any malware attacks.

FireEye has developed a very solid reputation as a cyber forensics organization, which is often called upon by other corporations to assist in tracking and shutting down botnet systems. In 2008, FireEye led the forensic investigation of the Srizbi botnet. The following year, it joined an effort to dismantle the Mega-D botnet, one of the largest in the world. In 2011, FireEye cooperated with Microsoft and the Federal Bureau of Investigation to destroy the Rustock botnet. These botnet destruction efforts have in turn created both a new revenue stream and a network of powerful companies interested in expanding FireEye's capabilities. Reflecting this fact, Dave DeWalt, the president of McAfee, joined the company as its CEO in 2012. Very quickly, the company began to expand, acquiring Mandiant for $1 billion in December 2013, and nPulse Technologies in May 2014. The company now has more than 1,000 employees and is regarded as one of the fastest-growing cyber security firms in the world.

Google, Inc.

Google is a massive multinational corporation that specializes in Internet search functions, advertising technology, cloud computing, and software development. It has moved into the hardware market, particularly through the creation of cell phones using the Android operating system. Google has also started to acquire companies specializing in providing Internet service. Several Google-owned websites are among the most visited in the world, and the original Google website (google.com) is the most-used website on the Internet. Google has become directly involved in a series of cyber conflicts, in part because their own software was hacked and used to target individuals and organizations in cyberspace, and in part because the

Google corporate leadership has become directly involved in social causes associated with rebellions in a number of states.

Google was founded in 1998 by Larry Page and Sergey Brin, who met as PhD students at Stanford University. In 2004, Google's initial public offering generated billions of dollars in stock purchases, massively expanding the operating capital of the company and facilitating its continual growth. Officially, the company's mission statement is "to organize the world's information and make it universally accessible and useful," a position that immediately made the company at odds with totalitarian regimes that refuse to even consider such an open approach to information. The company's unofficial slogan, "Don't be evil," might very well have given some of the same regimes pause, in part because the company refuses to explain its definition of evil.

Google began as an online search engine with a revolutionary approach to providing results. Page and Brin created a unique algorithm that factored in a website's connections to other sites as part of its prominence on the Internet, which in turn pushed it higher in the rankings provided for a search. Of course, providing such a useful service, while a nice gesture to the web-browsing public, did not generate the income necessary to keep the company's servers running. Thus, Google began to sell places at the top of the results list for any search, ironically allowing many companies to guarantee their businesses would be found, even though the standard search results would likely return the same webpages without a fee. Google also began to incorporate targeted advertising in the sidebars of its websites, based largely upon the search terms being utilized by an individual searching Google. Over time, Google refined its approach to commercialization of the website, including its decision to offer free e-mail accounts to web users (Gmail), so long as the user agreed to allow machine-searches of their e-mail message for targeted advertisements. Google has steadfastly claimed that the searching is entirely automated, although some users have complained of fears that Google employees might be personally searching Gmail accounts.

Mission statements and corporate mottoes aside, Google has been criticized for a number of significant policy decisions. In order to access the Chinese market, home to more Internet users than any other nation on earth, Google had to consent to a certain degree of censorship within the nation's borders, and to be the instrument of that censorship. Despite agreeing to this difficult position, Google discovered in 2009 that Chinese hackers had penetrated the source code and servers of Google, and used their position to spy on Google users who had expressed interest in Chinese dissident groups. Chinese hackers also targeted members of the exiled Tibetan government, including the Dalai Lama and his staff, using their penetration of Google networks. When the company learned of these intrusions, and of the exfiltration of Google source code to a Chinese-owned competitor, it unilaterally announced that it would no longer censor results in China, provoking a wave of cyber attacks as a result.

Google's ubiquity as both an e-mail source and Internet service provider has led to it being hailed as offering problems to some of the problems of cyber malfeasance, while ironically being used for other negative acts in cyberspace. Google's executive leadership has repeatedly indicated their belief that cloud computing is the future of networking and computer storage, and they have made the public familiar and comfortable with the concept through their e-mail system. Gmail can be accessed from virtually any terminal in the world, and messages sent on it are stored on one of millions of Google servers around the world. Google advertises that its Gmail service will always be free and will have unlimited data storage capacity, making it a tremendous resource freely offered. However, because of the technology involved and the way that Gmail transmits information to its users, researchers discovered in 2009 that certain organizations used Gmail as a form of dead-drop messaging. An ordinary e-mail message might be intercepted while in transit, making e-mail a particularly vulnerable form of technology for groups such as terror organizations. However, if more than one user has the same Gmail address and password, it becomes possible for them to share messages back and forth, by simply writing the message and then storing it in the message draft folder, or even the deleted messages folder. Each user can log in and check for messages, without actually transmitting the messages along unsecured and potentially vulnerable aspects of the Internet.

Google also shocked many users when former NSA contractor Edward Snowden revealed that NSA hackers had penetrated the Google system, possibly with a certain amount of acquiescence from the company, and could track users without obtaining any form of warrant. Critics have argued that Google's size and dominant market share have created a monopoly and an extremely powerful company. Further, they have claimed that Google unfairly avoids taxes by officially basing its operations in tax-haven countries despite keeping its headquarters in California, and that it has become extremely involved in political campaigns and funding, with one of the largest amounts of political donations for any corporation in the world. If information is the next great battlefield domain, as has been argued by a number of cyber theorists, Google has the potential to be the next great defense contractor, despite its continual statements that it has no interest in partnering with military operations. Despite those claims, Google has recently begun to acquire a number of robotics manufacturers, including Boston Dynamics, which has produced some of the most advanced robots currently fielded by the U.S. military.

Hayden, Michael

Michael Hayden (b. 1945) is a retired U.S. Air Force general who served as the 15th director of the National Security Agency (NSA) and the Central Intelligence Agency (CIA) under Presidents Bill Clinton, George W. Bush, and Barack

Obama. He is widely seen as one of the foremost experts on the ramifications of cyber developments upon intelligence collection, analysis, and operational utilization. Despite a reputation as a mild-mannered leader, Hayden has pushed strongly to expand the capabilities and authorities of the intelligence organizations he has led. He is currently a member of the Chertoff Group, a security consulting corporation founded by former secretary of homeland security Michael Chertoff.

Hayden joined the U.S. Air Force in 1969, after participating in the Reserve Officer Training Corps program at the University of Pittsburgh. He spent most of his uniformed career associated with some aspect of military intelligence, gradually rising through the ranks to assume command of the Air Intelligence Agency in 1996. In 1999, President Bill Clinton nominated Hayden to direct the NSA, an agency that had suffered from nearly a decade of reduced budgets and personnel cuts. Hayden quickly moved to revitalize the organization, both through revamping the leadership structure of the NSA and by updating its technological infrastructure. Many of the older members of NSA leadership chose to retire shortly after Hayden assumed the leadership position, in part due to financial inducements he introduced. The result was a younger, leaner NSA, with less experience but a greater interest in transparency within the organization and a much more casual relationship with the American public.

In the aftermath of the September 11, 2001, attacks, Hayden led the NSA in a massive effort to increase its responsibilities and capabilities. This not only included greater activities in the collection of signal intelligence from foreign sources, it also involved a much larger domestic surveillance role for the NSA than it had ever held. In theory, this was done to prevent further attacks against the homeland, but critics of the NSA program argued that it violated the Fourth Amendment protections of the U.S. Constitution, and that the NSA was engaged in illegal wiretapping activity with almost no oversight from the courts as required by the Foreign

Intelligence Surveillance Act of 1978. Despite these complaints, Hayden was named the principal deputy director of national intelligence in 2005, making him the highest-ranking intelligence official on active duty in the military. In 2006, President Bush nominated Hayden to succeed Porter Goss as the director of the Central Intelligence Agency. In that capacity, Hayden oversaw a major expansion of the CIA's use of remotely piloted vehicles (RPV), particularly armed variants of the MQ-1 Predator and MQ-9 Reaper.

Hayden's legacy in the intelligence community is twofold. He brought the uniformed and civilian intelligence organizations far closer together than they had been since the end of the Cold War, ostensibly to improve their function in the effort to find and destroy Al Qaeda. He also made major strides to enhance the intelligence agencies' opportunities to use kinetic attacks in the War on Terror, by allowing RPV strikes against suspected terrorist targets. These strikes, which have become a principal weapon in the War on Terror, have been the subject of enormous international criticism, in part because the intelligence agencies do not necessarily follow the Department of Defense regulations regarding the use of force. In the cyber realm, Hayden pushed to allow the NSA to engage in a much more aggressive approach to computerized attacks upon competitors' networks, rather than remaining focused solely upon a defensive mind-set.

Kaspersky, Yevgeniy "Eugene" Valentinovich

Eugene Kaspersky is a Russian information security specialist and founder of Kaspersky Lab, one of the leading commercial antivirus companies in the world. He is a prolific author and public speaker on cyber security issues. Kaspersky was born in Novorossiysk, in the former Soviet Union, in 1965. He showed a strong aptitude for mathematics and theoretical physics as a teenager and was chosen to attend a special scientific program at Moscow State University. He followed with a course of study at the Institute of Cryptography, Telecommunications, and Computer Science, a training facility run by the Russian military and KGB, where he majored in mathematical engineering. After graduation, Kaspersky began working as a computer science researcher, discovering the Cascade computer virus in 1989, and he helped to develop the AVP antivirus program, first released in 1992. When AVP was tested against other commercially available antivirus software, it came in first place in both virus detection and neutralization rates, in part because the software was kept separate from the antivirus database, making it more than a simple comparative system.

In 1997, Kaspersky and several of his colleagues, including his wife Natalya, founded the Kaspersky Lab, where Eugene Kaspersky served as the head of antivirus research for the next decade before becoming the company's CEO in 2007. The organization quickly developed into the largest privately held Internet security firm in the world, with operations in nearly every country on the planet and offices in more than 30 nations. Although he oversees the strategic direction of the company, he also remains current on technical details and contributes to the development of new products. His personal fortune is approximately $1 billion, although he lives in a fairly frugal fashion in a nondescript Moscow neighborhood.

Kaspersky has been extremely outspoken about the catastrophic possibilities associated with cyber attacks. He believes that cyber warfare will involve attacks upon critical infrastructure, which will have a devastating effect upon civilians who would not normally be targeted in a conventional conflict. To prevent such an outcome, Kaspersky is an ardent proponent of an international anti–cyber weapons treaty. In support of this idea, Kaspersky offers dozens of speeches per year in virtually any format. Despite the often intransigent stance of the Russian government, Kaspersky is a fervent supporter of international cooperation regarding cyber investigations, and believes that a universal standardization of cyber security principles and procedures would offer tremendous protection against cyber espionage, cyberterrorism, and cyber crime.

Libicki, Martin

Martin Libicki is a senior policy analyst at the RAND Corporation, specializing in how information technology contributes to and influences national security. He is a world-renowned expert in cyber security, cyber conflicts, and cyber war. Unlike many of the most well-known cyber experts in the world, Libicki absolutely refuses to advocate the use of offensive cyber capabilities, at least in public, and firmly believes that the possibilities of cyber technology to influence warfare has been greatly overstated. Instead, he argues that the capabilities of cyberspace are not directly correlated to the effects that can be achieved in the physical world through kinetic attack. Instead, the cyber domain lends itself to completely different capabilities, which, if harnessed correctly, can be of enormous value. When combined with kinetic attacks, cyber can serve as a force multiplier, but when taken alone, Libicki's belief is that its capabilities are relatively minimal. He also argues that states can take advantage of the misperceptions of other states when it comes to cyber, by developing robust cyber defenses that will serve as a significant deterrent against enemy attacks.

Prior to joining the RAND research team, Libicki served as a faculty member at the National Defense University. He has worked with the Defense Advanced Research Projects Agency (DARPA) on cyber research and its direct applications to current and future antiterrorism efforts. Libicki has been hired by the Federal Bureau of Investigation to conduct an information security analysis of the agency. He was also asked to assess the Central Intelligence Agency's In-Q-Tel program, and to offer an analysis of Al Qaeda's targeting strategies. Libicki holds a PhD in city and regional planning from the University of California, Berkeley, earned in 1978.

Libicki has published extensively upon the subjects of cyber power and information warfare. Many of his publications are available for free download from the RAND website (http://www.rand.com). His works have shown a graduate procession from an extremely conservative estimation of cyber capabilities to a gradual belief in the cyber domain's ability to influence the physical world. His book *What Is Information Warfare* examines the very notion of what information operations are and how they might influence other aspects of state-on-state violence. His 2001 work *Who Runs What in the Global Information Grid* is an excellent guide to the different forms of control that permeate the Internet, and how different forms of systemic control influence the actual dimensions of the World Wide Web. It also investigates the possibility of creating inter-operable command systems for the U.S. military, an objective that became highly desirable as a means to improve perfor-mance in the Global War on Terror. *New Challenges: New Tools for Defense Decisionmaking* was originally conceived as an advanced guide to decision making, but also served to illus-trate many of the fundamental changes in the U.S. military due to the end of the Cold War and the commencement of the Global War on Terror. *Conquest in Cyberspace: National Security and Information Warfare*, first published in 2007, chal-lenged the notion that conquest is even possible in cyberspace and reemphasized for decision makers that the cyber domain requires an entirely different mode of thinking for effective action. *Cyber Deterrence and Cyber War* makes his strongest case that cyber is more effective in a defensive mode, rather than an offensive one, in part because states can control their own defensive architecture, while the success or failure of an offensive position will always remain in doubt. Further, by maintaining a strong cyber defensive scheme, states may very well deter any form of cyber attack, thus avoiding being drawn into a potential conflict. *Crisis and Escalation in Cyberspace* builds upon the same theme, noting that cyber crises have the distinct potential to spill over in the physical world, making them far more dangerous.

Libicki has developed a very strong reputation for his keen analytical mind and his ardent desire to remain realistic in his assessments of cyber capabilities. At the same time, he has demonstrated an ability to evolve his thinking on cyber issues as the technology that underpins the cyber domain continues to improve. As such, Libicki is one of the few truly brilliant cyber theorists who has not become locked into a single mode of thought regarding the national utilization of cyber power.

Mandiant

Mandiant is a cyber security firm founded in 2004 by Kevin Mandia in Alexandria, Virginia. It was initially named Red Cliff Consulting and changed its name in 2006 as a rebranding effort. In 2011, the company received external funding that allowed it to expand to 300 employees and compete for much larger contracts with key elements of its industry. The company provides cyber security consulting and specialized threat detection and elimination software for financial institutions. In that capacity, Mandiant experts detected an advanced persistent threat (APT) emanating from the People's Republic of China. The APT appeared to target financial institutions through very targeted spearphishing campaigns, with the object of installing malware on corporate systems. Successful attacks could not only compromise the companies' financial records and investors' portfolios, but also expose flaws in their business practices and potentially create opportunities to defraud the targets of billions of dollars.

On February 18, 2013, Mandiant publicly released a major report documenting their findings from an investigation into attacks by PLA Unit 61398, the most aggressive cyber attack organization of the Chinese government. According to the report, the Chinese hackers had targeted hundreds of organizations for nearly a decade and had achieved remarkable success at infiltrating their systems and stealing enormous amounts of data. Mandiant provided all of the evidence of the attacks as a means to provoke a strong reaction from the United States and other victim governments. This evidence included a video posted to YouTube that showed a cyber intrusion by the APT perpetrators in real time. The company hoped its actions might curtail the Chinese cyber attacks, or at least force other target companies to improve their cyber security. It might also lead to an international agreement regarding the norms of acceptable behavior in cyberspace.

Mandiant's report caused an enormous stir in a number of circles. Within the cyber security world, many professionals had privately suspected the Chinese government, and PLA Unit 61398 in particular, of being a very active cyber espionage organization, but did not have the evidence necessary to make a public accusation. Mandiant's report may have contributed to the decision to bring a federal criminal complaint against the leaders of PLA 61398; five officers from the organization were indicted by a federal grand jury in 2014 for their cyber espionage activities. Mandiant's newfound notoriety also brought the attention of FireEye, a larger cyber security firm based in California. On December 30, 2013, FireEye purchased Mandiant, for a sum reportedly in excess of $1 billion, and incorporated Mandiant's operations into its own corporate structure.

McAfee, Inc.

McAfee is the largest computer security company in the world, and one of the pioneering developers of antivirus software. In 2010, it was purchased by the Intel Corporation for more than $7 billion, one of the largest computer mergers in history. The company was founded by British-American programmer John McAfee in 1987. Prior to that time, McAfee had worked

in a number of emerging computer corporations, defense contractors, and government agencies, including the National
Aeronautics and Space Administration (NASA), Univac, Xerox,
Computer Sciences Corporation, and Lockheed Aircraft Corporation. While working for Lockheed, McAfee was assigned to a
project working on the creation of some of the earliest antivirus
software. He recognized an unfulfilled niche in the computer
industry, resigned his position, and formed McAfee Associates
in 1987.

The company initially specialized in antivirus software but
soon began to branch into other aspects of computer security,
including encryption services. John McAfee left the company
in 1994 to pursue other programming interests, and thus
missed much of the exponential growth of the company's
assets. In 1997, McAfee Associates merged with Network
General, creating a new company, Network Associates. The
company continued to produce McAfee antivirus software
and, recognizing the value of the brand name, returned to the
name McAfee in 2004. In the past decade, McAfee has purchased dozens of smaller computer programming companies,
in the process acquiring a significant share of the encryption,
networking, and firewall markets. Intel's purchase of the company did not slow production of McAfee's flagship antivirus
program, although in early 2014, it was renamed Intel
Security. The decision came in the aftermath of a series of poor
reviews from industry publications, most of which found that
McAfee software provided an excellent spam filter but that its
antivirus capabilities had been superseded by competitors.
Further, while it did a relatively good job of detecting viruses,
if an infection reached a computer system, McAfee's software
did a poor job of actually removing the malware. Despite the
criticisms, McAfee researchers remain one of the top sources
of antivirus information in the world and have contributed to
the detection and negation of most of the largest worms and
viruses in recent history.

Microsoft Corporation

Microsoft Corporation is the largest software developing company in the world. Its flagship product, the Microsoft Windows operating system, controls a dominant share of the personal computer (PC) market on a global basis. Its Office suite of programs is also present on a majority of PC systems in the world and is used by billions of people on a daily basis. Recently, Microsoft has diversified its business offerings by moving into the computer hardware market as well as the video game console industry. Microsoft is one of the most valuable companies in the world, and arguably the most powerful high-technology corporation on the planet.

Microsoft was founded in 1975 by Bill Gates and Paul Allen, two childhood friends. Both had dropped out of college to begin careers as computer programmers, but the public release of the Altair 8800 microcomputer created an opportunity for the aspiring young software developers. They began with a BASIC interpreter program for the Altair system, and in 1980, won a contract with IBM to create a new operating system for the company's first entry into the PC market, named MS-DOS (Microsoft disk operating system). As the IBM market share quickly grew, the Microsoft products needed to power the machines grew at the same rate. Rather than simply cash in on its initial product, though, Microsoft proved both aggressive and innovative, releasing Microsoft Mouse in 1981 and in the process creating one of the ubiquitous pieces of computer hardware in use today. Allen left the company in 1983, after being diagnosed with Hodgkin's lymphoma, but remained a major stockholder in the corporation, which became a publicly traded company in 1986.

As IBM and its competitors continued to develop computer hardware, Microsoft expanded its operating system creations, which could be used on almost any computer platform, even those not produced by IBM. In 1985, the company built a user-friendly interface, Windows, that revolutionized the usability for computers in the personal and corporate environments. No longer was any programming expertise required to use a computer terminal, as the systems were designed to make their operation as simple as possible. The productivity of computers advanced exponentially with the release of Microsoft Office in 1990, a suite of programs including word-processing and spreadsheet programs. At the same time, the company continued to expand and improve its operating systems and other software offerings.

Microsoft's Windows revolutionized the computing industry, but it came at a price. Not only did its inclusion increase the price of every PC that contained Windows, but it also took up an increasingly large amount of storage space due to the ever-expanding size of the software's code. The size of the code also made sweeping it for programming errors and vulnerabilities an almost impossible task. Microsoft recognized that fact, and began a policy of releasing regular updates to patch and fix known vulnerabilities. Unfortunately, this solution required users to diligently update their computers on a regular basis, and those who did not do so became vulnerable to malware and exploitation of their systems.

Microsoft's dominance of the PC operating system market has made it a huge target for hackers, who spend enormous amounts of time and resources looking for vulnerabilities in Microsoft products. In the past two decades, substantial numbers of vulnerabilities have been exposed in the Office suite as well, creating a new vector by which hackers can attack other owners' computers. Critics have argued that Microsoft has done too little to identify and prevent potential vulnerabilities, preferring to rely upon other researchers, including hackers, to find the gaps in the software rather than doing it themselves. There is a financial aspect to the argument, in that updates are available only to owners of licensed copies of Microsoft products. Thus, the millions of pirated copies in use throughout the world cannot be updated, and hence are vulnerable to an uncountable number of malware programs.

Gates remains the chief technology advisor of Microsoft, having stepped down as CEO in 2000 and chairman of the board in 2014. In 2006, he began to transition from full-time work at Microsoft to part time, devoting more of his time and efforts to the Bill and Melinda Gates Foundation, a charity organization that has pioneered humanitarian causes in the developing world. Thanks to the success of his company, Gates became one of the richest people in the world, and according to some measures, the wealthiest. He remains one of the foremost innovators in computer programming in the industry and devotes a substantial amount of his time to advocating for greater computer security and efforts to prevent cyber warfare.

Mitnick, Kevin

Kevin is one of the earliest nationally famous American hackers, an author, and a computer security consultant. He has been arrested repeatedly for engaging in cyber crimes, and his cases have helped to define the U.S. law enforcement approach to hacking. He is one of the most notorious hackers in history, and an icon in the underground cyber community, although most of his criminal activities were facilitated by social engineering rather than creative software coding.

Mitnick was born in Los Angeles in 1963, and after graduating from high school, attended Pierce College and the University of Southern California, both located in the Los Angeles area. He began experimenting with social engineering as a teenager, convincing a friendly bus driver in Los Angeles to describe the function of the punch card system used by the bus network. Mitnick found he could ride the buses for free by plucking unused bus transfers from the trash cans near the stops and altering them with a store-bought ticket punch. As a teenager, Mitnick also became interested in computers and the idea of hacking. At age 16, Mitnick gained access to the computer network of the Digital Equipment Corporation

(DEC), which had no security systems beyond using an unlisted telephone number for modem access. Once Mitnick learned the correct number, he was able to access DEC's entire software archive, which he copied without permission. Mitnick also experimented with phreaking, a system of making free telephone calls using a whistle to simulate electronic commands to a telephone's switching equipment.

In 1988, Mitnick was arrested for stealing DEC's software and sentenced to 12 months in prison and three years of parole. During his parole period, Mitnick resumed his hacking activities, breaking into the Pacific Bell voice mail network, an intrusion detected by the system administrator. When a warrant was issued for his arrest, on the grounds that he had broken the terms of his parole, Mitnick fled to avoid returning to prison.

During Mitnick's flight, he began to specialize in computer attacks against the telecommunications industry, largely for his own gain. He communicated by cloning cellular phones, making it impossible to trace his location, and in the process of finding the necessary data to clone phones, Mitnick also stole computer software from the telephone companies. He exhibited many of the classic symptoms of addiction in his pursuit of computer intrusions, taking unnecessary risks that eventually contributed to his apprehension in Raleigh, North Carolina, in 1995. At the time of his arrest, Mitnick was the Federal Bureau of Investigation's most wanted criminal for computer crimes.

In 1999, Mitnick pled guilty to wire fraud, computer fraud, and interception of wire communications as part of a plea deal in U.S. federal court. When his punishment for breaking his parole and fleeing prosecution was added, Mitnick received a sentence of more than five years in a federal penitentiary. Most of that time was served while his case worked its way through the courts, with a substantial portion of it in solitary confinement out of a fear that Mitnick had the ability to control computers merely by whistling into a telephone receiver. If anything, this provision of his sentence simply demonstrated the ignorance of law enforcement and the judicial system, neither of which had a solid grasp of the mechanics of phreaking. He was released from prison in early 2000, again with a three-year parole period. During his parole, Mitnick was specifically barred from using any communications technology other than a landline telephone. His lawyers negotiated a reprieve on this issue, and the supervising court eventually granted Mitnick access to the Internet during his parole.

Mitnick became something of a cult hero within the hacking community, as many of his fellow hackers considered him a victim of overzealous prosecution and fear-mongering. While Mitnick undoubtedly broke into dozens of different computer networks, there is little evidence that he caused any damage or that he sought to enrich himself, beyond gaining access to the ability to freely communicate. Mitnick's autobiographical description of his activities, *The Art of Deception*, was published in 2002. In it, he claims that he obtained passwords, codes, and permissions through social engineering rather than by writing software or using code-cracking programs. If true, this claim would indicate that Mitnick is more of a skilled con artist than a hacker. Mitnick has been the subject of multiple books and a documentary film, all of which have contributed to his reputation within the hacker community.

Since completion of his parole, Mitnick has published two books on computer security, *The Art of Intrusion: The Real Stories behind the Exploits of Hackers, Intruders and Deceivers* (2005) and *Ghost in the Wires: My Adventures as the World's Most Wanted Hacker* (2011). He founded a computer security firm, Mitnick Security Consulting, that specializes in attacks-for-hire against corporate and private networks for the purpose of exposing security flaws so that they can be fixed before a malignant hacker exploits them. He is also the "Chief Hacking Officer" of KnowBe4, a security awareness training company that works with computer security officers to alert them to emerging cyber threats.

National Security Agency

The National Security Agency (NSA) is the premier U.S. intelligence agency tasked with signals intelligence (SIGINT) collection, decoding, and counterintelligence. Thus, in many ways, it is the foremost civilian cyber agency in the world. The NSA also holds responsibility for securing U.S. government communications systems against enemy intrusions. Like the more well-known Central Intelligence Agency (CIA), the NSA is authorized to utilize clandestine means to achieve its objectives, including bugging electronic systems, engaging in cyber espionage and sabotage, and potentially launching cyber attacks against both state and nonstate actors.

The NSA was formally created in 1952, although it grew out of several earlier organizations tasked with intercepting enemy signals and protecting American communications. These predecessor organizations included the U.S. Army's Cipher Bureau and Military Intelligence Branch, founded in 1917; the Signals Security Agency, created during World War II; and the Armed Forces Security Agency, established in 1949. For the first few decades after its founding, even the existence of the NSA was a closely guarded secret. Throughout the Cold War, the NSA gradually assumed an ever-increasing role in the attempt to collect useful information from electronic signals, using radio intercepts and satellites. During the investigations of the Watergate scandal, it was revealed that the NSA had routinely bugged the communications of President Richard Nixon's domestic political enemies, including prominent critics of the Vietnam War. In 1978, the U.S. legislature passed the Foreign Surveillance Act, a measure that severely limited the ability of intelligence agencies in the United States to collect SIGINT within the United States.

As computer technology rapidly expanded, the NSA became the lead agency for all forms of cyber espionage and counterintelligence activities on behalf of the U.S. government.

When the Cold War ended, most intelligence services in the United States, including the NSA, underwent drastic budget and personnel cuts. However, the NSA actually managed to expand its operations, largely due to the decrease in the price of computer equipment. Agency leadership argued for more resources on the grounds that the collection and analysis of SIGINT was far less costly, and more effective, than any attempts to develop human intelligence sources (HUMINT). Because encryption systems became increasingly more effective, the NSA was forced to engage in an effective cyber arms race, building up its own capabilities to keep pace with any potential competitors. It did so with very little government scrutiny, particularly in the aftermath of the September 11, 2001, terror attacks. During the War on Terror, the NSA essentially had a "blank check" to pursue any technology or data source that might aid in the attempt to destroy Al Qaeda. This led to a massive increase in the capabilities of the NSA, and very few limits on its surveillance targets.

The NSA has been accused of a number of actions that might violate domestic or international law, to include the collection of enormous volumes of "metadata" on U.S. users of cellular telephones; the bugging of foreign leaders' personal communication devices; and supplying collected information to domestic law enforcement agencies. Many of the programs of a questionable nature were revealed by Edward Snowden, a former NSA contractor who fled the country bearing the evidence needed to be an NSA "whistle-blower." Snowden alleged that the NSA was actively engaged in spying upon U.S. citizens, without any pretense of a legal warrant to do so; that it was attempting to monitor and record millions of telephone calls per day; and that it had built extremely detailed electronic dossiers on tens of millions of American citizens, linking their usage of technology and social media to create a massive database of personal profiles (Greenberg 2013). The Snowden revelations have provoked an enormous amount of scrutiny aimed toward an incredibly secretive organization, particularly from leaders of nations closely allied with the United States, who were appalled to discover that their personal conversations may have been recorded by the NSA (Poitras, Rosenbach, and Stark 2013).

Since at least 1998, the NSA has included an Office of Tailored Access Operations (TAO), a dedicated intelligence-gathering unit that can monitor, attack, and infiltrate foreign computer networks. Open-source records indicate that the TAO includes at least 1,000 dedicated hackers, designers, and engineers. Snowden leaked documents in 2013 and 2014 that suggest the TAO can break into most commonly used hardware and software with little effort, making it an extremely capable cyber warfare organization. Major U.S. telecommunications and Internet service providers have been accused of collaborating with the NSA to allow access to their data and networks as well as those of their customers, although none of the companies have confirmed such a direct link. Microsoft Corporation has also been accused of providing vulnerabilities suitable for exploitation to the NSA, before it issues patches to the public to close the vulnerabilities.

The NSA is currently led by Admiral Michael S. Rogers, who also serves as the head of U.S. Cyber Command (CYBERCOM). It is headquartered at Fort Meade, Maryland, where a classified number of employees numbering in the tens of thousands operate under a "black" budget, also of a classified amount. While technically, the NSA is under the direction of the Department of Defense, in practice, it operates as a hybrid military-intelligence organization with as much in common with the CIA as with the armed forces. It operates its own internal computer network system, akin to the DoD's NIPRNet and SIPRNet. The NSA also offers training and collaboration for other agencies tasked with training cyber warriors for the United States. Each year, the NSA offers cyber exercises that include an NSA "Red Team" that attempts to hack into sites being defended by teams of cyber experts. Most participants report that the NSA has always managed to break into all of the systems, and that the real challenge is simply to hold them off as long as possible and to learn from the experience. The NSA remains one of the most secretive organizations in the U.S. government, and barring further leaks from internal sources like Snowden, its activities are likely to remain highly classified and inaccessible to the public.

NATO Cooperative Cyber Defence Centre of Excellence

The NATO Cooperative Cyber Defence Center of Excellence (CCD COE) is located in Tallinn, Estonia, where it was founded in 2008. The organization was established to facilitate NATO cooperation in cyberspace, and to train NATO personnel in cyber security. The CCD COE also conducts research into cyber defense technology. Its location in Tallinn is largely a nod to the Russian hacking attacks upon Estonian cyber networks in 2007, and it serves as a symbolic reminder that an attack on any member of NATO, even through cyberspace, is considered an attack upon all members.

In 2003, the government of Estonia, one of the most wired nations on earth, proposed the creation of a collective cyber defense center, three years before Estonia joined NATO. Estonian cyber experts recognized the potential havoc that might be caused by a sustained cyber attack and, at the 2006 Riga Summit, pushed for an acknowledgment that international cooperation was needed to protect critical cyber infrastructure over the long term. When Russian hackers launched massive DDoS attacks against Estonian sites in 2007, the value of such attacks was amply demonstrated. In response, Estonia attempted, unsuccessfully, to invoke Article 5 of the NATO Charter, which might have triggered an alliance escalation against Russia.

Although NATO did not agree to enter the cyber conflict in 2007, the computer attacks demonstrated the need for a clarification of the alliance's policy regarding cyber attacks. During the 2008 NATO summit in Bucharest, the alliance announced that it would "provide a capability to assist allied nations, upon request, to counter a cyber attack." The establishment of the CCD COE was one key step to providing such a capacity for cyber responses. Not every member of NATO has chosen to join the operation of the CCD COE, but most of the major players have become involved to at least some extent. The organization's first goal is to improve the cyber interoperability of NATO networks, following the same patterns established for NATO standards of other communication gear. It also serves to create and refine NATO cyber doctrine, improve information security among the military networks of member states, allow cyber experimentation in a controlled environment, and establish the legal framework of military-related cyber activities. It has gradually become more involved with NATO exercises, supplying vital cyber expertise that had been largely marginalized in previous training operations.

People's Liberation Army Unit 61398 (China)

The People's Liberation Army (PLA) is the military organization of the People's Republic of China, which assumed control of the Chinese mainland in 1949 after a long and bloody civil war. Since that time, PLA units fought directly against the combined forces of the United States and the United Nations during the Korean War, provided assistance but did not engage in combat against the United States in the Vietnam War, and have fought a series of border skirmishes with India, the Soviet Union, and Vietnam. The PLA is by far the largest military organization in the world, with more than two million active duty and two million reserve duty personnel. It has the second-largest budget of any military, with an annual expenditure of over $130 billion. Unlike many militaries in the world, the PLA has direct responsibility for the cyber security of the Chinese nation and also takes the lead in launching cyber attacks devoted to espionage against rival governments and private corporations.

The PLA is organized into various bureaus and departments, with the Second Bureau, Third Department of the General Staff dedicated to cyber activity. Within the Third Department are organizations dedicated to virtually every aspect of cyber activities. PLA Unit 61398, based in Pudong, Shanghai, has been identified as one of the most active hacking organizations in the world, and is accused of carrying out advanced persistent threat campaigns against hundreds of Western targets, including defense contracting firms, financial corporations, and software engineers. It has been implicated in the creation of the GhostNet system, which largely targeted supporters of the Free Tibet movement and managed to infiltrate more than 1,000 computers in over 100 countries. Unit 61398 was probably culpable in Operation Aurora, Operation Shady RAT, and Operation Titan Rain, all of which were designed to exfiltrate enormous volumes of sensitive data from U.S. companies and military networks.

The activities of Unit 61398 have been discovered and analyzed by a number of sources, including the cyber security firm Mandiant, which released a report on the organization's activities in 2013. In the past three years, FireEye, which acquired Mandiant at the end of 2013, has tracked hundreds of targets attacked by Unit 61398, and estimates that the group has successfully hacked into the network operations of more than 1,000 organizations in just the last few years. The group attempts to maintain secrecy, but the malware implanted by its members communicates regularly with the servers housed in the same building as the PLA unit and tends to be active almost exclusively during business hours.

In early 2013, the *New York Times* publicly accused the PLA of attacking the newspaper's internal network and compromising its systems. In response, the editorial board decided to run a front-page article directly accusing the Chinese government of openly conducting cyber espionage and stealing billions of dollars' worth of trade secrets. This accusation provoked a massive denial operation from the Chinese government, which also

countered that the *New York Times* is hostile to Chinese interests and that its bias has led to unfair criticism in the public.
On May 19, 2014, a federal grand jury indicted five officers
from Unit 61398 on charges of stealing confidential business
information and intellectual property, as well as sabotage
of American corporate computer networks. Unsurprisingly,
the Chinese government has adamantly refused to extradite
the individuals or to cooperate with any attempts to investigate
the case.

PLA Unit 61398 is widely regarded as one of the most
prominent examples of state-sponsored cyber attacks. It has
devoted a substantial amount of time and effort to examining
and mapping the computer networks of infrastructure organizations in the United States, and has almost certainly managed
to place malware within those networks. Given the Chinese
government's determination to conduct wars by any means
available, and to place great emphasis upon winning the battle
for information, particularly in the cyber domain, it is likely
that probing attacks against American infrastructure serve a
preparatory function, and that the malware has created a
significant number of backdoors to allow rapid access to
Chinese hackers should they be ordered to sabotage or disrupt
American infrastructure.

Qiao Liang and Wang Xiangsui

Qiao Liang and Wang Xiangsui are two officers in the People's
Liberation Army (PLA) of China. They have developed a reputation as original thinkers and military theorists, due largely
to their authorship of *Unrestricted Warfare* when bother
were senior colonels in the PLA. This work, first published
in China in 1999 and soon translated into English and
French by the Chinese Foreign Broadcast Information
Service, addresses the issue of how China can potentially defeat
a technologically superior enemy through any means available. The authors saw a need for the work after watching the

American-led coalition that easily pushed Iraq out of Kuwait in the 1991 Persian Gulf War. They recognized that the Chinese military, while the largest in the world, simply did not have the ability to outmatch the United States in a conventional fight, even if the conflict remained confined to the Southeast Asian mainland. The Iraqi experience demonstrated that raw numbers provided little, if any, advantage when faced with an enemy decades advanced in technological development.

Qiao and Wang considered the United States to be a victim of its own success, in that its demonstrated conventional warfare superiority might deter some nations from engaging in a direct conflict, but would provoke other nations to investigate irregular warfare. To a certain extent, they were correct in this prediction, as demonstrated by the American struggles in Iraq and Afghanistan once the periods of conventional combat had been completed. In both locations, the United States proved completely unready for the challenges of counterinsurgency warfare, making potential adversaries of the future believe that American victory in a conflict was not a foregone conclusion.

Qiao and Wang coined the term "informatization" to describe their concept of modern and future warfare. To them, the primary struggle of future conflicts between highly developed states revolved around the collection, protection, and dissemination of information. Whichever nation in a war can do the best job of controlling the flow of information will hold a tremendous advantage over its opponents. They further argue that wars are not fought merely through military means. In modern societies, the military is inextricably connected with, and dependent upon, other organizations and networks. Thus, an attack upon a nation's economic infrastructure, for example, might have a much more telling effect than any effort to attack its fielded forces. They identified a number of other novel ways to attack a rival, many of which do not fit the traditional definition of warfare, but which might have devastating effects in their own right.

For example, Qiao and Wang suggested that "lawfare," essentially using international and nongovernmental legal organizations to change the rules of a conflict before any violence occurred, might prove a far more efficient use of resources than any attempt to design and build new military technology. They also argued that network-based attacks upon the energy infrastructure of a nation, such as cyber attacks on the electrical power grid, would have exponential effects that would reverberate throughout both the military and society as a whole. Without a trustworthy power supply, a nation would struggle to maintain its logistical apparatus needed for modern warfare. The logical inference from this point is that China, or any other nation interested in pursuing unrestricted warfare, might prepare for any potential conflict by attempting to hack into a rival's infrastructure control network, placing malware and trapdoors so that if a conflict erupted, they could trigger a massive failure through a fairly simple cyber operation.

Ironically, even though the purpose of the book was to determine how to win a conflict against a technologically advanced enemy, the authors also noted that it might be possible to close the gap of technological advance by using cyber espionage to gather as many technical and operational details about enemy equipment as possible. Over time, this would allow copies to be made of enemy technology, without the required investment of enormous resources and time to facilitate their native development. Many cyber security authors argue that Qiao and Wang inspired a massive offensive cyber campaign by the PLA with their suggestions in *Unrestricted Warfare.*

Qiao remains in the PLA, functioning largely in a strategic development role, although his exact position is not publicly disclosed. He has attained the rank of major general, and may be tapped for even higher responsibilities in the ongoing effort to modernize Chinese military technology, doctrine, and strategy. Wang retired from the PLA shortly after publication of his iconic work, and is now a professor at Beihang University in Beijing, formerly named Beijing University of Aeronautics and Astronautics (BUAA). This school specializes in the development of high-technology innovations for the PLA, including the effort to utilize materials stolen in cyber attacks against Western corporations and defense institutions and apply them to the Chinese military.

RAND Corporation

The RAND (Research and Development) Corporation is a think tank that provides strategic guidance, in-depth analysis, and policy examinations to the U.S. government, the U.S. military, and associated organizations. It was founded in 1948 as a collaborative partnership between the newly independent U.S. Air Force and the Douglas Aircraft Company, but has grown far beyond its initial size and mission. RAND still receives funds from the U.S. government, but has diversified to included finances from private donors, universities, and the health care industry, all of whom have benefitted from previous RAND analyses. RAND now operates as a nonprofit organization using more than $250 million in annual revenues.

When General of the Air Force Henry H. Arnold envisioned the creation of RAND, he expected it to serve as a means of developing very long-range technological projects. In this regard, Arnold thought that an independent agency would be best able to create major weapons improvements, including some projects on the order of the Manhattan Project that might revolutionize the nature of warfare. When the Douglas Aircraft Company became concerned that RAND's theoretical research would hinder the company's ability to bid on major defense procurement projects, RAND was spun off into a separate organization. Since that time, RAND has served in more of an advisory and analysis capacity, rather than in direct pursuit of hard research objectives, which has remained with other government and private agencies. RAND's current mission statement is "to help improve policy and decision making through research and analysis."

RAND's early contributions included major projects of systems analysis for the space program, computer science, and developing artificial intelligence. RAND's researchers were instrumental in developing both the theoretical concept and the actual structure of the Internet, and have helped in the long-range planning for its improvement and governance. Most of RAND's research directly involves national security in some fashion, although it has also done major long-term studies for other aspects of the U.S. government. RAND has served as a magnet for top talent, with more than 30 Nobel Prize winners working with the organization in some fashion. Much of RAND's national security research is highly classified, but every piece of unclassified research is posted on the RAND website for free public access.

Rogers, Michael S.

Admiral Michael S. Rogers is the commander of the U.S. Cyber Command (CYBERCOM) and the director of the National Security Agency (NSA). He assumed command of both from General Keith Alexander on April 3, 2014. Prior to assuming control of the U.S. Department of Defense's largest and best-resourced cyber warfare center, Rogers commanded the Tenth Fleet and the U.S. Fleet Cyber command, the U.S. Navy's primary cyber warfare organizations.

Rogers was born and raised in Chicago, but attended Auburn University in Alabama, where he participated in the Naval Reserve Officers Training Corps (NROTC) program. As a surface-warfare officer, his first duties in the navy were in naval gunfire support operations, and he saw combat actions near Grenada, Lebanon, and El Salvador during the 1980s. After five years of service, Rogers shifted his focus within the Navy to cryptology, moving into one of the most highly classified fields within the U.S. military. Although cryptology is extremely important to the military's operations, it does not usually provide many opportunities for career advancement when compared to the more visible and glamorous command opportunities within the fleet. Nevertheless, he stayed within the specialty and advanced much faster than his peers, primarily due to his interest in remaining up to date on the most advanced computer encryption capabilities.

In 2003, the United States led a coalition that invaded Iraq, both to depose President Saddam Hussein and to search for weapons of mass destruction (WMDs). Prior to the invasion, the United States coordinated a massive information operations campaign against the Iraqi military, characterized by calls to officers' cell phones, e-mails to service members, and broadcast interruptions on military networks. In every case, the recipients were instructed to park their military vehicles in specific formations that would be visible from the air as a signal that they would not offer resistance. Those units that complied saw their vehicles destroyed by airpower attacks, but were not themselves targeted by coalition aircraft. Rogers, who served on the Joint Staff in the preparation of the invasion, has been given much of the credit for this massive campaign.

In 2007, Rogers was named the commander of the military intelligence program for the Pacific Command (PACOM), headquartered in Hawaii. Two years later, he was tapped to head the entire military intelligence program for the Joint Chiefs of Staff, followed by an assignment to command the U.S. Fleet Cyber Command. His star continued its meteoric rise in 2014, when President Barack Obama nominated Rogers to command CYBERCOM and direct the NSA. The position included a promotion to four-star rank, the highest level currently in use by the U.S. military. Rogers assumed command over CYBERCOM and NSA as the organizations were dealing with the fallout from revelations by Edward Snowden that the NSA had engaged in a massive surveillance campaign that targeted both American citizens and international political leaders.

Some observers expected Alexander to essentially take the blame for the programs before his departure, and thought that Rogers would denounce the programs and vow to change the way his organizations collect data. Instead, Rogers has been relatively silent about the procedures of CYBERCOM and the NSA, allowing a pair of court cases to determine whether the data collection was illegal. In July 2014, two federal courts ruled that the NSA had not broken any laws in its operations, although it was suggested that further oversight by the judicial system might be warranted in the future.

Russian Business Network (RBN)

The Russian Business Network (RBN) is one of the largest cyber crime organizations in the world. It offers hosting services for a wide variety of illegal websites, including ones that specialize in identity theft, credit card fraud, and child pornography. It also collaborates with the largest spam operators and malware distributers in cyberspace. The RBN was registered in St. Petersburg, Russia, in 2006, and quickly grew into an international criminal network. Many of its activities have proven impossible to trace by global authorities, in part because the Russian government turns a blind eye to the RBN's activities, as long as it does not target Russian interests or institutions (Krebs 2007).

In addition to providing hosting services for illicit networks, the RBN also serves as a clearinghouse for cyber mercenaries, offering up enormous botnet resources for rental that can then be used in DDoS attacks. Businesses that have criticized the RBN for its practices have encountered an almost endless stream of attacks originating from the RBN's servers, which are housed on hundreds of networks in dozens of countries. The massive DDoS attacks on Estonia in 2007 and Georgia in 2008 may have been initiated by the RBN, possibly with some degree of government collusion. There is some evidence that the RBN's founder, who is known only by his online nickname "Flyman," may be related to a powerful Russian politician, which would account for some of the protections that the RBN has been able to claim from the Russian government (Warren 2007).

Snowden, Edward

Edward Snowden is a former contractor for the National Security Agency (NSA) who is responsible for one of the largest breaches of classified documents in American history. In 2013, he released hundreds of classified documents that showed the NSA had engaged in several massive surveillance programs, including efforts to collect data on American citizens and to penetrate the classified networks of allied nations. Snowden has been charged with violations of the Espionage Act and theft of government property and, if convicted, could face decades of imprisonment should he return to U.S. soil. As of this writing, Snowden lived in Russia, which granted him temporary asylum on August 1, 2013. He had applied for, but not received, asylum from the governments of more than 40 countries.

Snowden was born in 1983 in Elizabeth City, North Carolina. He did not complete high school, but did earn a GED through the Anne Arundel Community College in Maryland. After a brief enlistment in the U.S. Army, Snowden began to work as a computer security specialist, obtaining a position as a computer systems administrator with the Central Intelligence Agency (CIA) in 2006. In that capacity, he was posted to Geneva, Switzerland, where he claimed he witnessed CIA efforts to compromise a Swiss banker by setting him up for a drunk-driving charge. In 2012, Snowden accepted a position working for Dell Corporation as an NSA contractor, stationed at Yokota Air Base in Japan. He consulted with government and military leaders on how to effectively secure computer networks from international intrusions. At the same time, he began to download classified documents to removable data devices, using his Top Secret/Secure Classified Information clearance to obtain access.

In 2013, Snowden accepted a position with security contractor Booz Allen, a job that he claims to have pursued for the express purpose of obtaining classified documents. There is substantial argument over whether Snowden used passwords and access illegally obtained from coworkers, or whether he simply had all the necessary permissions to access the more than 200,000 documents that he downloaded and later leaked to a variety of outlets. By all accounts, Snowden has an enormous talent for finding creative ways to break into classified computer networks, a skill that caused his employers to hire him in spite of clearly falsified credentials on his employment applications. Many of the educational qualifications he provided to potential employers were transparently incorrect. Snowden received his security clearance after a private corporation, U.S. Investigations Services (USIS), filed documentation that he had passed a background check. In 2014, the U.S. Department of Justice filed fraud charges against USIS, alleging that the company failed to actually investigate individuals, and instead simply falsified reports on the subjects it was paid to examine.

Snowden has claimed in a series of interviews with several media outlets that he attempted to use internal channels to challenge the constitutionality of the NSA programs, but that his supervisors refused to investigate the legal issues, or simply covered up any potential problems. The NSA has repeatedly claimed that there is no evidence that Snowden attempted to use the proper procedures to report his concerns. In any event, in late 2012, Snowden contacted Glenn Greenwald of *The Guardian* and began negotiations to leak sensitive documents. In early 2013, he contacted documentary filmmaker Laura Poitras and expanded his leaking activities, followed shortly by contacting Barton Gellman of the *Washington Post*. When the first articles based upon his leaks appeared in early June 2013, Snowden was in Hong Kong. On June 22, the U.S. State

Department revoked Snowden's passport, hoping to prevent him from leaving Hong Kong before he could be extradited to stand trial in the United States. The next day, Snowden boarded a flight to Moscow, where he became stranded at the airport due to his lack of a Russian visa and his revoked passport. After nearly six weeks, Snowden received a one-year temporary asylum.

The extent of Snowden's leaks is not currently certain, with some estimates that he downloaded up to two million documents. His computer skills ensure that he has the capability to hide his tracks and store his stolen materials in any number of digital locations. He has gradually leaked his materials to a variety of news organizations, beginning with revelations of the classified surveillance programs that he found unconstitutional. His leaks began with documents related to the NSA's PRISM program, a systematic attempt to access Americans' Google and Yahoo accounts. Snowden's revelations have not been limited to American surveillance programs; he has also revealed classified information about British, Australian, and Canadian programs of a similar nature. Snowden demonstrated that the NSA had constructed a massive telephone calls database that gathered contact information for millions of calls each day, and that included the transfer of call data from Verizon to the U.S. government. He claimed that during his time as an NSA contractor, he had the ability to look into anyone in the world, for virtually any reason, stating "I, sitting at my desk, could wiretap anyone, from you or your accountant, to a federal judge or even the president, if I had a personal email."

Snowden also informed the public that many of the standard forms of commercially available encryption did little to stop NSA snooping, as the agency could crack them with little effort. The NSA became heavily involved in social networks and online gaming communities, most notably Second Life and World of Warcraft, as a means of gathering information about specific users. It also took great pains to collect a database of sexual activities involving any potential radical elements of

American society, in case future efforts to discredit such individuals proved necessary.

Perhaps the most damaging leaked information that Snowden provided was ample evidence that U.S. intelligence agencies had spied on the personal communication devices and accounts of dozens of national leaders around the world, including some of the closest allies of the United States. In particular, German chancellor Angela Merkel took personal umbrage at the discovery that the NSA had tapped her personal cell phone. The NSA's collection efforts went well beyond national security issues, and crossed over into economic and industrial espionage, precisely the types of activities that the U.S. government had protested when they were practiced by the Chinese government. While it is impossible to accurately measure the effect of Snowden's revelations upon U.S. diplomatic relations, his leaks have certainly damaged the American government's relationships with its counterparts around the globe.

The reaction to Snowden's leaks has been mixed. Many press outlets have hailed his efforts as an example of necessary transparency, while officials from U.S. intelligence agencies have called his actions cowardly and traitorous. Some have claimed that Snowden's leaks have helped terror organizations by showing them the NSA's collection methods, thus allowing them to change their communications to avoid interception. In January 2014, President Barack Obama announced a series of fundamental changes to the NSA's surveillance programs, a decision that was almost certainly forced by the Snowden leaks. Libertarian groups have called for a presidential pardon, or at least clemency for Snowden, on the grounds that he had exposed illegal and unacceptable government interference in the lives of American citizens.

Regardless of Snowden's motivations and intentions, his revelations have triggered a national debate about the role of intelligence agencies in the collection of surveillance data, and what level of monitoring of the domestic American population is acceptable. In December 2013, two court cases related to Snowden's leaks created even more controversy. In *Klayman v. Obama*, a federal judge ruled that the NSA's bulk collection of telephone metadata was unconstitutional, and that the government had unlawfully monitored the communications of the plaintiff, Larry Klayman, for harassment purposes. Less than two weeks later, the American Civil Liberties Union (ACLU) lost a case, *ACLU v. Clapper*, filed against James Clapper, the director of national intelligence. In that case, the ACLU argued that the entire program was unconstitutional. The judge found that the value of the surveillance outweighed the privacy claims, and therefore the program was legal.

Perhaps the greatest irony of Snowden's activities is that they will likely provoke many nations and private companies to devote significantly more effort to cyber security. While the NSA and other state-sponsored intelligence agencies will still likely have the ability to penetrate many, if not most, computer networks, the casual collection of enormous volumes of data is likely to become at least somewhat more difficult in response to the Snowden revelations. Snowden has received dozens of whistle-blowing and public-service awards for his actions, and has participated in a number of prominent technology-conference speaking engagements via Internet teleconference. Snowden remains a controversial figure in the debate over national security, the right to privacy, and the role of intelligence agencies in the collection of information about individual citizens.

Symantec Corporation

Symantec Corporation is a technology company founded in Sunnyvale, California, in 1982 by Gary Hendrix. It is one of the largest computer security firms in the world, the producer of Norton Antivirus software, and one of the most trusted certificate authorities on the Internet. Symantec also offers storage, backup, and cloud computing capabilities for corporations and private individuals. It employs more than 20,000 individuals around the world, including some of the top threat detection analysts in the computer industry.

Hendrix used a National Science Foundation grant to found Symantec, intending initially to focus upon the development of artificial intelligence. They began by creating database and natural language–processing programs, but made the unfortunate decision to write their software to be compatible with the minicomputers designed by the Digital Electronic Corporation (DEC), rather than the IBM personal computer systems. When DEC collapsed, the Symantec products had no marketability, and the company was in a dangerous financial position, although its experts had developed a substantial knowledge base in a very new field. Symantec merged with C&E Software in 1984 and began to offer a pair of new products, "The Intelligent Assistant" natural language system and "Q&A," a database and word-processing program. The company still faced enormous hurdles and was forced to very aggressively market its software to avoid bankruptcy.

Despite its modest beginnings and early struggles, Symantec began to capture market share and increased sales, and continued to move into new areas of software development. In 1989, Symantec programmers began to develop an antivirus program, in part because it might create new partnership opportunities with Microsoft. In 1990, Symantec purchased Peter Norton Computing, already a producer of antivirus software, and merged its internal efforts into the existing Norton Antivirus program. This wildly successful venture soon accounted for more than 80 percent of Symantec's revenues, allowing the company to continue acquiring smaller computer firms and to drop its underperforming products. In 2004, Symantec merged with Veritas, the largest software industry merger in history at that time. In 2010, Symantec acquired Verisign, a major authentication business that issues trust certificates upon which Internet security depends.

In recent years, Symantec has had substantial turmoil in its leadership, with a series of short-lived CEOs running the company. Several vulnerabilities have been detected in Symantec antivirus and other software utilities, some of which make a computer vulnerable for exploitation by DDoS attacks. The company has been publicly accused of using scare tactics to convince computer users to purchase more expensive software to prevent or remove malware from infected machines. Symantec has also been targeted repeatedly by hacker organizations, at least two of which have publicly released sections of software code for proprietary Symantec programs. Verisign's network was breached in 2010, although the company kept that information secret for nearly two years and has never clarified which systems had been penetrated. The intrusion and the lack of transparency has led some system administrators to declare Verisign certificates untrustworthy. Given the very large market share held by Verisign, this means that a significant amount of doubt and mistrust has been sown over a large swath of the Internet, where reputation and trustworthiness are the keys to a functional business relationship.

Syrian Electronic Army

The Syrian Electronic Army (SEA) is an informal group of hackers that claim to support the Syrian government and its president, Bashar al-Assad. Their chosen methods tend toward relatively unsophisticated brute-force attacks, including DDoS and website defacements. They have targeted a wide variety of victims, including political dissidents within Syria, media outlets reporting upon conditions in the ongoing Syrian civil war, and human rights groups that accuse the Syrian government of violations. The SEA is the foremost Arab hacking group in the world, and it has launched a number of attacks against Israeli targets without the need for a specific provocation. Its relationship to the Syrian government has not been determined, although most indications are that the SEA is not a state-sponsored group, and that it more closely resembles an ideological cyber militia.

Members of the SEA include technologically savvy young hacktivists, possibly including some who are of Syrian descent but not actually living in Syria. The group has repeatedly managed to take over Twitter feeds from major media outlets, providing a very broad platform for its rather juvenile approach to hacktivism. Most of these accounts have been compromised via straightforward phishing activities. Some of the biggest successes of the group involved capturing control of the Reuters and Associated Press news agencies' Twitter feeds, which were used to send out false information about the Syrian civil war. Multiple news organizations picked up on the false information and reported it, assuming the news agencies would provide further information to back the reports. In addition to hacking, the group has launched DDoS attacks against some of the largest media organizations in the world, with limited success, and has conducted spam campaigns to spread pro-Syrian propaganda. The Facebook pages of President Barack Obama and President Nicolas Sarkozy have both been flooded by SEA commentary, taking advantage of the open comments feature common to many public figures' Facebook accounts.

Because most of the SEA's cyber intrusions have been to conduct website defacements or to spread misinformation, they have not developed a destructive reputation as of yet. However, in 2014, they managed to successfully infiltrate the servers of eBay, PayPal, and Facebook, suggesting that their capacity for misdeeds may be growing. In each case, the SEA claimed it had done so to demonstrate its abilities, not to conduct any form of cyber crime. When President Obama considered sending direct assistance to Syrian rebels in 2013, the SEA renewed its propaganda campaign, including a successful temporary seizure of the U.S. Marine Corps recruitment website. Although most of their attacks have been irritating rather than damaging, the SEA is an interesting group because they demonstrate that cyber warfare capabilities are not determined solely by the resources of a nation, and that access to the skills necessary for cyber attacks is not difficult to generate, even for a small nation embroiled in a civil war.

Tenenbaum, Ehud "Udi"

Ehud Tenenbaum, known in hacking circles as "The Analyzer," is an Israeli-born cyber criminal who perpetrated one of the earliest systematic intrusion campaigns against the computer networks of the U.S. Department of Defense and other government agencies. He was born in Ramat HaSharon, Israel, in 1979, and showed an early interest in computer technology as well as a knack for software code writing. He soon formed a small online hacker group that he led in a series of intrusion campaigns against the National Aeronautics and Space Administration (NASA), the Department of Defense, the Israeli Knesset, and a series of international academic institutions. Tenenbaum and his comrades set their sights high, aiming for some of the most secure and confidential networks in the world, including an attack upon the Israel Defense Force's classified network.

At times, Tenenbaum has trended toward hacktivism, including a series of attacks against the networks and servers of Hamas, the Palestinian terrorist organization based in the Gaza Strip that has sworn to eradicate Israel. On several occasions, Tenenbaum has claimed to have destroyed the Hamas website, although it is more likely that he only managed to knock it offline for a short period of time, as it remains in operation. Tenenbaum's group came to the notice of the Pentagon in 1998, which misinterpreted his group's cyber penetrations as a sophisticated Iraqi hacking campaign. The attacks prompted a massive interdepartmental investigation involving the Federal Bureau of Investigations, the U.S. Air Force Office of Special Investigations, NASA, the U.S. Department of Justice, the National Security Agency, and the Central Intelligence Agency. After an enormous investment of resources, the investigation, code-named "Solar Sunrise," revealed the involvement of

Tenenbaum, operating from Israel where such computer intrusions were not yet illegal, and two California teenagers, where they were against the law.

The Israeli police eventually arrested Tenenbaum for penetrating Israeli networks, but refused to extradite him to the United States for prosecution in an American court. He pled guilty, but offered a statement that his goal was to demonstrate the poor cyber security of the systems that he attacked, ostensibly to help improve their defenses. After a short stint in an Israeli prison, Tenenbaum founded an information security company, 2XS. In this regard, he followed the stereotypical attempt of a teenage hacker to monetize his previous criminal activities by offering to test cyber defenses in exchange for a fee. However, Tenenbaum found that running a cyber security business did not offer the type of lucrative rewards that he thought his talents should bring, and he once again turned to cyber crime. In 2008, Tenenbaum and a few of his hacker colleagues were arrested in Montreal and charged with credit card fraud, based upon hacking into financial corporations' networks to steal the numbers, which were then sold to other criminal groups for duplication and exploitation. Canada agreed to extradite Tenenbaum to the United States, where he pled guilty to the offense in exchange for cooperating with a larger cyber investigation and was sentenced to time already served. Tenenbaum continues to offer his refined hacking skills as a freelance cyber security expert.

U.S. Cyber Command

U.S. Cyber Command (CYBERCOM) is a military organization designed to unify the individual military services' efforts at cyber warfare into a single organization, placed under the control of U.S. Strategic Command (STRATCOM). In theory, this allows a combined effort at cyber defense against enemy cyber attacks. It also enables a coherent offensive strategy, should one be desired by U.S. political leaders, within the cyber domain. The joint nature of the organization will allow the military to reduce redundancies and increase information-sharing between the services, but it might also create a "group-think" effect rather than allowing diverse approaches to be presented and pursued.

The genesis of CYBERCOM began in 2006, when the U.S. Air Force unilaterally announced an intention to assume the leadership role in U.S. military efforts in cyberspace. Not surprisingly, the other services saw the Air Force effort as an attempt to preemptively assume control over a domain of interest to all of the services. Previous service rivalries reemerged, with accusations that the Air Force would prioritize its own interests with little regard for the needs or desires of the other services. Similar arguments had already marred effective cooperation in the application of air power in the Afghan and Iraq wars, with the Army accusing the Air Force of shirking its responsibilities for close air support of ground troops, and the Navy complaining that the Air Force minimized the utility and contributions of naval aviators. While the concept of unifying cyber operations generated a positive response, the other services had no interest in surrendering their cyber assets to Air Force control. After two years of bureaucratic infighting, the Air Force essentially dropped its proposal that it should run the entire effort, paving the way for a joint, unified command.

On June 23, 2009, Secretary of Defense Robert M. Gates directed the creation of a joint organization tasked with overseeing the military cyber effort. More than a year later, Air Force lieutenant general Keith Alexander presented a plan to Congress, outlining a new military organization. At the time of his submission, Alexander served as the director of the National Security Agency (NSA), a position he retained until his retirement from active duty in May 2014. His plan was accepted with minimal modifications, and not surprisingly, Alexander was named the first commander of the new unit. To signify the importance of the organization, he received a promotion to full general, one of only 38 officers in the U.S. military to hold four-star rank. He assumed control of Cyber Command at its new headquarters, located at Fort Meade, Maryland, collocated with the NSA. By blending the NSA and CYBERCOM, the Department of Defense essentially combined the cyber efforts of both the uniformed and civilian organizations dedicated to computerized warfare, and united them under a single leader. While this might have helped to synchronize the nation's approach to cyber warfare, it also blurred the line between military and nonmilitary assets. It further created the risk of groupthink and an inability to develop creative solutions to cyber challenges, in part due to the inherently formal nature of the military rank structure.

On April 5, 2014, Admiral Michael S. Rogers assumed command of CYBERCOM. Rogers's selection demonstrated the important principle that the unified command did not inherently belong to one service. The actual missions, responsibilities, and authorizations for Cyber Command are still in development as the young organization begins to assume control over the vast cyber assets held by the military. Chief among its subordinate organizations are the Second Army, the Tenth Fleet, and the Twenty-fourth Air Force, each of which has primary responsibility for its respective service's cyber efforts. As Cyber Command continues to expand and develop, it is likely to assert an increasing role in the development of a U.S. national cyber strategy, the first iteration of which was released in July 2011. Unsurprisingly, many of the most important aspects of Cyber Command's activities remain highly classified aspects of the national defense infrastructure.

WikiLeaks

WikiLeaks is an organization dedicated to the publication of secret information, government leaks, and classified data, often from anonymous sources. Ostensibly created to hold governments accountable for their actions, WikiLeaks has largely served to publish enormous amounts of classified communications with little regard for the ramifications of its dissemination of the information. It has mainly hurt Western democracies, which tend to have a more open information-access system and fewer controls upon its potential leakers. Further, those nations are less likely to take drastic action against employees who release classified data or their families, while totalitarian regimes rarely self-impose such restrictions. That said, WikiLeaks does not specifically target governments or nongovernmental institutions, so much as it serves as an anonymous clearinghouse for leaks. The organization claims that it carefully vets each document before publication or release, and that it has never been the victim of a misattributed or false leak, largely on the grounds that traditional media sources provide ample opportunities for such data.

WikiLeaks was founded in 2006 by a small group of mostly unidentified activists. The most public founder of WikiLeaks, Julian Assange, has taken credit for the inspiration, original coding, and philosophy of WikiLeaks, although hundreds of unpaid volunteers have been associated with the website and organization. Prior to 2010, WikiLeaks operated as a traditional wiki, allowing users to post and modify content. However, in 2010, the group decided to retain full control over the site, ostensibly to maintain fidelity in the documents being leaked. In the same year, WikiLeaks began to receive an enormous volume of classified material from an unknown U.S. source, eventually revealed to be Private Bradley Manning, including hundreds of thousands of confidential diplomatic cables from decades of State Department records. These releases caused enormous embarrassment for the U.S. government, which immediately banned federal employees from accessing the WikiLeaks site, even from home computers. Out of fear that the United States might take a far more punitive action, WikiLeaks publicly released an "insurance file" under a presumably unbreakable encryption key, with the implied threat that the password to the file would be released should anything happen to the website or to Assange. Four larger insurance files followed under encryption. To date, while the files have been copied to countless servers and computers, the passphrases have not been released, and the encryption has not been broken.

Due to its facilitating the release of classified information, WikiLeaks has become the target of a number of governments, cyber organizations, and corporations. A number of court judgments against WikiLeaks have resulted in orders to shut down the site, but it is hosted on dozens of mirror sites and under multiple different domain names, making it almost impossible to close down by court order. WikiLeaks has also been subjected to massive DDoS attacks, with similar failed results due to its redundancy. Its server hosts are in nations with extremely strong legal protections for press agencies, making a diplomatic agreement to close the website by force highly unlikely to succeed. In 2010, WikiLeaks actually released a U.S. Department of Defense counterintelligence report that offered suggestions for how to deter WikiLeaks from further disclosures, a sure gesture of contempt for the U.S. government.

One of the few mechanisms that has produced some success against WikiLeaks has been an effort to shut down its funding stream. The organization began as a self-funded effort, but the cost of servers and website hosting led the founders to solicit donations from the global public. In 2010, PayPal, MasterCard, and Visa all voluntarily shut down donations to the site, on the ground that they did not wish to facilitate illegal activities, although they offered no proof that WikiLeaks had technically broken any laws. While this prevented certain donations, millions of dollars have been donated to the organization via direct bank transfers. Each major disclosure of classified data has triggered a surge in donations to the site, despite the best efforts of the governments that feel targeted by its disclosures. One final attempt to shut down WikiLeaks was conducted by directly attacking Assange, who became the target of a criminal probe for sexual assault in Sweden.

Assange claimed the prosecution was political, rather than criminal, and obtained political asylum from the nation of Ecuador. Since 2012, he has resided in the Ecuadorian embassy in London, under threat of arrest and extradition if he leaves the grounds.

References

Abella, Alex. 2009. *Soldiers of Reason: The RAND Corporation and the Rise of the American Empire.* Boston: Mariner Books.

"About Symantec." 2014. Retrieved from http://www .symantec.com/about/profile/.

"Admiral Michael S. Rogers." 2014. United States Navy Biography. Retrieved from http://www.navy.mil/navydata/ bios/navybio.asp?bioID=434.

"Anonymous (Internet Group)." 2014. *New York Times.* Retrieved from http://topics.nytimes.com/top/reference/ timestopics/organizations/a/anonymous_internet_group/ index.html.

Auletta, Ken. 2001. *World War 3.0: Microsoft and Its Enemies.* New York: Random House.

Auletta, Ken. 2010. *Googled: The End of the World as We Know It.* New York: Penguin.

Bamford, James. 2009. *The Shadow Factory: The Ultra-Secret NSA from 9/11 to the Eavesdropping on America.* Norwell, MA: Anchor.

Belfiore, Michael. 2009. *The Department of Mad Scientists: How DARPA Is Remaking Our World, from the Internet to Artificial Limbs.* New York: HarperCollins.

"Biography—15th Director." 2012. National Security Agency. Retrieved from http://www.nsa.gov/about/leadership/bio _hayden.shtml.

"Biography—16th Director." 2012. National Security Agency. Retrieved from http://www.nsa.gov/about/leadership/bio _alexander.shtml.

"Biography—17th Director." 2014. Retrieved from https:// www.nsa.gov/about/leadership/bio_rogers.shtml.

Blane, John V., ed. 2002. *Cyberwarfare: Terror at a Click.* New York: Novinka Books.

Bradley, Tony. 2013. "In Their Own Words: Kaspersky Lab CEO and Cofounder Eugene Kaspersky." *Forbes,* September 23. Retrieved from http://www.forbes.com/sites/ tonybradley/2013/09/23/in-their-own-words-kaspersky -lab-cofounder-and-ceo-eugene-kaspersky/.

Brenner, Joel. 2011. *America the Vulnerable: Inside the New Threat Matrix of Digital Espionage, Crime, and Warfare.* New York: Penguin Press.

Brenner, Susan W. 2009. *Cyberthreats: The Emerging Fault Lines of the Nation State.* New York: Oxford University Press.

Clarke, Richard A., and Robert K. Knake. 2010. *Cyber War: The Next Great Threat to National Security and What to Do about It.* New York: HarperCollins.

"Corporate Factsheet: McAfee." 2014. Retrieved from http:// www.mcafee.com/us/resources/brochures/br-mcafee-fact -sheet.pdf.

"DARPA: Creating and Preventing Strategic Surprise." 2014. Defense Advanced Research Projects Agency website. Retrieved from http://www.darpa.mil.

Defense Information Systems Agency. 2014. Retrieved from http://www.disa.mil/.

"Dmitri Alperovitch." 2013. *Foreign Policy.* Retrieved from http://www.foreignpolicy.com/2013_global_thinkers/ public/alperovitch.

Domscheit-Berg, Daniel. 2011. *Inside WikiLeaks.* London: Crown Publishers.

FireEye. 2014. Retrieved from http://www.fireeye.com/.

Fleck, John. 2005. "Battle against Hackers Costs Employee Job." *Albuquerque Journal*, September 15, 2005.

Foley, Mary Jo. 2008. *Microsoft 2.0: How Microsoft Plans to Stay Relevant in the Post-Gates Era.* New York: Wiley.

"Gates Establishes U.S. Cyber Command, Names First Director." 2010. *Air Force Net*, May 21, 2010. Retrieved from http://archive.today/20120722051608/http://www.af.mil/news/story.asp?id=123205791.

Gibbs, Nancy. 2006. "Thinker, Briefer, Soldier, Spy." *Time*, May 15.

"Global Information Grid (GIG) Bandwidth Expansion (GIG-BE)." 2011. *GlobalSecurity.org*. Retrieved from http://www.globalsecurity.org/intell/systems/gig-be.htm.

Goodell, Jeff. 1996. *The Cyberthief and the Samurai.* New York: Dell.

Greenberg, Andy. 2013. "NSA Secretly Admitted Illegally Tracking Thousands of 'Alert List' Phone Numbers for Years." *Forbes*, September 10.

Greenwald, Glen. 2014. *No Place to Hide: Edward Snowden, the NSA, and the U.S. Surveillance State.* New York: Metropolitan Books.

Gurnow, Michael. 2014. *The Edward Snowden Affair: Exposing the Politics and Media behind the NSA Scandal.* Indianapolis, IN: Blue River Press.

Harris, Shane. 2013. "The Cowboy of the NSA." *Foreign Policy*, September 9. Retrieved from http://www.foreignpolicy.com/articles/2013/09/08/the_cowboy_of_the_nsa_keith_alexander?page=0,2.

"Jeffrey Carr." 2014. *O'Reilly Radar.* Retrieved from http://radar.oreilly.com/jeffc.

Kramer, Franklin D., Stuart H. Starr, and Larry K. Wentz, eds. 2009. *Cyberpower and National Security.* Dulles, VA: Potomac Books.

Krebs, Brian. 2007. "Shadowy Russian Firm Seen as Conduit for Cybercrime." *Washington Post,* October 13.

Levy, Steven. 2011. *In the Plex: How Google Thinks, Works, and Shapes Our Lives.* New York: Simon & Schuster.

Libicki, Martin C. 2007. *Conquest in Cyberspace: National Security and Information Warfare.* New York: Cambridge University Press.

Libicki, Martin C. 2009. *Cyberdeterrence and Cyberwar.* Santa Monica, CA: RAND Corporation.

Libicki, Martin C. 2012. *Crisis and Escalation in Cyberspace.* Santa Monica, CA: RAND Corporation.

Mandiant. 2013. "APT1: Exposing One of China's Cyber Espionage Units." http://intelreport.mandiant.com/ Mandiant_APT1_Report.pdf.

"Martin C. Libicki." 2014. RAND Corporation website. Retrieved from http://www.rand.org/about/people/l/libicki _martin_c.html.

Mediati, Nick. 2012. "McAfee Internet Security 2012 Review: Uneven Protection, Sluggish Speeds." *PC World,* January 30.

Messmer, Ellen. 2013. "Symantec CEO on Reorg: 'Our System is Just Broken.'" *Computer World,* January 24. Retrieved from http://www.computerworld.com/article/ 2494630/cloud-computing/symantec-ceo-on-reorg—our -system-is-just-broken-.html.

Mitnick, Kevin. 2012. *Ghost in the Wires: My Adventures as the World's Most Wanted Hacker.* Boston: Back Bay.

Mitnick, Kevin, and William Simon. 2003. *Art of Deception: Controlling the Human Element of Security.* New York: Wiley.

Morris, Adam. 2013. "Julian Assange: The Internet Threatens Civilization." *Salon*, April 30. Retrieved from http://www.salon.com/2013/04/30/tk_5_partner_15/.

Nicks, Denver. 2012. *Private: Bradley Manning, WikiLeaks, and the Biggest Exposure of Official Secrets in American History.* Chicago: Chicago Review Press.

North Atlantic Treaty Organization Cooperative Cyber Defence Centre of Excellence, Tallinn, Estonia. 2010. Retrieved from http://www.ccdcoe.org/tallinn-manual.html.

Olson, Parmy. 2012. *We Are Anonymous: Inside the Hacker World of LulzSec, Anonymous, and the Global Cyber Insurgency.* New York: Little, Brown.

Palmer, Maija. 2012. "A Tech Tycoon Who Values Privacy." *Financial Times.* September 25.

Perlroth, Nicole, and David E. Sanger. 2014. "FireEye Computer Security Firm Acquires Mandiant." *New York Times*, January 2.

Poitras, Laura, Marcel Rosenbach, and Holger Stark. 2013. "Ally and Target: U.S. Intelligence Watches Germany Closely." *Der Spiegel*, September 16.

Qiao Liang and Wang Xiangsui. 1999. *Unrestricted Warfare.* Translated by the Foreign Broadcast Information Service. Beijing: People's Liberation Army Literature and Arts Publishing House.

Rashid, Famida Y. 2012. "Security Think Tank Analyzes How International Law Applies to Cyber War." *Security Week*, September 2. Retrieved from http://www.securityweek.com/security-think-tank-analyzes-how-international-law-applies-cyber-war.

"Richard Clarke." 2013. Belfer Center for Science and International Affairs, Harvard University. Retrieved from http://belfercenter.ksg.harvard.edu/experts/1621/richard_clarke.html.

"Richard Clarke Biography." 2005. *Encyclopedia of World Biography.* Retrieved from http://www.notablebiographies. com/news/Ca-Ge/Clarke-Richard.html#b.

Rid, Thomas. 2013. *Cyber War Will Not Take Place.* New York: Oxford University Press.

Rosenzweig, Paul. 2013. *Cyber Warfare: How Conflicts in Cyberspace Are Challenging American and Changing the World.* Santa Barbara, CA: Praeger Security International.

Singer, P. W., and Allan Friedman. 2014. *Cybersecurity and Cyberwar.* New York: Oxford University Press.

"Solar Sunrise." 2011. GlobalSecurity.org. Retrieved from http://www.globalsecurity.org/military/ops/solar-sunrise -htm.

Sterling, Bruce. 2009. "The Project Grey Goose Cyberwar Report. *Wired*, August 3.

Stone, Brad, and Michael Riley. 2013. "Mandiant: The Go-To Security Firm for Cyber-Espionage Attacks." *Business Week*, February 7. Retrieved from http://www.businessweek.com/ articles/2013-02-07/mandiant-the-go-to-security-firm-for -cyber-espionage-attacks.

"35 Innovators under 35." 2013. *MIT Technology Review.* Retrieved from http://www.technologyreview.com/lists/ innovators-under-35/2013/.

Thomas, Douglas. 1999. "Life Not Kosher for Mitnick." *Wired*, August 18.

Thornburgh, Nathan. 2005. "The Invasion of the Chinese Superspies." *Time*, August 29.

Trounson, Rebecca. 1998. "Hacker Case Taps into Fame, Fury." *Los Angeles Times*, April 27.

Vaidhyanathan, Siva. 2011. *The Googlization of Everything (and Why We Should Worry).* Berkeley: University of California Press.

Vijayan, Jaikumar. 2007. "Q&A: Reverse Hacker Describes His Ordeal." *Computerworld,* February 26.

"A Walk on the Dark Side." 2007. *The Economist,* August 30. Retrieved from http://www.economist.com/node/9723768.

Wallace, James. 1993. *Hard Drive: Bill Gates and the Making of the Microsoft Empire.* New York: HarperBusiness.

Ware, Willis H., ed. 2008. *RAND and the Information Evolution: A History in Essays and Vignettes.* Santa Monica, CA: RAND Corporation.

Warren, Peter. 2007. "Hunt for Russia's Web Criminals." *The Guardian,* November 15.

This chapter offers examples of some of the attempts made by national decision-makers to set boundaries upon the conduct of cyber warfare. It focuses heavily, though not entirely, upon the United States and its allies. This is partially because the United States is more dependent upon cyber power than any other nation, and partially because the United States is one of the few nations that publicly releases its government's policies. As a leader in the cyber domain, the United States has the unique opportunity to shape the nature of future cyber conflicts, and to potentially establish boundaries for cyber warfare that might mitigate its worst aspects before they are experienced.

Excerpts from the North Atlantic Treaty (1949)

Estonia joined the North Atlantic Treaty Organization (NATO) in 2006, one of the dozen states that joined the alliance after the end of the Cold War. In 2007, Estonia's cyber domain was overwhelmed by massive DDoS attacks from Russian hacktivists who may have been operating under the instructions of the Russian government. Estonia attempted to invoke Article 5 of the North

---

General Keith B. Alexander, head of U.S. Cyber Command, before testimony in Congress on June 18, 2013. Alexander addressed revelations that the National Security Agency has collected private citizens' phone and Internet records as part of a massive antiterrorism cyber initiative. (AP Photo/J. Scott Applewhite)

Atlantic Treaty, which might have triggered a substantial escala-
tion in the brewing conflict. However, the NATO Security
Council decreed that the cyber attacks did not constitute an "armed
attack" because they had not injured anyone or caused substantial
property damage. One year later, NATO announced the creation
of a Cooperative Cyber Defence Centre of Excellence, headquar-
tered in Tallinn, Estonia.

Article 4

The Parties will consult together whenever, in the opinion of
any of them, the territorial integrity, political independence or
security of any of the Parties is threatened.

Article 5

The Parties agree that an armed attack against one or more of
them in Europe or North America shall be considered an attack
against them all and consequently they agree that, if such an
armed attack occurs, each of them, in exercise of the right of
individual or collective self-defence recognised by Article 51 of
the Charter of the United Nations, will assist the Party or
Parties so attacked by taking forthwith, individually and in concert with the other Parties, such action as it deems necessary,
including the use of armed force, to restore and maintain the
security of the North Atlantic area.

Any such armed attack and all measures taken as a result
thereof shall immediately be reported to the Security Council.
Such measures shall be terminated when the Security Council
has taken the measures necessary to restore and maintain
international peace and security.

Source: North Atlantic Treaty Organization. Retrieved from
http://www.nato.int/cps/en/natolive/official_texts_17120.htm.

Remarks of President Barack Obama on Securing the Nation's Cyber Infrastructure, Washington, D.C., May 29, 2009

Barack Obama's first presidential election campaign harnessed the power of cyberspace in ways that no candidate had ever done before, including using the Internet for unprecedented amounts of fund-raising and directly communicating with supporters. In this major policy speech, President Obama outlined his plan to improve the cyber security of the United States through several major steps to protect U.S. cyber networks. Although critics argued that the president's plan did not do nearly enough to protect the nation's cyber infrastructure, it still represented a major shift in the federal approach to cyber security and defensive preparations for cyber war.

It's long been said that the revolutions in communications and information technology have given birth to a virtual world. But make no mistake: This world—cyberspace—is a world that we depend on every single day. It's our hardware and our software, our desktops and laptops and cell phones and Blackberries that have become woven into every aspect of our lives.

It's the broadband networks beneath us and the wireless signals around us, the local networks in our schools and hospitals and businesses, and the massive grids that power our nation. It's the classified military and intelligence networks that keep us safe, and the World Wide Web that has made us more interconnected than at any time in human history.

So cyberspace is real. And so are the risks that come with it.

It's the great irony of our Information Age—the very technologies that empower us to create and to build also empower those who would disrupt and destroy. And this paradox—seen and unseen—is something that we experience every day.

It's about the privacy and the economic security of American families. We rely on the Internet to pay our bills, to bank, to shop, to file our taxes. But we've had to learn a whole new vocabulary just to stay ahead of the cyber criminals who would do us harm—spyware and malware and spoofing and phishing and botnets. Millions of Americans have been victimized, their privacy violated, their identities stolen, their lives upended, and their wallets emptied. According to one survey, in the past two years alone cyber crime has cost Americans more than $8 billion.

I know how it feels to have privacy violated because it has happened to me and the people around me. It's no secret that my presidential campaign harnessed the Internet and technology to transform our politics. What isn't widely known is that during the general election hackers managed to penetrate our computer systems. To all of you who donated to our campaign, I want you to all rest assured, our fundraising website was untouched. (Laughter.) So your confidential personal and financial information was protected.

But between August and October, hackers gained access to emails and a range of campaign files, from policy position papers to travel plans. And we worked closely with the CIA— with the FBI and the Secret Service and hired security consultants to restore the security of our systems. It was a powerful reminder: In this Information Age, one of your greatest strengths—in our case, our ability to communicate to a wide range of supporters through the Internet—could also be one of your greatest vulnerabilities.

This is a matter, as well, of America's economic competitiveness. The small businesswoman in St. Louis, the bond trader in the New York Stock Exchange, the workers at a global shipping company in Memphis, the young entrepreneur in Silicon Valley—they all need the networks to make the next payroll, the next trade, the next delivery, the next great breakthrough. E-commerce alone last year accounted for some $132 billion in retail sales.

But every day we see waves of cyber thieves trolling for sensitive information—the disgruntled employee on the inside, the lone hacker a thousand miles away, organized crime, the industrial spy and, increasingly, foreign intelligence services. In one brazen act last year, thieves used stolen credit card information to steal millions of dollars from 130 ATM machines in 49 cities around the world—and they did it in just 30 minutes. A single employee of an American company was convicted of stealing intellectual property reportedly worth $400 million. It's been estimated that last year alone cyber criminals stole intellectual property from businesses worldwide worth up to $1 trillion.

In short, America's economic prosperity in the 21st century will depend on cybersecurity.

And this is also a matter of public safety and national security. We count on computer networks to deliver our oil and gas, our power and our water. We rely on them for public transportation and air traffic control. Yet we know that cyber intruders have probed our electrical grid and that in other countries cyber attacks have plunged entire cities into darkness.

Our technological advantage is a key to America's military dominance. But our defense and military networks are under constant attack. Al Qaeda and other terrorist groups have spoken of their desire to unleash a cyber attack on our country—attacks that are harder to detect and harder to defend against. Indeed, in today's world, acts of terror could come not only from a few extremists in suicide vests but from a few key strokes on the computer—a weapon of mass disruption.

In one of the most serious cyber incidents to date against our military networks, several thousand computers were infected last year by malicious software—malware. And while no sensitive information was compromised, our troops and defense personnel had to give up those external memory devices—thumb drives—changing the way they used their computers every day.

And last year we had a glimpse of the future face of war. As Russian tanks rolled into Georgia, cyber attacks crippled Georgian government websites. The terrorists that sowed so much death and destruction in Mumbai relied not only on guns and grenades but also on GPS and phones using voice-over-the-Internet.

For all these reasons, it's now clear this cyber threat is one of the most serious economic and national security challenges we face as a nation.

It's also clear that we're not as prepared as we should be, as a government or as a country. In recent years, some progress has been made at the federal level. But just as we failed in the past to invest in our physical infrastructure—our roads, our bridges and rails—we've failed to invest in the security of our digital infrastructure.

No single official oversees cybersecurity policy across the federal government, and no single agency has the responsibility or authority to match the scope and scale of the challenge. Indeed, when it comes to cybersecurity, federal agencies have overlapping missions and don't coordinate and communicate nearly as well as they should—with each other or with the private sector. We saw this in the disorganized response to Conficker, the Internet "worm" that in recent months has infected millions of computers around the world. . . .

From now on, our digital infrastructure—the networks and computers we depend on every day—will be treated as they should be: as a strategic national asset. Protecting this infrastructure will be a national security priority. We will ensure that these networks are secure, trustworthy and resilient. We will deter, prevent, detect, and defend against attacks and recover quickly from any disruptions or damage. . . .

First, working in partnership with the communities represented here today, we will develop a new comprehensive strategy to secure America's information and communications networks. To ensure a coordinated approach across government, my Cybersecurity Coordinator will work closely with my Chief Technology Officer, Aneesh Chopra, and my Chief Information Officer, Vivek Kundra. To ensure accountability in federal agencies, cybersecurity will be designated as one of my key management priorities. Clear milestones and performances metrics will measure progress. And as we develop our strategy, we will be open and transparent, which is why you'll find today's report and a wealth of related information on our Web site, www.whitehouse.gov.

Second, we will work with all the key players—including state and local governments and the private sector—to ensure an organized and unified response to future cyber incidents. Given the enormous damage that can be caused by even a single cyber attack, ad hoc responses will not do. Nor is it sufficient to simply strengthen our defenses after incidents or attacks occur. Just as we do for natural disasters, we have to have plans and resources in place beforehand—sharing information, issuing warnings and ensuring a coordinated response.

Third, we will strengthen the public/private partnerships that are critical to this endeavor. The vast majority of our critical information infrastructure in the United States is owned and operated by the private sector. So let me be very clear: My administration will not dictate security standards for private companies. On the contrary, we will collaborate with industry to find technology solutions that ensure our security and promote prosperity.

Fourth, we will continue to invest in the cutting-edge research and development necessary for the innovation and discovery we need to meet the digital challenges of our time. And that's why my administration is making major investments in our information infrastructure: laying broadband lines to every corner of America; building a smart electric grid to deliver energy more efficiently; pursuing a next generation of air traffic control systems; and moving to electronic health records, with privacy protections, to reduce costs and save lives.

And finally, we will begin a national campaign to promote cybersecurity awareness and digital literacy from our boardrooms to our classrooms, and to build a digital workforce for the 21st century. And that's why we're making a new commitment to education in math and science, and historic investments in science and research and development. Because it's not enough for our children and students to master today's technologies—social networking and e-mailing and texting and blogging—we need them to pioneer the technologies that will allow us to work effectively through these new media and allow us to prosper in the future. So these are the things we will do.

Let me also be clear about what we will not do. Our pursuit of cybersecurity will not—I repeat, will not include—monitoring private sector networks or Internet traffic. We will preserve and protect the personal privacy and civil liberties that we cherish as Americans. Indeed, I remain firmly committed to net neutrality so we can keep the Internet as it should be—open and free.

Source: *Public Papers of the Presidents of the United States: Barack Obama*, Book I, 724–28. Washington DC: Government Printing Office, 2009. Available online at http://www.gpo.gov/fdsys/pkg/PPP-2009-book1/pdf/PPP-2009-book1-Doc-pg724.pdf.

Excerpts of Secretary of State Hillary Clinton on Internet Freedom, Washington, D.C., January 21, 2010

Secretary of State Hillary Clinton delivered these remarks before a gathering of Internet freedom activists, U.S. political leaders, and international visitors. Her remarks demonstrate both the U.S. resolve to protect its own cyberspace and a belligerent approach to any nations that have a different view of the importance of Internet freedom. Her remarks were interpreted by some authoritarian governments as a deliberate effort by the United States to undermine their control of the Internet in their nations, and a call to arms for insurgents in China, Iran, and North Korea to use the Internet as a means to communicate with fellow rebels and increase their resistance to the government forces.

The spread of information networks is forming a new nervous system for our planet. When something happens in Haiti or Hunan, the rest of us learn about it in real time—from real people. And we can respond in real time as well. Americans eager to help in the aftermath of a disaster and the girl trapped in the supermarket are connected in ways that were not even imagined a year ago, even a generation ago. That same principle applies to almost all of humanity today. As we sit here, any of you—or maybe more likely, any of our children—can take out the tools that many carry every day and transmit this discussion to billions across the world.

Now, in many respects, information has never been so free. There are more ways to spread more ideas to more people than at any moment in history. And even in authoritarian countries, information networks are helping people discover new facts and making governments more accountable.

During his visit to China in November, for example, President Obama held a town hall meeting with an online component to highlight the importance of the internet. In response to a question that was sent in over the internet, he defended the right of people to freely access information, and said that the more freely information flows, the stronger societies become. He spoke about how access to information helps citizens hold their own governments accountable, generates new ideas, encourages creativity and entrepreneurship. The United States belief in that ground truth is what brings me here today.

Because amid this unprecedented surge in connectivity, we must also recognize that these technologies are not an unmitigated blessing. These tools are also being exploited to undermine human progress and political rights. Just as steel can be used to build hospitals or machine guns, or nuclear power can either energize a city or destroy it, modern information networks and the technologies they support can be harnessed for good or for ill. The same networks that help organize movements for freedom also enable al-Qaida to spew hatred and incite violence against the innocent. And technologies with the potential to open up access to government and promote transparency can also be hijacked by governments to crush dissent and deny human rights.

In the last year, we've seen a spike in threats to the free flow of information. China, Tunisia, and Uzbekistan have stepped up their censorship of the internet. In Vietnam, access to popular social networking sites has suddenly disappeared. And last Friday in Egypt, 30 bloggers and activists were detained. One member of this group, Bassem Samir, who is thankfully no longer in prison, is with us today. So while it is clear that the spread of these technologies is transforming our world, it is still unclear how that transformation will affect the human rights welfare of the world's population.

On their own, new technologies do not take sides in the struggle for freedom and progress, but the United States does. We stand for a single internet where all of humanity has equal access to knowledge and ideas. And we recognize that the world's information infrastructure will become what we and others make of it. Now this challenge may be new, but our responsibility to help ensure the free exchange of ideas goes back to the birth of our republic.

There are many other networks in the world. Some aid in the movement of people or resources, and some facilitate exchanges between individuals with the same work or interests. But the internet is a network that magnifies the power and potential of all others. And that's why we believe it's critical that its users are assured certain basic freedoms. Freedom of expression is first among them. This freedom is no longer defined solely by whether citizens can go into the town square and criticize their government without fear of retribution. Blogs, emails, social networks, and text messages have opened up new forums for exchanging ideas, and created new targets for censorship. As I speak to you today, government censors somewhere are working furiously to erase my words from the records of history. But history has already condemned these tactics.

Some countries have erected electronic barriers that prevent their people from accessing portions of the world's networks. They've expunged words, names, and phrases from search engine results. They have violated the privacy of citizens who engage in non-violent political speech. These actions contravene the Universal Declaration of Human Rights, which tells us that all people have the right "to seek, receive and impart information and ideas through any media and regardless of frontiers." With the spread of these restrictive practices, a new information curtain is descending across much of the world. And beyond this partition, viral videos and blog posts are becoming the samizdat of our day.

As in the dictatorships of the past, governments are targeting independent thinkers who use these tools. In the demonstrations that followed Iran's presidential elections, grainy cell phone footage of a young woman's bloody murder provided a digital indictment of the government's brutality. We've seen reports that when Iranians living overseas posted online criticism of their nation's leaders, their family members in Iran were singled out for retribution. And despite an intense campaign of government intimidation, brave citizen journalists in Iran continue using technology to show the world and their fellow citizens what is happening inside their country. In speaking out on behalf of their own human rights, the Iranian people have inspired the world. And their courage is redefining how technology is used to spread truth and expose injustice.

Some nations, however, have co-opted the internet as a tool to target and silence people of faith. Last year, for example, in Saudi Arabia, a man spent months in prison for blogging about Christianity. And a Harvard study found that the Saudi Government blocked many web pages about Hinduism, Judaism, Christianity, and even Islam. Countries including Vietnam and China employed similar tactics to restrict access to religious information.

Now, just as these technologies must not be used to punish peaceful political speech, they also must not be used to persecute or silence religious minorities. Now, prayers will always travel on higher networks. But connection technologies like the internet and social networking sites should enhance individuals' ability to worship as they see fit, come together with people of their own faith, and learn more about the beliefs of others. We must work to advance the freedom of worship online just as we do in other areas of life.

A connection to global information networks is like an on-ramp to modernity. In the early years of these technologies, many believed they would divide the world between haves and have-nots. But that hasn't happened. There are 4 billion cell phones in use today. Many of them are in the hands of market vendors, rickshaw drivers, and others who've historically lacked access to education and opportunity. Information networks have become a great leveler, and we should use them together to help lift people out of poverty and give them freedom from want.

Now, we have every reason to be hopeful about what people can accomplish when they leverage communication networks and connection technologies to achieve progress. But make no mistake—some are and will continue to use global information networks for darker purposes. Violent extremists, criminal cartels, sexual predators, and authoritarian governments all seek to exploit these global networks. Just as terrorists have taken advantage of the openness of our societies to carry out their plots, violent extremists use the internet to radicalize and intimidate. As we work to advance freedoms, we must also work against those who use communication networks as tools of disruption and fear.

Governments and citizens must have confidence that the networks at the core of their national security and economic prosperity are safe and resilient. Now this is about more than petty hackers who deface websites. Our ability to bank online, use electronic commerce, and safeguard billions of dollars in intellectual property are all at stake if we cannot rely on the security of our information networks.

States, terrorists, and those who would act as their proxies must know that the United States will protect our networks.

Those who disrupt the free flow of information in our society or any other pose a threat to our economy, our government, and our civil society. Countries or individuals that engage in cyber attacks should face consequences and international condemnation. In an internet-connected world, an attack on one nation's networks can be an attack on all. And by reinforcing that message, we can create norms of behavior among states and encourage respect for the global networked commons.

Source: U.S. Department of State. Retrieved from http://www .state.gov/secretary/20092013clinton/rm/2010/01/135519.htm.

Excerpts from the *Tallinn Manual on the International Law Applicable to Cyber Warfare, Draft,* NATO Cooperative Cyber Defence Centre of Excellence, 2010

In 2010, NATO's Cooperative Cyber Defence Centre of Excellence, headquartered at Tallinn, Estonia, invited experts in international law, cyber security, and information technology to draft a manual of rules for cyber warfare. While the manual is not binding on even the member states of NATO, it does offer a means to open discussion on the creation of international law governing cyber conflict. In this regard, it follows the long history of international laws of armed conflict that began through similar international conferences. This manual seeks to apply the laws of physical warfare to the cyber domain, but also recognizes that some aspects of cyber war, including the means of attack and the individuals involved, differ markedly from the physical world.

Rule 5. A State shall not knowingly allow the cyber infrastructure located in its territory or under its exclusive governmental control to be used for acts that adversely and unlawfully affect other States.

Rule 6. A State bears international legal responsibility for a cyber operation attributable to it and which constitutes a breach of international obligation.

Rule 7. The mere fact that a cyber operation has been launched or otherwise originates from governmental cyber infrastructure is not sufficient evidence for attributing the operation to that State but is an indication that the State in question is associated with the operation.

Rule 8. The fact that a cyber operation has been routed via cyber infrastructure located in a State is not sufficient evidence for attributing the operation to that State.

Rule 9. A State injured by an internationally wrongful act may resort to proportionate countermeasures, including cyber countermeasures, against the responsible state.

Rule 10. A cyber operation that constitutes a threat or use of force against the territorial integrity or political independence of any State, or that is in any other manner inconsistent with the purposes of the United Nations, is unlawful.

Rule 11. A cyber operation constitutes a use of force when its scale and effects are comparable to non-cyber operations rising to the level of a use of force.

Rule 16. The right of self-defence may be exercised collectively. Collective self-defence against a cyber operation amounting to an armed attack may only be exercised at the request of the victim-State and within the scope of the request.

Rule 20. Cyber operations executed in the context of an armed conflict are subject to the law of armed conflict.

Rule 28. Mercenaries involved in cyber operations do not enjoy combatant immunity or prisoner of war status.

Rule 29. Civilians are not prohibited from directly participating in cyber operations amounting to hostilities but forfeit their protection from attacks for such time as they so participate.

Rule 30. A cyber attack is a cyber operation, whether offensive or defensive, that is reasonably expected to cause injury or death to persons or damage or destruction to objects.

Rule 31. The principle of distinction applies to cyber attacks.

Rule 32. The civilian population as such, as well as individual civilians, shall not be the object of cyber attack.

Rule 36. Cyber attacks, or the threat thereof, the primary purpose of which is to spread terror among the civilian population, are prohibited.

Rule 51. A cyber attack that may be expected to cause incidental loss of civilian life, injury to civilians, damage to civilian objects, or a combination thereof, which would be excessive in relation to the concrete and direct military advantage anticipated is prohibited.

Rule 61. Cyber operations that qualify as ruses of war are permitted.

Rule 66. (a) Cyber espionage and other forms of information gathering directed at an adversary during an armed conflict do not violate the law of armed conflict. (b) A member of the armed forces who has engaged in cyber espionage in enemy-controlled territory loses the right to be a prisoner of war and may be treated as a spy if captured before re-joining the armed forces to which he or she belongs.

Rule 77. Prisoners of war and interned protected persons shall not be compelled to participate in or support cyber operations directed against their own country.

Rule 84. Diplomatic archives and communications are protected from cyber operations at all times.

Rule 85. Collective punishment by cyber means is prohibited.

Rule 93. A neutral State may not knowingly allow the exercise of belligerent rights by the parties to the conflict from cyber infrastructure located in its territory or under its exclusive control.

Source: North Atlantic Treaty Organization Cooperative Cyber Defence Centre of Excellence, Tallinn, Estonia. Retrieved from http://www.ccdcoe.org/tallinn-manual.html.

Excerpts of "International Strategy for Cyberspace," May 2011

Many Western nations, the United States included, make their national security strategies available to the public. Of course, these strategy documents offer more of a general guide to the nation's priorities and goals than a practical examination of how those goals will be reached. Nevertheless, the U.S. cyberspace strategy is an important example that clarifies not only how the American government envisions the needs of the international cyberspace community, but what underpins its understanding of the interaction of nations. Take note that while much of the document is extremely optimistic regarding the future of the Internet, there is a lightly veiled threat that any form of cyber attack may provoke a kinetic retaliation from the United States. Further, the American conception that all of the people of the world should have free, open access to the Internet, and should be granted liberty and privacy in its use, is anathema to the totalitarian regimes of the world that abhor the idea of open information-sharing among their subject populations. As the United States tries to push such a vision on a global scale, it is essentially sowing the seeds of revolt among those populations.

The Future We Seek

The cyberspace environment that we seek rewards innovation and empowers individuals; it connects individuals and strengthens communities; it builds better governments and expands accountability; it safeguards fundamental freedoms and enhances personal privacy; it builds understanding, clarifies norms of behavior, and enhances national and international security. To sustain this environment, international collaboration is more than a best practice, it is a first principle.

Our Goal

The United States will work internationally to promote an *open, interoperable, secure, and reliable* information and communications infrastructure that supports international trade and commerce, strengthens international security, and fosters free expression and innovation. To achieve that goal, we will build and sustain an environment in which *norms of responsible behavior* guide states' actions, sustain partnerships, and support the rule of law in cyberspace.

Stability through Norms

The United States will work with like-minded states to establish an environment of expectations, or norms of behavior, that ground foreign and defense policies and guide international partnerships. The last two decades have seen the swift and unprecedented growth of the Internet as a social medium; the growing reliance of societies on networked information systems to control critical infrastructures and communications systems essential to modern life; and increasing evidence that governments are seeking to exercise traditional national power through cyberspace. These events have not been matched by clearly agreed-upon norms for acceptable state behavior in cyberspace. To bridge that gap, we will work to build a consensus on what constitutes acceptable behavior, and a partnership among those who view the functioning of these systems as essential to the national and collective interest.

The Role of Norms

In other spheres of international relations, shared understandings about acceptable behavior have enhanced stability and provided a basis for international action when corrective measures are required. Adherence to such norms brings predictability to state conduct, helping prevent the misunderstandings that could lead to conflict.

The development of norms for state conduct in cyberspace does not require a reinvention of customary international law, nor does it render existing international norms obsolete.

Long-standing international norms guiding state behavior—in times of peace and conflict—also apply in cyberspace. Nonetheless, unique attributes of networked technology require additional work to clarify how these terms apply and what additional understandings might be necessary to supplement them. We will continue to work internationally to forge consensus regarding how norms of behavior apply to cyberspace, with the understanding that an important first step in such efforts is applying the broad expectations of peaceful and just interstate conduct to cyberspace.

The Basis for Norms

Rules that promote order and peace, advance basic human dignity, and promote freedom in economic competition are essential to any international environment. These principles provide a basic roadmap for how states can meet their traditional international obligations in cyberspace and, in many cases, reflect duties of states that apply regardless of context. The existing principles that should support cyberspace norms include:

- *Upholding Fundamental Freedoms:* States must respect fundamental freedoms of expression and association, online as well as off.
- *Respect for Property:* States should in their undertakings and through domestic laws respect intellectual property rights, including patents, trade secrets, trademarks, and copyrights.
- *Valuing Privacy:* Individuals should be protected from arbitrary or unlawful state interference with their privacy when they use the Internet.
- *Protection from Crime:* States must identify and prosecute cybercriminals, to ensure laws and practices deny criminals safe havens, and cooperate with international criminal investigations in a timely manner.

– *Right of Self-Defense:* Consistent with the United Nations Charter, states have an inherent right to self-defense that may be triggered by certain aggressive acts in cyberspace.

Deriving from these traditional principles of interstate conduct are responsibilities more specific to cyberspace, focused in particular on preserving global network functionality and improving cybersecurity. Many of these responsibilities are rooted in the technical realities of the Internet. Because the Internet's core functionality relies on systems of trust (such as the Border Gateway Protocol), states need to recognize the international implications of their technical decisions, and act with respect for one another's networks and the broader Internet. Likewise, in designing the next generation of these systems, we must advance the common interest by supporting the soundest technical standards and governance structures, rather than those that will simply enhance national prestige or political control. Emerging norms, also essential to this space, include:

– *Global Interoperability:* States should act within their authorities to help ensure the end-to-end interoperability of an Internet accessible to all.
– *Network Stability:* States should respect the free flow of information in national network configurations, ensuring they do not arbitrarily interfere with internationally interconnected infrastructure.
– *Reliable Access:* States should not arbitrarily deprive or disrupt individuals' access to the Internet or other networked technologies.
– *Multi-stakeholder Governance:* Internet governance efforts must not be limited to governments, but should include all appropriate stakeholders.
– *Cybersecurity Due Diligence:* States should recognize and act on their responsibility to protect information

infrastructures and secure national systems from damage or misuse.

While cyberspace is a dynamic environment, international behavior in it must be grounded in the principles of responsible domestic governance, peaceful interstate conduct, and reliable network management. As these ideas develop, the United States will foster and participate fully in discussions, advancing a principled approach to Internet policy-making and developing shared understandings appropriate to each issue.

Defense: Dissuading and Deterring

The United States will defend its networks, whether the threat comes from terrorists, cybercriminals, or states and their proxies. Just as importantly, we will seek to encourage good actors and dissuade and deter those who threaten peace and stability through actions in cyberspace. We will do so with overlapping policies that combine national and international network resilience with vigilance and a range of credible response options. In all our defense endeavors, we will protect civil liberties and privacy in accordance with our laws and principles.

Defense Objective

The United States will, along with other nations, encourage responsible behavior and oppose those who would seek to disrupt networks and systems, dissuading and deterring malicious actors, and reserving the right to defend these vital national assets as necessary and appropriate.

Dissuasion

Protecting networks of such great value requires robust defensive capabilities. The United States will continue to strengthen our network defenses and our ability to withstand and recover from disruptions and other attacks. For those more sophisticated attacks that do create damage, we will act on well-developed response plans to isolate and mitigate disruption to our machines, limiting effects on our networks, and potential cascade effects beyond them.

Strength at Home

Ensuring the resilience of our networks and information systems requires collective and concerted national action that spans the whole of government, in collaboration with the private sector and individual citizens. For a decade, the United States has been fostering a culture of cybersecurity and an effective apparatus for risk mitigation and incident response. We continue to emphasize that systematically adopting sound information technology practices—across the public and private sectors—will reduce our Nation's vulnerabilities and strengthen networks and systems. We are also making steady progress towards shared situational awareness of network vulnerabilities and risks among public and private sector networks. We have built new initiatives through our national computer security incident response team to share information among government, key industries, our critical infrastructure sectors, and other stakeholders. And we continually seek new ways to strengthen our partnership with the private sector to enhance the security of the systems on which we both rely.

Strength Abroad

This model of defense has been successfully shared internationally through education, training and ongoing operational and policy relationships. Today, through existing and developing collaborations in the technical and military defense arenas, nations share an unprecedented ability to recognize and respond to incidents—a crucial step in denying would-be attackers the ability to do lasting damage to our national and international networks. However, a globally distributed network requires globally distributed early warning capabilities. We must continue to produce new computer security incident response capabilities globally, and to facilitate their interconnection and enhanced computer network defense. The United States has a shared interest in assisting less developed nations to build capacity for defense, and in collaboration with our partners, will intensify our focus on this area. Building relationships with friends and allies will increase collective security across the international community.

Deterrence

The United States will ensure that the risks associated with attacking or exploiting our networks vastly outweigh the potential benefits. We fully recognize that cyberspace activities can have effects extending beyond networks; such events may require responses in self-defense. Likewise, interconnected networks link nations more closely, so an attack on one nation's networks may have impact far beyond its borders.

In the case of criminals and other non-state actors who would threaten our national and economic security, domestic deterrence requires all states have processes that permit them to investigate, apprehend, and prosecute those who intrude or disrupt networks at home and abroad. Internationally, law enforcement organizations must work in concert with one another whenever possible to freeze perishable data vital to ongoing investigations, to work with legislatures and justice ministries to harmonize their approaches, and to promote due process and the rule of law—all key tenets of the Budapest Convention on Cybercrime.

When warranted, the United States will respond to hostile acts in cyberspace as we would to any other threat to our country. All states possess an inherent right to self-defense, and we recognize that certain hostile acts conducted through cyber-space could compel actions under the commitments we have with our military treaty partners. We reserve the right to use all necessary means—diplomatic, informational, military, and economic—as appropriate and consistent with applicable international law, in order to defend our Nation, our allies, our partners, and our interests. In so doing, we will exhaust all options before military force whenever we can; will carefully weigh the costs and risks of action against the costs of inaction; and will act in a way that reflects our values and strengthens our legitimacy, seeking broad international support whenever possible.

Military: Preparing for 21st Century Security Challenges

Since our commitment to defend our citizens, allies, and inter-ests extends to wherever they might be threatened, we will:

— *Recognize and adapt to the military's increasing need for reliable and secure networks.* We recognize that our armed forces increasingly depend on the networks that support them, and we will work to ensure that our military remains full equipped to operate even in an environment where others might seek to disrupt its systems, or other infrastructure vital to national defense. Like all nations, the United States has a compelling interest in defending its vital national assets, as well as our core principles and values, and we are committed to defending against those who would attempt to impede our ability to do so.

— *Build and enhance existing military alliances to confront potential threats in cyberspace.* Cybersecurity cannot be achieved by any one nation alone, and greater levels of international cooperating are needed to confront those actors who would seek to disrupt or exploit our networks. This effort begins by acknowledging that the interconnected nature of networked systems of our closest allies, such as those of NATO and its member states, creates opportunities and new risks. Moving forward, the United States will continue to work with the militaries and civilian counterparts of our allies and partners to expand situational awareness and shared warning systems, enhance our ability to work together in times of peace and crisis, and develop the means and method of collective self-defense in cyberspace. Such military alliances and partnerships will bolster our collective deterrence capabilities and strengthen our ability to defend the United States against state and non-state actors.

— *Expand cyberspace cooperation with allies and partners to increase collective security.* The challenges of cyberspace also create opportunities to work in new ways with allied and partner militaries. By developing a shared understanding of standard operating procedures, our armed forces can enhance security through coordination and greater information exchange; these engagements will diminish misperceptions about military activities and the potential for escalatory behavior. Dialogues and best practice exchanges to enhance partner capabilities, such as digital forensics, work force development, and network penetration and resiliency testing will be important to this effort. The United States will work in close partnership with like-minded states to leverage capabilities, reduce collective risk, and foster multi-stakeholder initiatives to deter malicious activities in cyberspace.

Moving Forward

The benefits of networked technology should not be reserved to a privileged few nations, or a privileged few within them. But connectivity is no end unto itself; it must be supported by a cyberspace that is open to innovation, interoperable the world over, secure enough to earn people's trust, and reliable enough to support their work.

Thirty years ago, few understood that something called the Internet would lead to a revolution in how we work and live. In that short time, millions now owe their livelihoods—and even their lives—to advances in networked technology. A billion more rely on it for everyday forms of social interaction. This technology propels society forward, accomplishing things previous generations scarcely thought possible. For our part, the United States will continue to spark the creativity and imagination of our people, and those around the world. We cannot know what the next great innovation will be, but are committed to realizing a world in which it can take shape and flourish.

This strategy is a roadmap allowing the United States Government's departments and agencies to better define and coordinate their role in our international cyberspace policy, to execute a specific way forward, and to plan for future implementation. It is a call to the private sector, civil society, and end-users to reinforce these efforts through partnership, awareness, and action. Most importantly, it is an invitation to other states and peoples to join us in realizing this vision of prosperity, security, and openness in our networked world. These ideals are central to preserving the cyberspace we know, and to creating, together, the future we seek.

Source: White House documents, including *International Strategy for Cyberspace: Prosperity, Security, and Openness in a Networked World*, May 2011 (retrieved from http://www.whitehouse.gov/sites/default/files/rss_viewer/international_strategy_for_cyberspace.pdf).

Excerpts of Secretary of Defense Leon Panetta on Cybersecurity, October 11, 2012

Secretary of Defense Leon Panetta, speaking to the Business Executives for National Security, laid out both the current capabilities of the U.S. Department of Defense and its short-term priorities for the cyberspace domain. In his speech, he suggested that the United States had largely solved the fundamental attribution problem for cyber attacks, while also noting the incredible vulnerabilities of American infrastructure and the failure of private companies to undertake even the most basic cyber security precautions. Unlike many leaders in comparable positions, Panetta seems optimistic that cyber defense and deterrence are both technically feasible and fiscally possible.

Cyberspace has fundamentally transformed the global economy. It's transformed our way of life, providing two billion people across the world with instant access to information to communication, to business opportunities. Cyberspace is the new frontier, full of possibilities to advance security and prosperity in the 21st century. And yet, with these possibilities also come new perils and new dangers. The Internet is open. It's highly accessible, as it should be. But that also presents a new terrain for warfare. It is a battlefield of the future where adversaries can seek to do harm to our country, to our economy, and to our citizens. I know that when people think of cybersecurity today, they worry about hackers and criminals who prowl the internet, steal people's identities, steal sensitive business information, steal even national security secrets. Those threats are real and they exist today. But the even greater danger—the danger facing us in cyberspace goes beyond crime and it goes beyond harassment. A cyber attack perpetrated by nation states or violent extremist groups could be as destructive as the terrorist attack on 9/11. Such a destructive cyber-terrorist attack could virtually paralyze the nation.

Let me give you some examples of the kinds of attacks that we have already experienced. In recent weeks, as many of you know, some large U.S. financial institutions were hit by so-called Distributed Denial of Service attacks. These attacks delayed or disrupted services on customer websites. While this kind of tactic isn't new, the scale and speed with which it happened was unprecedented. But even more alarming is an attack that happened two months ago when a very sophisticated virus called Shamoon infected computers in the Saudi Arabian State Oil Company Aramco. Shamoon included a routine called a "wiper," coded to self-execute. This routine replaced crucial systems files with an image of a burning U.S. flab. But it also put additional garbage data that overwrote all the real data on the machine. More than 30,000 computers that it infected were rendered useless and had to be replaced. It virtually destroyed 30,000 computers. Then just days after this incident, there was a similar attack on RasGas of Qatar, a major energy company in the region. All told, the Shamoon virus was probably the most destructive attack that the private sector has seen to date.

These attacks mark a significant escalation of the cyber threat, and they have renewed concerns about still more destructive scenarios that could unfold. For example, we know that foreign cyber actors are probing America's critical infrastructure networks. They are targeting the computer control systems that operate chemical, electricity, and water plants and those that guide transportation throughout this country. We know of specific instances where intruders have successfully gained access to these control systems. We also know that they are seeking to create advanced tools to attack these systems and cause panic and destruction and even loss of life.

An aggressor nation or extremist group could use these kinds of cyber tools to gain control of critical switches. They could, for example, derail passenger trains or even more dangerous, derail trains loaded with lethal chemicals. They could contaminate the water supply in major cities or shutdown the power grid across large parts of the country. The most destructive scenarios involve cyber actors launching several attacks on our critical infrastructure at one time, in combination with a physical attack on our country. Attackers could also seek to disable or degrade critical military systems and communication networks. The collective result of these kinds of attacks could be a cyber Pearl Harbor, an attack that would cause physical destruction and the loss of life. In fact, it would paralyze and shock the nation and create a new, profound sense of vulnerability.

The Department of Defense, in large part through the capabilities of the National Security Agency, NSA, has developed the world's most sophisticated system to detect cyber intruders and attackers. We are acting aggressively to get ahead of this problem, putting in place measures to stop cyber attacks dead in their tracks. We are doing this as part of a broad whole of government effort to confront cyber threats.

The Department of Defense also has a role. It is a supporting role but it is an essential role. And tonight, I want to explain what that means. But first let me make clear what it does not mean. It does not mean that the Department of Defense will monitor citizens' personal computers. We're not interested in personal communications or in e-mails or in providing the day to day security of private and commercial networks. That is not our goal. That is not our job. That is not our mission. Our mission is to defend the nation. We defend. We deter, and if called upon, we take decisive action to protect our citizens. In the past, we have done so through operations on land and at sea, in the skies and in space. In this century, the United States military must help defend the nation in cyberspace as well. If a foreign adversary attacked U.S. soil, the American people have every right to expect their national defense forces to respond. If a crippling cyber attack were launched against our nation, the American people must be protected. And if the Commander in Chief orders a response, the Defense Department must be ready to obey that order and to act.

To ensure that we fulfill our role to defend the nation in cyberspace, the department is focusing upon three main tracks.

One, developing new capabilities. Two, putting in place the policies and organizations we need to execute our mission. And three, building much more effective cooperation with industry and our international partners.

First, developing new capabilities. DoD is investing more than $3 billion annually in cybersecurity because we have to retain that cutting edge capability in the field. Following our new defense strategy, the department is continuing to increase key investments in cybersecurity even in an era of fiscal restraint. Our most important investment is in skilled cyber warriors needed to conduct operations in cyberspace. Just as DoD developed the world's finest counterterrorism force over the past decade, we need to build and maintain the finest cyber force and operations. We're recruiting, we're training, the best and the brightest in order to stay ahead of other nations. It's no secret that Russia and China have advanced cyber capabilities. Iran has also undertaken a concerted effort to use cyberspace to its advantage. Moreover, DoD is already in an intense daily struggle against thousands of cyber actors who probe the Defense Department's networks, millions of times a day. Throughout the innovative efforts of our cyber operators, we've been trying to enhance the department's cyber defense programs. These systems rely on sensors, they rely on software to hunt down the malicious codes before it harms our systems. We actively share our own experience defending our systems with those running the nation's critical private sector networks. In addition to defending the department's networks, we also help deter attacks. Our cyber adversaries will be far less likely to hit us if they know that we will be able to link to the attack or that their effort will fail against our strong defenses. The department has made significant advances in solving a problem that makes deterring cyber adversaries more complex, the difficulty of identifying the origins of that attack. Over the last two years, DoD has made significant investments in forensics to address this problem of attribution and we're seeing the returns on that investment. Potential aggressors should be aware that the United States has the capacity to locate them and to hold them accountable for their actions that may try to harm America.

But we won't succeed in preventing a cyber attack through improved defenses alone. If we detect an imminent threat that will cause significant, physical destruction in the United States or kill American citizens, we need to have the option to take action against those who would attack us to defend this nation when directed by the president. For these kinds of scenarios, the department has developed the capability to conduct effective operations to counter threats to our national interests in cyberspace. Let me be clear that we will only do so to defend our nation, to defend our interests, to defend our allies and we will only do so in a manner that is consistent with the policy principles and legal frameworks that the department follows for other domains including the law of armed conflict.

Which brings me to the second area of focus, policies and organization. Responding to the cyber threat requires the right policies and organizations across the federal government. For the past year, the Department of Defense has been working very closely with other agencies to understand where are the lines of responsibility when it comes to cyber defense. Where do we draw those lines? And how do those responsibilities get executed? As part of that effort, the department is now finalizing the most comprehensive change to our rules of engagement in cyberspace in seven years. The new rules will make clear that the department has a responsibility, not only to defend DoD's networks, but also to be prepared to defend the nation and our national interests against an attack in or through cyberspace. These new rules make the department more agile and provide us with the ability to confront major threats quickly.

Three years ago, the department took a major step forward by establishing the United States Cyber Command, under the leadership of General Keith Alexander, a four-star officer who also serves as the director of the National Security Agency. Cyber Command has matured into what I believe is a world-class organization. It has the capacity to conduct a full range of missions inside cyberspace. The threat picture could be quickly shared with DoD's geographic and functional combatant commanders, with DHS, with FBI and with other agencies in government. After all, we need to see an attack coming in order to defend against that attack. And we're looking at ways to strengthen Cyber Command as well. We must ensure that it has the resources, that it has the authorities, that it has the capabilities required to perform this growing mission. And it must also be able to react quickly to events unfolding in cyberspace and help fully integrate cyber into all of the department's plans and activities.

And finally, the third area is to build stronger partnerships. As I've made clear, securing cyberspace is not the sole responsibility of the United States military or even the sole responsibility of the United States government. The private sector, government, military, our allies—all share the same global infrastructure and we all share the responsibility to protect it. Therefore, we are deepening cooperation with our closest allies with the goal of sharing threat information, maximizing shared capabilities and determining malicious activities. The president, the vice president, Secretary of State and I have made cyber a major topic of discussion in nearly all of our bilateral meetings with foreign counterparts. I recently met with our Chinese military counterparts just a few weeks ago. As I mentioned earlier, China is rapidly growing its cyber capabilities. In my visit to Beijing, I underscored the need to increase communication and transparency with each other so that we could avoid a misunderstanding or a miscalculation in cyberspace. This is in the interest of the United States, but it's also in the interest of China.

Ultimately, no one has a greater interest in cybersecurity than the businesses that depend on a safe, secure and resilient global, digital infrastructure. Particularly those who operate the critical networks that we must help defend. To defend those networks more effectively, we must share information between the government and the private sector about threats in cyberspace. We've made real progress in sharing information with the private sector. But very frankly, we need Congress to act to ensure that this sharing is timely and comprehensive.

Companies should be able to share specific threat information with the government, without the prospect of lawsuits hanging over their head. And a key principle must be to protect the fundamental liberties and privacy in cyberspace that we are all duty bound to uphold. Information sharing alone is not sufficient. We've got to work with the business community to develop baseline standards for our most critical private-sector infrastructure, our power plants, our water treatment facilities, our gas pipelines. This would help ensure that companies take proactive measures to secure themselves against sophisticated threats, but also take common sense steps against basic threats. Although awareness is growing, the reality is that too few companies have invested in even basic cybersecurity. The fact is that to fully provide the necessary protection in our democracy, cybersecurity legislation must be passed by the Congress. Without it, we are and we will be vulnerable.

Source: U.S. Department of Defense transcripts. Retrieved from http://www.defense.gov/transcripts/transcript.aspx?tran scriptid=5136.

Excerpts from U.S. Department of Defense, Defense Science Board, Task Force Report: "Resilient Military Systems and the Advanced Cyber Threat," January 2013

In June 2011, the Defense Science Board (DSB) was tasked with examining the current state of cyber security in the Department of Defense and offering recommendations for how the DoD could improve its cyber posture. The extensive report, of which excerpts are below, paints a grim picture of the cyber conditions confronting the DoD, and concedes that there will be extensive penetrations of the U.S. cyber network even if all of the recommendations are carried out. Further, it is telling that the DSB considers it an important aspiration for the United States to rise to the level of worthy competitor in the cyber domain. The DSB views the potential of cyber warfare, which it believes will be a part of every future conflict, to present an existential threat to the nation matched only by the danger of nuclear weapons.

The United States cannot be confident that our critical Information Technology (IT) systems will work under attack from a sophisticated and well-resourced opponent utilizing cyber capabilities in combination with all of their military and intelligence capabilities (a "full spectrum" adversary). While this is also true for others (e.g. Allies, rivals, and public/private networks), this Task Force strongly believes the DoD needs to take the lead and build an effective response to measurably increase confidence in the IT systems we depend on (public and private) and at the same time decrease a would-be attacker's confidence in the effectiveness of their capabilities to compromise DoD systems. We have recommended an approach to do so, and we need to start now!

While DoD takes great care to secure the use and operation of the "hardware" of its weapon systems, these security practices have not kept up with the cyber adversary tactics and capabilities. Further, the same level of resource and attention is not spent on the complex network of information technology (IT) systems that are used to support and operate those weapons or critical cyber capabilities embedded within them. This Task Force was asked to review and make recommendations to improve the resilience of DoD systems to cyber attacks and to develop a set of metrics that the Department could use to track progress and shape investment priorities.

Over the past 18 months, the Task Force received more than 50 briefings from practitioners and senior officials throughout the DoD, Intelligence Community (IC), commercial practitioners, academia, national laboratories, and policymakers. As a result of its deliberations, the Task Force concludes that:

- The cyber threat is serious, with potential consequences similar in some ways to the nuclear threat of the Cold War
- The cyber threat is also insidious, enabling adversaries to access vast new channels of intelligence about critical U.S. enablers (operational and technical; military and industrial) that can threaten our national and economic security
- Current DoD actions, though numerous, are fragmented. Thus, DoD is not prepared to defend against this threat
- DoD red teams, using cyber attack tools which can be downloaded from the Internet, are very successful at defeating our systems
- U.S. networks are built on inherently insecure architectures with increasing use of foreign-built components
- U.S. intelligence against peer threats targeting DoD systems is inadequate
- With present capabilities and technology it is not possible to defend with confidence against the most sophisticated cyber attacks
- It will take years for the Department to build an effective response to the cyber threat to include elements of deterrence, mission assurance and offensive cyber capabilities

The DoD, and its contractor base are high priority targets that have sustained staggering losses of system design information incorporating years of combat knowledge and experience. Employing reverse engineering techniques, adversaries can exploit weapon system technical plans for their benefit. Perhaps even more significant, they gained insight to operational concepts and system use (e.g., which processes are automated and which are person controlled) developed from decades of U.S. operational and developmental experience—the type of information that cannot simply be recreated in a laboratory or factory environment. Such information provides tremendous benefit to an adversary, shortening time for development of countermeasures by years.

In addition, there is evidence of attacks that exploit known vulnerabilities in the domestic power grid and critical infrastructure systems. DoD, and the United States, is extremely reliant on the availability of its critical infrastructure.

Recent DoD and U.S. interest in counterfeit parts has resulted in the identification of widespread introduction of counterfeit parts into DoD systems through commercial supply chains. Since many systems use the same processors and those processors are typically built overseas in untrustworthy environments, the challenge to supply chain management in a cyber-contested environment is significant.

DoD is in the process of institutionalizing a Supply Chain Risk Management (SCRM) strategy that prioritizes scarce security resources on critical mission systems and components, provides intelligence analysis to acquisition programs and incorporates vulnerability risk mitigation requirements into system designs.

The success of DoD red teams against its operational systems should also give pause to DoD leadership. During exercises and testing, DoD red teams, using only small teams and a short amount of time, are able to significantly disrupt the "blue team's" ability to carry out military missions. Typically, the disruption is so great, that the exercise must be essentially reset without the cyber intrusion to allow enough operational capability to proceed. These stark demonstrations contribute to the Task Force's assertion that the functioning of DoD's systems is not assured in the presence of even a modestly aggressive cyber attack.

The benefits to an attacker using cyber exploits are potentially spectacular. Should the United States find itself in a full-scale conflict with a peer adversary, attacks would be expected to include denial of service, data corruption, supply chain corruption, traitorous insiders, kinetic and related non-kinetic attacks at all altitudes from underwater to space. U.S. guns, missiles, and bombs may not fire, or may be directed against our own troops. Resupply, including food, water, ammunition, and fuel may not arrive when or where needed. Military Commanders may rapidly lose trust in the information and ability to control U.S. systems and forces. Once lost, that trust is very difficult to regain.

The impact of a destructive cyber attack on the civilian population would be even greater with no electricity, money, communications, TV, radio, or fuel (electrically pumped). In a short time, food and medicine distribution systems would be ineffective, transportation would fail or become so chaotic as to be useless. Law enforcement, medical staff, and emergency personnel capabilities could be expected to be barely functional in the short term and dysfunctional over sustained periods. If the attack's effects were reversible, damage could be limited to an impact equivalent to a power outage lasting a few days. If an attack's effects cause physical damage to control systems, pumps, engines, generators, controllers, etc., the unavailability of parts and manufacturing capacity could mean months to years are required to rebuild and reestablish basic infrastructure operation.

The DoD should expect cyber attacks to be part of all conflicts in the future, and should not expect competitors to play by our version of the rules, but instead apply their own rules (e.g. using surrogates for exploitation and offense operations, sharing IP with local industries for economic gain, etc.).

Recommendations:

1. Protect the Nuclear Strike as a Deterrent (for existing nuclear armed states and existential cyber attack).

2. Determine the Mix of Cyber, Protected-Conventional, and Nuclear Capabilities Necessary for Assured Operation in the Face of a Full-Spectrum Adversary.

3. Refocus Intelligence Collection and Analysis to Understand Adversarial Cyber Capabilities, Plans and Intentions, and to Enable Counterstrategies.

4. Build and Maintain World-Class Cyber Offensive Capabilities (with appropriate authorities).

5. Enhance Defenses to Protect Against Low and Mid-Tier Threats.

6. Change DoD's Culture Regarding Cyber and Cyber Security.

7. Build a Cyber Resilient Force.

The network connectivity that the United States has used to tremendous advantage, economically and militarily, over the past 20 years has made the country far more vulnerable than ever to cyber attacks. At the same time, our adversaries are far more capable of conducting such attacks. The DoD should expect cyber to be part of all future conflicts, especially against near-peer and peer adversaries. This Task Force believes that full manifestation of the cyber threat could even produce existential consequences to the United States, particularly with respect to critical infrastructure. To maintain global stability in the emerging area of cyber warfare, the United States must be, and be seen as, a worthy competitor in this domain.

This Task Force developed a set of recommendations that, when taken in whole, creates a strategy for DoD to address this broad and pervasive threat. Cyber is a complicated domain and must be managed from a systems perspective. There is no silver bullet that will reduce DoD cyber risk to zero. While the problem cannot be eliminated, it can and must be determinedly managed through the combination of deterrence and improved cyber defense. Deterrence is achieved with offensive cyber, some protected-conventional capabilities, and anchored with U.S. nuclear weapons. This strategy removes the requirements to protect all of our military systems from the most advanced cyber threats, which the Task Force believes is neither feasible nor affordable.

It will take time to build the capabilities necessary to prepare and protect our country from the cyber threat. *We must start now!*

Source: U.S. Department of Defense, Defense Science Board. *Task Force Report: Resilient Military Systems and the Advanced Cyber Threat.* January 2013. Retrieved from http://www.acq .osd.mil/dsb/reports/ResilientMilitarySystems.CyberThreat.pdf.

Statement of General Keith B. Alexander, Commander, United States Cyber Command, before the Senate Committee on Armed Services, March 12, 2013

General Keith B. Alexander, the director of the National Security Agency and the commander of U.S. Cyber Command, gave a prepared statement to the U.S. Senate Committee on Armed Services. In that statement, he laid out the basic tenets of U.S. cyber policy and the current state of affairs in the cyber domain. This excerpt, entitled "The Strategic Landscape," clarifies the role of U.S. Cyber Command in the American national defense structure. It pays particular attention to the threats that currently confront the United States in the cyber domain.

U.S. Cyber Command operates in a dynamic and contested environment that literally changes its characteristics each time someone powers on a networked device. Geographic boundaries are perhaps less evident in cyberspace, but every server, fiber-optic line, cell tower, thumb drive, router, and laptop is owned by someone and resides in some physical locale. In this way cyberspace resembles the land domain—it is all owned, and it can be reshaped. Most networked devices, for example, are in private hands, and their owners can deny or facilitate others' cyber operations by how they manage and maintain their networks and devices. Cyberspace as an operating environment also has aspects unique to it. Events in cyberspace can seem to happen instantaneously. Data can appear to reside in multiple locations. There is a great deal of anonymity, and strongly encrypted data are virtually unreadable. In cyberspace, moreover, sweeping effects can be precipitated by states, enterprises, and individuals, with the added nuance that such cyber actors can be very difficult to identify. The cyber landscape also changes rapidly with the connection of new devices and bandwidth, and with the spread of strong encryption and mobile devices. Despite the unique characteristics of cyberspace, states still matter because they can affect much of the physical infrastructure within their borders. Convergence is our watchword; our communications, computers, and networks are merging into one digital environment as our political, economic, and social realms are being re-shaped by the rush of innovation.

In this environment that is both orderly and chaotic, beneficial and perilous, we at USCYBERCOM have to focus on actors who possess the capability—and possibly the intent—to harm our nation's interests in cyberspace or to use cyber means to inflict harm on us in other ways. Unfortunately, the roster of actors of concern to us is growing longer and growing also in terms of the variety and sophistication of the ways they can affect our operations and security.

State actors continue to top our list of concerns. We feel confident that foreign leaders believe that a devastating attack on the critical infrastructure and population of the United States by cyber means would be correctly traced back to its source and elicit a prompt and proportionate response. Nonetheless, it is possible that some future regime or cyber actor could misjudge the impact and the certainty of our resolve.

We have some confidence in our ability to deter major state-on-state attacks in cyberspace but we are not deterring the seemingly low-level harassment of private and public sites, property, and data. As former Secretary of Defense Panetta explained to an audience in New York last October, states and extremist groups are behaving recklessly and aggressively in the cyber environment. Such attacks have been destructive to both data and property. The Secretary mentioned, for example, the remote assaults last summer on Saudi Aramco and RasGas, which together rendered inoperable—and effectively destroyed the data on—more than 30,000 computers. We have also seen repressive regimes, desperate to hold on to power in the face of popular resistance, resort to all manner of cyber harassment on both their opponents and their own citizens caught in the crossfire. Offensive cyber programs and capabilities are growing, evolving, and spreading before our eyes; we believe it is only a matter of time before the sort of sophisticated tools developed by well-funded state actors find their way to non-state groups or even individuals. The United States has already become a target. Networks and websites owned by Americans and located here have endured intentional, state-sponsored attacks, and some have incurred damage and disruption because they happened to be along the route to another state's overseas targets.

Let me draw your attention to another very serious threat to U.S. interests. The systematic cyber exploitation of American companies, enterprises, and their intellectual property continued unabated over the last year. Many incidents were perpetrated by organized cybercriminals. Identity and data theft are now big business, netting their practitioners large profits and giving rise to an on-line sub-culture of markets for stolen data and cyber tools for stealing more. Much cyber exploitation activity, however, is state-sponsored. Foreign government–directed cyber collection personnel, tools, and organizations are targeting the data of American and western businesses, institutions, and citizens. They are particularly targeting our telecommunications, information technology, financial, security, and energy sectors. They are exploiting these targets on a scale amounting to the greatest unwilling transfer of wealth in history. States and cybercriminals do not leave empty bank vaults and file drawers behind after they break-in—they usually copy what they find and leave the original data intact—but the damage they are doing to America's economic competitiveness and innovation edge is profound, translating into missed opportunities for U.S. companies and the potential for lost American jobs. Cyber-enabled theft jeopardizes our economic growth.

We at USCYBERCOM work closely with our interagency partners to address these threats.

We must also watch potential threats from terrorists and hacktivists in cyberspace. The Intelligence Community and others have long warned that worldwide terrorist organizations like al Qaeda and its affiliates have the intent to harm the United States via cyber means. We agree with this judgment, while noting that, so far, their capability to do so has not matched their intent. This is not to downplay the problem of terrorist use of the Internet. Al Qaeda and other violent extremist groups are on the Web proselytizing, fundraising, and inspiring imitators. We should not ignore the effectiveness with which groups like al Qaeda and its affiliates radicalize ever larger numbers of people each year—on more continents. The Federal Bureau of Investigation and other agencies cite instances in which would-be terrorists found motivation and moral support for suicide attacks at jihadist websites and chat rooms. This is an especially serious and growing problem in areas of hostilities where our troops and personnel are deployed. Another threat that is not growing as fast as we might have feared, on the other hand, is that of hacktivists with a cause or a grievance that leads them to target U.S. government and military networks. Our vulnerabilities to this sort of disruption remain, but 2012 saw fewer such incidents than 2011.

Source: United States Department of Defense transcripts. Retrieved from http://www.defense.gov/home/features/2013/0713_cyberdomain/docs/Alexander%20testimony%20March%202013.pdf.

6 Resources

The resources summarized and analyzed in this chapter are some of the most readily available and influential works discussing the short history of cyber warfare. It is not all-encompassing; rather, it is designed to be a starting point for the novice interested in developing a solid grounding in the key controversies within cyberspace. The works range from traditional books and articles to Internet projects and cyber e-zines, demonstrating the wide variety of potential sources to examine for a greater understanding of cyber conflict.

Print Resources

Armistead, Leigh, ed. 2007. *Information Warfare: Separating Hype from Reality.* Washington, DC: Potomac Books.

> As the title suggests, this book is designed to clarify what the actual capabilities of information warfare are, and to eliminate outlandish scenarios that have come to dominate the public discussion of cyber warfare. The book argues that cyberterrorism, in particular, has been overblown by media attention and has gained an undeserved reputation as a threat to the general public. The authors

Police officer Kim Jae-pil of South Korea's Cyber Terror Response Center shows seized hard drives that were used in a wave of cyber attacks against the agency's headquarters in Seoul. North Korea's spy agencies are suspected of perpetrating the attacks. (AP Photo/Ahn Young-joon) suggest that because there have been no widespread incidents of cyberterrorism, it is impossible to adequately plan for their possible use in the future. They believe that hackers and terror groups are simply too divergent from one another to form a useful partnership, as neither can offer much of interest to the other. Further, terror organizations are not developing sophisticated cyber capabilities on their own, and as a result, their available methods are limited to brute-force DDoS attacks and minor website defacements. The book offers the key point that hacktivists should not be equated with terrorists, in part because their goal is not to inject fear into the public discourse. Although hacktivists often portray themselves as engaged in civil disobedience for a legitimate cause, the same could be argued about many of the less-violent terror organizations that operate in the world, at least to third parties who have no interest in their agendas.

Arquilla, John, and David Ronfeldt. 1996. "The Advent of Netwar." Santa Monica, CA: RAND Corporation.

This report, originally prepared for the U.S. Secretary of Defense, argues that netwar (networked warfare) should be considered at the opposite end of the conflict spectrum from cyber warfare. According to Arquilla and Ronfeldt, a netwar consists of two or more highly networked states engaging in a high-intensity conflict, while a cyber war is more likely to be part of a low-intensity conflict, possibly involving a nonstate actor. In a netwar, the primary goal of each belligerent is to disrupt, degrade, or destroy the enemy's networks, bringing down their entire capacity to resist by eliminating key aspects of their military capabilities.

The ideas presented in this report reflected the influence of network operations in the Persian Gulf War and borrow somewhat from the air power theories of John Warden and John Boyd. Arquilla and Ronfeldt see networks as inherently adaptable, flexible, versatile, and opportunistic in their offensive capacities. Network defenses benefit by being redundant, robust, and resilient. If networks have a key vulnerability, it is in their need for extensive communications between different aspects of the network—creating a potential vulnerability to cyber attack. The authors believe the United States would likely benefit from netwar, and they predicted that developing netwar capabilities would make the United States unchallengeable on the conventional battlefield. This prediction held true in 2003, when American-led coalition forces quickly invaded Iraq and overthrew its government, using a much smaller force to accomplish a much greater mission than the one pursued in the Gulf War only 12 years earlier.

Arquilla, John, and David Ronfeldt, eds. 1997. *In Athena's Camp*. Santa Monica, CA: RAND Corporation.

Arquilla and Ronfeldt's *In Athena's Camp* makes the argument that the 1990s bore a great resemblance to the 1920s regarding military assumptions and behaviors. In both decades, too many military professionals assumed that the era of warfare had essentially ended, not realizing that they were actually simply in an interwar period. In the aftermath of World War I, this led to a major demilitarization in the Western democracies, which then left them completely unprepared to counter the rise of Nazi Germany. In the 1990s, the collapse of the Soviet Union and the end of the Cold War had a similar effect, with many Western nations expecting a massive "peace dividend" that left them vulnerable to terror attacks in the early twenty-first century.

This volume relies heavily upon metaphorical explanations of modern warfare. The title suggests that Athena, the ancient Greek goddess of wisdom who entered the world fully armed and armored, more closely signifies the patron of modern conflict than Ares, the Greek god of war, who held a reputation for violence unmitigated by rationality. To the authors, cyber warfare is really about information dominance, a claim that allows them to proclaim the Mongols to be the original cyber warriors, despite their prominence eight centuries before the first computer. The Mongols excelled at deception and surprise attacks by overwhelming force at a decisive point, something that Western military forces pursue as a matter of doctrine. The writers also rely heavily upon a comparison of strategic board games, arguing that modern warfare resembles Go much more than it resembles a chess match.

The authors contend that information dominance will be the most important component of military conflicts in the future, and that belligerents with a more accurate picture of the battlefield will have an almost insurmountable advantage. Cyber networks offer both a means to transmit and analyze said information, and also a way to attack the enemy's understanding of the situation being faced. The ongoing revolution in cyber capabilities, they argue, is forcing a redesign of military organizations, which in turn heavily influence the development of doctrine and strategy. Those nations that do the best job of adapting to the new operating environment will flourish on the battlefields of the twenty-first century, while those that fail to adapt will find themselves marginalized and increasingly irrelevant in the great power politics of the new century.

Arquilla, John, and David Ronfeldt. 1992. *Cyberwar Is Coming!* Santa Monica, CA: RAND Corporation.

This short think piece is one of the foundational writings about cyber war. In addition to coining the terms "cyberwar" and "netwar," Arquilla and Ronfeldt predicted a revolution in information technology that would fundamentally change warfare. They considered it not just as an enabler, but also a way to fundamentally alter the ways of thinking and types of conflict practiced by military professionals. They argued that cyber capabilities require major changes in the organization of entities, and they force the redistribution of power within organizations, usually to weaker actors. The U.S. military demonstrated the key role of information dominance in the Persian Gulf War, enabling a complete rout of one of the largest militaries in the world, at a minimal cost to U.S. and coalition forces.

Interestingly, Arquilla and Ronfeldt correctly assumed that the adoption of cyber war would trigger the use of much smaller ground forces, with air power tasked with blinding the enemy and supplying information to theater commanders. Their biggest miscalculation was the assumption that the United States would primarily fight wars as a defender rather than an aggressor, a prediction that proved completely false in the ensuing two decades.

Bateman, Robert L., III, ed. 1999. *Digital War: A View from the Front Lines.* Novato, CA: Presidio Press.

In this volume, Bateman organizes eight U.S. Army officers who all seek to illustrate how computers and digital networks have begun to influence military operations, particularly in, but not limited to, the U.S. Army. The work makes the argument that a revolution in military affairs is underway and will allow for a far more effective and efficient army if it can be well managed. The book is a mixture of nonfiction, no-nonsense accounts of a networked military organization, and somewhat silly and speculative fictional pieces about an imagined future.

Unlike some similar volumes, Bateman's work includes some efforts to note the potential drawbacks of becoming too dependent upon or burdened by technology, particularly at the tactical level. As Daniel P. Bolger notes, it is impossible for troops to fight carrying 140 pounds of gear; thus, to use all of the cyber resources available, something will have to be taken out of the inventory. Unfortunately, the U.S. Army has a tendency to keep piling more gear onto its soldiers, making them highly vulnerable to a lightly armed, nimble opponent that eschews the high-technology gear in favor of mobility and firepower. Given the relative fragility of many cyber systems, Bolger believes they should largely be relegated to the strategic level of warfare, and that troops in the field should be allowed to benefit from the information supplied by cyber operations without having to carry out said operations in the field.

The digital revolution may enable an entirely new approach to warfare, but it also means there will be a great deal more scrutiny of military operations, on almost an instant basis, thanks to the media's ability to engage in the same level of information-gathering and delivery as the military it is covering. The military cannot expressly control the media in a Western democracy, but must be aware of its influence and role. These prescient arguments have been amply demonstrated in the conflicts in Iraq and Afghanistan, where journalists have become a ubiquitous feature of the conflict, and their reports, increasingly filed through digital means, have made the war accessible to anyone with an Internet connection.

Bousquet, Antoine. 2009. *The Scientific Way of Warfare: Order and Chaos on the Battlefields of Modernity.* New York: Columbia University Press.

Bousquet argues that the dominant scientific paradigms of an era have determined the Western way of warfare for the past few centuries. He defines the key periods as mechanistic, thermodynamic, electromagnetic, and cybernetic, with a gradually emerging new period he terms "chaoplexic." The current cybernetic era, in his view, is dominated on the battlefield by computers, greater automation in weapon systems, and the centralization of warfare. The key to modern military victory lies in information dominance, as the belligerent who best controls the flow of accurate information holds an insurmountable advantage in combat. The shrinking response times between an idea and its action being carried out have led strategists to dream of an era of omniscience, when total knowledge of the conditions of the battlefield becomes possible. Of course, such knowledge will be far too great for a single human being to grasp, and thus humanity might be on a path to outsourcing its military leadership and command to specialized computers that can process all of the necessary information and react immediately to the changing conditions. This, in turn, drives a push for autonomous weapons, distributed networks that can offer both positive and negative feedback, and the independent emergence of extremely complex systems without direct control by a single leader.

Bowden, Mark. 2011. *Worm: The First Digital World War.* New York: Atlantic Monthly Press.

Bowden specializes in the examination of a single, discrete operation in a conflict. His previous works include *Black Hawk Down* and *Killing Pablo*. In *Worm*, he analyzes the effort to control a single piece of malware, Conficker, whose creators and purpose remain a mystery to this day. Conficker was a very effective worm that managed to infect 12 million computers in a short period of time, uniting them into a single massive botnet. Such a widespread botnet could potentially be used to launch massive denial of service attacks, or might be used to copy and transmit information from the host computers. Its detection prompted the creation of a massive international group, calling itself "the cabal," that brought together academics, industry cyber security professionals, and government officials to fight its distribution. Their efforts caught the attention of Conficker's creators, who upgraded the worm in an effort to counter the cabal's work.

Bowden considers the Conficker incident to be a digital war, as cyber combatants struggled to outfox one another in the digital environment. Others have considered Conficker to simply be an act of digital piracy, cyber crime, or cyberterrorism. More than anything, the Conficker experience demonstrated the need for a dedicated organization that can bring together resources to fight against such cyber attacks. It also highlighted the unserious attitude of the U.S. government toward cyber security, as political appointees with little or no knowledge of the subject continue to be the most important decision-makers in the cyber policy realm.

Brenner, Joel. 2011. *America the Vulnerable: Inside the New Threat Matrix of Digital Espionage, Crime, and Warfare.* New York: Penguin Press.

Brenner, the former senior counsel and inspector general of the National Security Agency, is in a uniquely qualified position to offer his opinions regarding the cyber security of the United States and the interconnected nature of crime, espionage, and conflict in the cyber domain. Unfortunately, the requirements of national security preclude him from sharing all of his knowledge, as one might expect, although he somewhat suggests that virtually any secret belonging to the U.S. government is readily available to talented hackers, particularly if they are sponsored by rival nations. Brenner notes the key relationships between privacy, security, and transparency, which apply to the cyber domain at least as much as they do to the physical world. He contends that the problem of cyber security is so challenging that it might be insurmountable, and thus that total transparency may be inevitable, regardless of the consequences for personal and government privacy.

Brenner, like many other knowledgeable authors, argues that the U.S. government has not taken cyber security very seriously, a fact that has undermined its ability to protect national secrets and infrastructure from enemy intrusions. However, he also notes that government agencies like the NSA have played an important role in pushing for increased cyber transparency, ironically making the United States more vulnerable to enemies while at the same time allowing greater intrusions by the government into the lives of the citizenry. Unlike most authors, Brenner argues that cyber crime, espionage, and warfare are all directly connected to one another and cannot be considered separate problems. He envisions the United States becoming embroiled in an international crisis in the near future and discovering that it cannot project power through military might due to failures in cyber capabilities. An enemy might be able to hinder U.S. logistics and communications through cyber attacks, which would make military operations difficult. More ominously, an enemy might be able to place the U.S. homeland at risk, a situation that no enemy nation has achieved in two centuries. This vulnerability is due primarily to decisions made by American political and corporate leaders, who have placed too many systems into the global cyber network, making them logical targets for enemy cyber attacks.

Brenner's biggest lesson for the reader is that computer users cannot be trusted to engage in effective security measures. Thus, the entire Internet and all of the hardware upon it need to be redesigned to make security a fundamental part of the architecture, rather than a patchwork of security software programs. Quite frankly, he believes that given a choice between convenience and security, users will almost inevitably choose convenience, a decision that places every other user of the network at risk due to their laziness and carelessness. While the massive alteration of the entire computer network would cost enormous resources, he points out that cyber crime and espionage are already draining the U.S. economy of billions of dollars per year and growing at an exponential rate. If nothing is done, the United States will be doomed to fall behind the nations that have chosen to place a top priority on developing cyber capabilities, most notably China and Russia, and will not be able to recover its position as the principal hegemon of economic and military might in the world.

Brenner, Susan W. 2009. *Cyberthreats: The Emerging Fault Lines of the Nation State.* New York: Oxford University Press.

Brenner's argument is that cyberwar is by definition a subtle and erosive process, which is completely at odds with the overt and destructive nature of warfare in the physical world. She also notes that in the cyber domain, the dominant legal concepts of warfare for more than three centuries, namely *jus ad bello* and *jus in bello*, will not function in the same manner. *Jus ad bello* refers to the circumstances in which a nation may justifiably undertake war, while *jus in bello* governs the types of actions in war that can be considered ethical and legal. One key example is the attempt to spare civilians, whenever possible, from the ravages of warfare. In exchange for this consideration, civilians agree not to engage in armed conflict. However, in the cyber realm, civilians may be the most important combatants, and it is almost impossible to protect civilians from potential harm through cyber attack.

To Brenner, there is little practical difference between cyber crime, cyberterrorism, and cyber war, and the delineations between them revolve primarily around motivations. Cybercriminals engaged in cyber attacks for the traditional purposes of crime, primarily material enrichment. Cyberterrorists launch cyber attacks to coerce a government or a population for political purposes, using fear as a primary motivator. Cyber war has many of the same characteristics, in that a nation might expect to gain some form of enrichment from the attacks, and will certainly seek to coerce an enemy, either to concede a goal or to not take a specific action.

Brenner believes that the future of global conflict will not be limited to states, a consideration amply demonstrated by the international nature of violent extremist groups such as Al Qaeda. She argues that war will gradually devolve into a contest between nonstate actors, with guerrillas and mercenary armies taking the place of state-funded forces. In the cyber domain, the same pattern will occur, and in fact the greater incorporation of cyber capabilities into warfighting will only speed the process. Because the cyber domain has no geographic boundaries and cannot be defended in the same manner as a traditional state, the physical concepts of state interaction will gradually erode due to increased reliance upon the cyber domain. She coins the term "cyb3rchaos" to encompass the dystopian future of cyber crime, cyberterrorism, and cyber war. For the United States and Western democracies, the erosive process will provide a particularly thorny problem, and their clear divisions between law enforcement and military spheres of activity are likely to disappear. Further, civilians will become more involved in both the law enforcement and military processes, in part because they are not excluded from enemy cyber attacks.

Brennan offers a potential prescription to policy makers in the United States for a means to counter some of the worst effects of bringing the cyber domain into state conflicts. She suggests the creation of a Cyber Security Agency that can blend civil-military efforts in the cyber domain, although to make such a combination of efforts possible, it might be necessary to repeal or heavily modify the 1878 *posse comitatus* law. Of course, the increased reliance of the Department of Defense upon contractor personnel might allow for such a combined effort without formally merging civilian cyber warriors into the DoD. More than anything, Brennan reminds her readers that to create a better system in the new reality of cyber dominance, they must abandon efforts to transfer existing concepts into the cyber domain, and instead determine the defining principles of cyberspace before attempting to set the rules of international interaction in the new environment.

Campen, Alan D., and Douglas H. Dearth. 2000. *CyberWar 3.0: Human Factors in Information Operations and Future Conflict.* Fairfax, VA: AFCEA International Press.

This collection of essays presents a snapshot of the cyber war picture in 2000, and the theoretical portions of the work still have utility to the modern researcher. According to the authors, in the twenty-first century, conflicts have become increasingly shaped by both information warfare and hence cyber warfare. Even with the constraints of the cyber domain, however, there are lessons to be gleaned from classical strategists, in particular Sun Tzu and Basil Liddell-Hart, both of whom advocated an indirect approach to the destruction of the enemy. By definition, the cyber domain enables such an indirect approach and, in fact, essentially requires it for any strategic effect. The authors define and discuss the concept of a revolution in military affairs (RMA), a change in military operations that provides an enormous advantage to adopters and that makes all preceding approaches to conflict dangerously obsolete. Cyber warfare makes the notions of perception management and psychological warfare particularly important, as the ability to control an enemy's access to information, and to influence the enemy's thinking, provides a nearly insurmountable advantage in war. Thus, military organizations of the future will need to place special emphasis upon the protection of their own critical infrastructures from cyber attack, and must spend an inordinate amount of time and resources considering the most vulnerable element of any cyber network: the human operators.

Campen, Alan D., Douglas H. Dearth, and R. Thomas Goodden. 1996. *Cyberwar: Security, Strategy, and Conflict in the Information Age.* Fairfax, VA: AFCEA International Press.

This volume collects a series of cyber war articles from *SIGNAL* magazine into a single volume. The publisher, the Armed Forces Communication and Electronics Association, is dedicated to providing the most current information about communications technology. While the articles are technologically obsolete due to their age, they provide a solid theoretical foundation for many of the elements of cyber warfare. Further, the articles do a remarkably good job of predicting the near-term future of cyber conflict, and they are old enough that their predictions can be effectively evaluated. The work demonstrates that even in 1996, there was a solid understanding of the ongoing revolution in military affairs being created by cyber issues, at least among experts. This proves the point that such revolutions do not simply happen in the blink of an eye—they can be detected, shaped, and reacted to over time. Thus, their results are not a foregone conclusion, a point that the authors make when attempting to shape the debate over future cyber activities.

Carr, Jeffrey. 2009. *Inside Cyber Warfare: Mapping the Cyber Underworld.* Sebastopol, CA: O'Reilly Media.

Jeffrey Carr's *Inside Cyber Warfare* is a thorough examination of the recent events characterized by some as cyber warfare. Much of it is informed by the findings of Project Grey Goose, a series of open-source investigations conducted by volunteers. Carr's central argument is that cyber warfare is largely the activity of nonstate groups, although they may operate in conjunction with state entities. He sees cyber crime as the laboratory in which the tools of cyber war are created, although he notes that cyber crime should not be considered an act of war, in part due to the motivations of the actors involved. Carr notes that the price of entry into the underworld of the cyber domain is far lower than that of any other form of warfare, particularly with the broad availability of toolkits that can perform many of the basic cyber attacks without any knowledge or sophistication on the part of the user.

Carr also makes the interesting point that third-world nations represent an enormous potential resource for cyber warriors. Most third-world computers use a form of the Windows operating system, but most users cannot afford to pay for a legal copy of the software. Thus, pirated copies are the norm, which means that their users cannot download patches and software updates to eliminate vulnerabilities in their computer systems. This matters, he argues, because it makes them perfect targets for the assembly of botnets. As more areas of the world become connected to the Internet via wireless or fiber-optic means, each of these potential zombie computers becomes a weapon for controllers in more advanced nations.

Carr's work also investigates whether or not cyber attacks can be constituted as an act of war. He argues that they can, but only under certain circumstances. Not all cyber attacks rise to that level, most are more irritating than devastating. To be an act of war, a cyber attack would need to cause substantial physical damage or inflict fatalities, and even then, it might not be an act of war, but it might be more accurately characterized as a criminal or terrorist event. If cyber war occurs, though, it will not follow the methods of warfare in the physical world, but it will still be bounded by many of the norms of warfare. Chief among these are the principles of necessity and distinction, each of which may be difficult to translate to the cyber realm. By design, Carr's work raises as many questions as it answers, but it is an excellent in-depth study of many of the cyber conflicts that have gone largely ignored by Western scholars and media outlets.

Clarke, Richard A., and Robert K. Knake. 2010. *Cyber War: The Next Great Threat to National Security and What to Do about It.* New York: HarperCollins.

Clarke served in the White House for four presidential administrations, including a stint as the national coordinator for security, infrastructure protection, and counterterrorism under President Bill Clinton. In that role, he sought to undertake a massive improvement for the security of the nation's cyber networks, with little success. Political intransigence, a refusal by decision-makers to study the problems and understand the potential risks of inaction, the potential costs associated with his program, and the resistance of major Internet service providers all combined to prevent any major effort to improve security on the U.S. Internet. This work is designed to present the dangers associated with inaction to the U.S. population, in the hope of producing political pressure on the federal government to take decisive action, without which, Clarke contends, the United States will remain incredibly vulnerable to cyber espionage, cyber crime, and cyber attacks in support of military operations.

Clarke and Knake argue that the massive, ongoing cyber espionage efforts of competitor nations, most notably Iran and China, have undermined not just the military advantages of the nation, but also the economic advantages that underpin the entire American national power structure. They begin by demonstrating the scope of the problem and the ways in which cyber attacks have already been utilized in support of, or in place of, military attacks in the physical world. They then lay out the current structure of the modern Internet, and the key vulnerabilities of a system that was never designed to link billions of computers and users into a single network of information and commerce. Clarke and Knake suggest that the very first objectives of the U.S. government's cyber policy should be a so-called "Defensive Triad," consisting of an attempt to stop malware at the "backbone ISPs" that supply the vast majority of cyber traffic; a major security upgrade of the nation's electric grid; and a serious attempt to secure and protect the Department of Defense computer networks and the weapons that are dependent upon them. They also argue that the United States should adopt a leadership position in the negotiation of an international agreement to outlaw or at least regulate the use of cyber attacks in international conflicts, and to prevent the spread of cyber crime. Finally, a major effort to completely redesign both the hardware and the software that underpin the Internet, with security as the foremost consideration, might eliminate the problems of cyber espionage, cyber crime, and cyber war once and for all.

Halpin, Edward, Philippa Trevorrow, David Webb, and Steve Wright, eds. 2006. *Cyberwar, Netwar and the Revolution in Military Affairs.* New York: Palgrave Macmillan.

This volume has a wide variety of perspectives offered by authors, ranging from the idea that the United States leads the world in information warfare capabilities, to the notion that it is by far the most vulnerable nation on earth to such attacks. An essay by Geoffrey Darnont illustrates the problems with the term "cyberwar" that arise from trying to apply the classical definitions of warfare, in part because cyber attacks do not involve weapons, are not limited to states, and may not result in material harm, even if they do significant damage to data. To Darnont, many of the commonly held beliefs about legal behavior in warfare do not apply to cyberspace, in part because they simply do not translate well to the cyber domain. Two excellent essays by Fanourios Pantelogiannis and Chris Wu examine the cyber capabilities and intentions of Russia and China, respectively. Both note that their objects of study do not follow the American patterns regarding the use of cyber assets to support kinetic attacks, and will instead pursue network capabilities that more closely match their own societies. While neither foresaw how heavily Russia and China would invest in cyber, their general explanation of the Russian and Chinese approaches to the field have proven remarkably prescient.

Kramer, Franklin D., Stuart H. Starr, and Larry K. Wentz, eds. 2009. *Cyberpower and National Security*. Dulles, VA: Potomac Books.

This work is a collection of essays examining the strategic implications of cyberpower for national security, written by a veritable who's who of cyber strategists, theorists, and practitioners. They argue that the United States is the key actor in the international cyber dimension, and that if cyber accords are to be created, they will not function without U.S. acquiescence, and possibly U.S. leadership. The work is broken into six parts, beginning with the "Foundations of Cyberpower." This section includes an overview and the necessary definitions that underpin the overall work, as well as a number of direct policy recommendations that could guide the development of a U.S. cyber strategy. The next section provides a deeper examination of the component parts of cyberspace, and how cyber operations relate to the other elements of society. The military use of cyberspace, with an emphasis upon cyber deterrence, constitutes the third portion of the book. This section examines the issues unique to military operations in cyberspace, including how computer networks might be used to facilitate physical attacks upon enemy systems.

The fourth section develops the theme of information operations that can be conducted through cyberspace, including propaganda and psychological operations, as well as espionage activities that are currently being pursued by dozens of nations. Strategic problems are the subject of the fifth section, with an emphasis upon the twin problems of criminal activity and cyber terrorism. This section also includes an examination of the ways in which nations other than the United States pursue their developments in cyberspace, and how each nation's approach reflects national priorities and shared assumptions. The final section of the work covers institutional issues, including the possibility of global governance of cyberspace, the establishment of laws that might limit cyber activities, and how cyberspace has become intimately tied to infrastructure, which has created opportunities for economic savings through efficiency, but also made infrastructure more vulnerable to cyber attack. The authors conclude the work by pushing for the U.S. government to study not just the capabilities of potential cyber enemies, but also the cultural beliefs that guide the cyber activities of rivals. Understanding their approaches to cyber can help define their objectives and methodology, making the job of countering their moves within the domain, and deterring cyber aggression, a far easier proposition.

Libicki, Martin C. 2007. *Conquest in Cyberspace: National Security and Information Warfare.* New York: Cambridge University Press.

Libicki argues that the notion of cyber conquest has largely been overhyped, because the possibility of seizing and holding control of an enemy's cyber assets is extremely difficult. In Libicki's estimation, cyber assets might actually serve more of a deterrent against enemy activity than an offensive weapon, in part due to the incorrect assumptions that many policy makers hold regarding the utility of cyber weapons. While seizing an enemy system and maintaining control over it for an extended period is virtually impossible, destruction or corruption of information is far more likely. In this case, though, backup servers that are not directly connected to the same network can offset many of the dangers of data loss, and mitigate the effects of such a loss. Libicki also discusses the concept of "friendly conquest" through the cyber domain, by which he means the use of cyber assets in information operations to influence the opinions of enemies, either in a positive or a negative fashion. A positive example would include creating a more favorable view of the attacker in the target population, through the planting of biased information and the illusion of popular consensus. A negative example could include sowing discord among allies, by creating the impression through the cyber domain that they are working at cross-purposes. Libicki concludes the work by noting that advantages in the cyber domain tend to be transitory in nature, meaning that even the term "conquest" is a misnomer for the cyber realm.

Libicki, Martin C. 2009. *Cyberdeterrence and Cyberwar.* Santa Monica, CA: RAND Corporation.

This book is the culmination of Libicki's study of cyber issues on behalf of the U.S. Air Force. It examines the political and policy dimensions of cyber conflicts, and whether it is possible to deter cyber attacks, either through a robust cyber defense or the ability to counterattack through cyberspace. Libicki argues that the fundamental problem with cyber systems is that they have inherent security flaws and are connected to the Internet, making those flaws accessible to outsiders. He sees cyber attacks as inherently untrustworthy and uncertain of success, and believes that even the most successful attacks will only have a temporary effect of frustrating enemy computer operators. The threat of a "cyber Pearl Harbor," in Libicki's estimation, has been blown completely out of proportion and should not be allowed to hinder rational utilization of the cyber domain. He sees cyber warfare as inherently indecisive, in that the longer it is conducted, the more likely the enemy will be able to identify weaknesses in their computer systems and repair them.

Libicki makes an extensive comparison between cyber and nuclear warfare, in part to demonstrate the scale of destruction made possible by each. Whereas cyber attacks tend to weaken over time, as the opponent figures out how to counter their effects, nuclear weapons maintain their destructive capability, with the last bomb causing just as much damage as the first one used. Further, the deterrence capabilities of nuclear weapons have been proven for decades—nuclear devices have not been detonated in anger since 1945. Determining attribution in a nuclear war is not difficult—in cyber war, it can be an almost impossible proposition. If the common understanding is that cyber attacks are cheap, and cyber defenses are expensive, an attacker may choose to launch constant cyber intrusions with impunity, secure in the notion that they will not be proven to be the source of the attacks, or that they have far less to lose than their original target in any protracted cyber conflict. Libicki concludes that the creation and maintenance of substantial cyber defenses has a deterrent effect and, at the same time, can block all but the most well-financed attacks, essentially creating a filter that makes the attribution problem much easier in the event that an attack succeeds and causes enough damage to provoke a response.

Libicki, Martin C. 2012. *Crisis and Escalation in Cyberspace.* Santa Monica, CA: RAND Corporation.

Libicki's *Crisis and Escalation in Cyberspace* discusses the management of cyber crises at every stage of their development. He argues that cyber crises, which might be triggered by deliberate cyber attacks, cyber crime, or cyber espionage, are increasingly probable in the near future. However, unlike crises that arise from the physical world, the general norms of behavior for reacting to and managing cyber crises have not been established and do not follow the same rules of logical as crises in the physical world. To manage a cyber crisis, policy makers must understand the fundamental difference between the cyber domain and the physical world, and how actions in each might influence future actions in the other. Many of the commonly held assumptions about state relations in the physical world do not transfer well to the cyber domain, where correctly identifying an actor can present a very challenging problem. Thus, the parameters of a cyber crisis are likely to be much more difficult to define, and that uncertainty can lead to defensive reactions, including violent outbursts.

The instability of cyber crises is largely due to misperceptions about the actions or intents of other states. Libicki believes it is possible to create and adhere to new norms of cyber behavior, which might in turn produce a new level of stability. Efforts to defuse a crisis, rather than use it as an opportunity for escalation, might also serve to reduce the threat of cyber crises, although defusing such scenarios requires patience, practice, and forbearance that might create domestic pressure upon the state that is attempting to prevent an escalation. To Libicki, controlling the narrative of a crisis is extremely important, and may present the greatest challenge of all to a state caught off-guard by a cyber attack. However, it is key for states to be transparent in the messages they are attempting to send, as attempts to rely upon signaling, a well-established practice in diplomatic circles, can prove disastrous in the cyber domain. Libicki concludes this work by arguing that the creation of robust cyber defenses might serve to both deter attackers and prevent cyber crises from growing beyond a manageable stage. Offensive cyber capabilities, on the other hand, should be held in reserve when possible, and should never be employed without a careful consideration of the potential escalations that they might trigger from their target.

Marvel, Elisabette M., ed. 2010. *China's Cyberwarfare Capability.* New York: Nova Science Publishers, 2010.

This collection of essays is designed to evaluate the progress of the People's Republic of China in creating a military force capable of engaging in cyber warfare. It is based entirely on open sources, which somewhat limits the ability of the authors to be certain of China's capabilities, but which also allows readers to easily consult the same sources and draw their own conclusions. Around the turn of the century, the Chinese government decided to pursue a major cyber modernization effort, one that would allow a shift from a regional focus to a global power projection capability. No longer would the Chinese mainland fixate upon the island of Taiwan; rather, China would harness its national resources to assume a lead position in the cyber domain. To facilitate this dominance, the Chinese government decided to utilize computer network exploitation, gathering as much data as possible from rival nations via cyber espionage. This would allow China to catch up in its military technology programs, while at the same time creating "blind spots" in enemy information-gathering, which might then be exploited by kinetic attack.

Unlike many nations, China has chosen to create a full information warfare doctrine, linking cyber attack and electronic warfare into a single General Staff department, and placing cyber defense and signal intelligence collection together in a separate department. China plans to use cyber warfare on a wide scale in any future conflict, with the primary target the enemy's C4ISR assets. Chinese doctrine considers information dominance as the primary first objective in a conflict. To enable its cyber operations in such a future war, the People's Liberation Army has launched a massive espionage campaign through the cyber domain, including attempts to penetrate and exploit the networks of private corporations. Should China become engaged in a war with the United States, it will unleash a massive attack upon the Department of Defense's NIPRNet and logistics networks, using pathways already established by the prewar cyber intrusions. Attacks on the classified DoD network will accompany the campaign, primarily through brute-force attacks against servers tasked with carrying SIPRNet and JWICS traffic, rather than any attempt to decrypt materials on these classified networks.

Guiding the Chinese cyber doctrine is a deliberate ambiguity about what types of cyber activities it considers to be acts of war. While the Chinese government routinely denies any cyber attacks upon Western networks, it likens the cyber domain to nuclear warfare, in that cyber attacks might operate as a deterrent to enemy activities in the physical world. The Chinese certainly understand that detection of their culpability in cyber attacks might bring international condemnation, but they calculate that the potential gains far outweigh the risks, and they trust that attribution through definitive proof is unlikely. In keeping with the Chinese approach to modern warfare, which relies upon mass armies that can overwhelm an enemy through sheer numbers, the Chinese cyber doctrine calls for the use of information warfare "militias," civilians that will voluntarily engage in cyber warfare on behalf of the nation. As long as the United States and other Western nations remain complacent about cyber security, Chinese intrusions will continue, and will further the Chinese goal to become the equal of any Western nation in military technology and power projection capabilities, preferably before engaging in any open conflict.

Poroshyn, Roman. 2013. *Stuxnet: The True Story of Hunt and Evolution.* Denver, CO: Outskirts Press, 2013.

This short volume is a thorough examination of the history of the Stuxnet virus. According to Poroshyn, there are many misunderstandings associated with the history of the virus. Notably, he argues that the circumstances surrounding the discovery of the virus make no sense, in that it was missed by every major computer security company in the world and then serendipitously discovered by a previously obscure computer firm in Belorussia named VirusBlokAda. Poroshyn considers this evidence that the virus was not discovered so much as unmasked, a deliberate decision that changed the function of Stuxnet from a cyber weapon into a propaganda and psychological tool. Having already done significant damage to the Iranian uranium enrichment program, Stuxnet's sudden publicity led Iranian nuclear engineers to question the security of their system and to take the entire program offline as a means to stop further damage. Poroshyn also argues that many of the common conceptions about Stuxnet are incorrect, particularly the assumptions about the source of the virus. In his estimation, there are simply too many obvious clues that the program should be attributed to Israel, making him suspect that the software is not an Israeli product, but instead is an extremely elaborate framing attempt, although he does not go so far as to name the creator.

Qiao Liang and Wang Xiangsui. 1999. *Unrestricted Warfare*. Translated by the Foreign Broadcast Information Service. Beijing: People's Liberation Army Literature and Arts Publishing House.

Unrestricted Warfare was written by two colonels in the People's Liberation Army (PLA) of China, who sought to solve the fundamental problem of how to defeat a technologically superior enemy in a modern war. Their investigation was prompted by the U.S.-led coalition invasion of Kuwait and Iraq in 1991, when the Iraqi army, the fourth-largest in the world, was routed with seemingly little effort. To Qiao and Wang, the worst strategy for a war with the United States would be to accede to the Americans' desire for a conventional war limited to military resources and objectives. Such a conflict would inherently favor the United States and its allies, even if it is fought on the enemy's home soil. Instead of participating in such an unfair fight, the authors investigated other means of waging a conflict against such a powerful foe, using unexpected methods to undermine the enemy's strongest resources while husbanding one's own forces and resources. Although the text was made readily available online, a Panamanian publishing house printed an English translation of the work subtitled "China's Master Plan to Destroy America." While this addition to the title might have stimulated additional sales of the work, it also conveyed a substantial misunderstanding of the purpose of the work, particularly because it was coupled with a cover image of the World Trade Center after being struck by aircraft on September 11, 2001.

To Qiao and Wang, the most important commodity in any conflict is not airplanes, ships, guns, or even manpower; it is information, without which a modern military cannot function. Denying the United States access to information could provide an enormous advantage, but by itself, it will not be enough to create the conditions for victory. Thus, attacks upon the underpinnings of the U.S. military might are a necessary aspect of any conflict with the American government. The United States possesses the world's largest economy, and its government uses economic resources as a major advantage in conflicts. The resources provided by the American economy offer the opportunity for massive technological development, and for a military force that possesses the best logistics system in the world. In turn, the logistics system allows American forces to fight with enormous firepower, as they assume they can resupply ammunition and other consumables even at the highest rates of consumption.

To offset the technological advantages of the United States, Qiao and Wang advocated a massive espionage campaign, targeting not just the government, but also private corporations that contribute to defense. Computer attacks on financial institutions might introduce a degree of instability to the economy, while efforts to penetrate the research networks at universities and private corporations might stimulate the expansion of the Chinese economy and foster a massive growth of Chinese manufacturing capabilities. Peacetime hacking attempts upon the American cyber infrastructure might make wartime cyber campaigns far easier and more effective, in part because Chinese hackers would have already mapped the systems they wished to disrupt, degrade, or destroy.

This work has often been regarded as the inspiration for a Chinese national effort to offset technological and economic inferiority through the largest cyber espionage campaign in history. Some critics have argued that Qiao and Wang effectively advocated terrorism as an effective and acceptable form of warfare, a move that would essentially signal that the Chinese government had no interest in following any of the laws of armed conflict. In practice, the authors discussed the concept of terrorism and why it might be an attractive form of warfare to some potential belligerents, particularly if they fought at a major disadvantage; but they did not actually recommend terror attacks be carried out by the Chinese military or affiliated groups. They did expressly push for a blurring of the lines between civilian and military objectives, which could also potentially upset the current international legal framework that guides the legitimacy of military operations, but did so mostly by noting that there is far less delineation between military and civilian endeavors in the modern era than there was at the time that the most important legal boundaries of warfare were set.

Reveron, Derek S., ed. 2012. *Cyberspace and National Security: Threats, Opportunities, and Power in a Virtual World.* Washington, DC: Georgetown University Press.

Reveron argues that cyber war has not happened as of 2012, but that it is increasingly likely as cyber capabilities continue to develop faster than security protocols. Overall, this book is one of the regular updates of cyber information that come out almost every year, which put together the full picture of the current cyber environment. This volume has an excellent mix of technical, popular, and theoretical information, making it a valuable resource for any researcher of cyber warfare.

One of the authors, Steven Bucci, makes a strong case that the combination of terrorism and cybercrime will be the biggest cyber threat of the near future. Because many terror organizations are well funded, they certainly have the resources necessary to develop extensive cyber networks. Although training cyber warriors requires extensive education, time, and practice, a number of major cyber crime organizations can be expected to essentially work as cyber mercenaries, providing instant cyber capabilities if their price is met. Many of the contributors agree that the term "cyber war" is problematic, largely on the grounds that if a cyber attack has no inherent violence, it cannot be considered an act of war. They note that no human has yet died as a direct result of a cyber attack, and until such a death occurs, calling cyber activities war may be premature.

The book is particularly valuable for the insights that it offers on the nature of cyber warfare programs in several nations. It notes that the cyber "heavyweights" are not necessarily the most advanced nations in terms of military might or economic heft, but rather are the states that have devoted themselves to harnessing the power of the new domain. Thus, the obvious choices of the United States, China, and Russia are joined by the less-expected Middle Eastern nations of Israel and Iran. Even though there have been few formal declarations of the norms governing the cyber realm, certain expectations have arisen about acceptable behavior. According to these authors, Stuxnet violated the taboos of the cyber domain, in part because it had the potential to harm far more than its presumed target, the Iranian nuclear program.

The sections on China and Russia offer important caveats regarding the largest cyber rivals of the United States. Russia is not particularly skilled as a nation when it comes to technological development, and has little domestic industry dedicated to the production of computers and related electronics. Thus, it has to rely almost entirely upon imports to fuel its cyber program. Nevertheless, the Russian government has aggressively pushed for a cyber war capability, while the Russian criminal syndicates have leaped into the cyber domain and used computers to carry out far-reaching attacks for economic gains. As long as the Russian cyber criminals do not target any interests within Russia, they are tolerated, and possibly encouraged, by the Russian government. The influx of foreign capital through criminal enterprises has helped to fuel other Russian economic initiatives in an indirect fashion.

China has used the Internet to make the control of its far-flung provinces much easier. This has solved many of the traditional problems with governance in China, including the slow speed of communications from the rural areas to the urban centers of government. In addition, the government has become increasingly obsessed with censorship of both domestic and international sources. In this regard, web access is a dual-edged sword. The Internet potentially creates an enormous avenue for "undesirable" information to flood into the country, but it also offers a control point for the government, which has become very skilled at monitoring communications within its borders. The Chinese government has demonstrated a conspicuous paranoia about Western control of the Internet and, as a result, has put enormous efforts into diplomatic efforts to make ICANN a United Nations system. Both the Russian and Chinese governments obviously view the Internet in a radically different fashion from that of the U.S. government, something that American strategists should keep in mind when they are devising cyber war policies.

Rid, Thomas. 2013. *Cyber War Will Not Take Place.* New York: Oxford University Press.

Rid's work is a very up-to-date study that firmly argues that cyber war has not yet occurred, and will not occur in the future. According to Rid, the concept of warfare inherently calls for violence, while cyber attacks offer the possibility of achieving the same goals without the use of destructive kinetic attacks. He believes the term "cyber war" is terribly misleading, because it implies a form of destruction that may no longer be required in state conflicts if cyber attacks become the norm. However, he also believes that cyber is more valuable in three key activities that are not war, but might be associated with it. Specifically, he believes that cyber assets are most effective when they are used for sabotage, espionage, and subversion, rather than outright warfare.

Like Martin Libicki, Rid sees attribution as an almost insurmountable problem, and one that directly conflicts with the use of cyber weapons for war. Specifically, he argues that states do not engage in the coercion of other states through indirect means and anonymous attacks. Thus, if a state wished to use cyber warfare as a means to compel an enemy to surrender, or to deter an enemy from a specific action, the state would need to do so through overt means. The roles of sabotage, espionage, and subversion, on the other hand, are traditional covert activities that a state might attempt without any desire to be recognized as the actor.

Rid believes that the United States is the most powerful cyber actor, although it is also the nation must vulnerable to cyber attack due to pathetic attention to security measures. He proves his point by providing an extensive overview of cyber attacks throughout history and their effects. In his discussion of Stuxnet, he directly blames the United States and Israel for the worm, largely on the basis of their perceived benefit from temporarily halting the Iranian nuclear program. He notes that such a programming effort could not be successful without extreme supporting preparations, including direct intelligence collection about the system architecture of the Iranian nuclear program. Such intelligence operations are so expensive that they require the resources of a nation-state as well as insider help from one or more members of the program being targeted. Rid sees China as the most active nation regarding cyber espionage, as its government has decided upon a path of constant cyber intrusions to gather any military or economic data that can be found, largely in pursuit of greater economic and military hegemony.

Schiller, Craig A., Jim Binkley, David Harley, Gadi Evron, Tony Bradley, Carsten Willems, and Michael Cross, eds. 2007. *Botnets: The Killer Web App.* Canada: Syngress Publishing.

This volume provides an overview of the botnet concept, written when it had been in operation for only a few years. It shows the rapid rise of botnet systems, with specific large-scale examples to demonstrate their utility and pernicious capabilities. It also walks through how botnets can be created, ways they infect other computers, what activities they enable, and the roles they play in both spam and phishing operations. In addition to a walkthrough of the most common botnets in 2007, including SDBot, RBot, Agobot, Spybot, and Mytob, this work also shows the most effective means for system administrators to detect and counter botnets.

The authors are dedicated to the creation and propagation of the Ourmon program, a system designed to detect and prevent botnets from invading computer networks. In pursuit of that noble goal, they assembled intelligence resources for organizations that might be targets of botnets. They also showed the then-current responses to botnets, including the very real dangers associated with trying to track or counter a botmaster, who would likely turn his botnet against the investigator in retaliation. Even in 2007, the authors estimated that 100 million computers were infected by at least one botnet, with as many as 350,000 held by a single controller. While the work has portions that are overly technical for the lay reader, it is still a useful resource to develop an in-depth understanding of the botnet concept, which has grown in both size and sophistication, but which still operates on the same principles.

Singer, P. W., and Allan Friedman. 2014. *Cybersecurity and Cyberwar.* New York: Oxford University Press.

Singer and Friedman's work aims to create an easy guide to the layperson for the current state of affairs regarding cyber conflict. It blends a thorough understanding of the general concepts of cyber warfare with an accessible explanation of how these issues can affect the day-to-day lives of ordinary readers who are not security professionals. Their fundamental argument is that computers have completely revolutionized the organization and function of human societies, and even though this has created a new avenue for conflict and criminal activity, the rewards of the computer revolution far outweigh the risks. They believe that if computer users have a basic understanding of computer security, they will be relatively well armed to remain safe in cyberspace.

This is one of the most engaging and easily understood recent works on cybersecurity and cyber war, and it does an exceptional job of providing both the overview of the concepts and the specific examples that readers may have noted in media reports. Singer and Friedman have a knack for connecting to their audience through shared cultural experiences, including the incorporation of popular films, television programs, and social media activities to illustrate their larger points. Unlike many of the competing works on the subject, this volume provides an easy entry point to the subject, with carefully supplied and practical definitions supplementing the broad analysis of cyber security.

Stiennon, Richard. 2010. *Surviving Cyber War*. Lanham, MD: Government Institutes Publishing.

Unlike many researchers, Stiennon argues that the United States has gotten serious about preparing for cyberwar, although a number of steps still need to be taken to prevent potential enemies from winning a conflict in cyberspace. To Stiennon, the first step the United States must take is to start holding individuals accountable for allowing cyber breaches, in both government and corporate settings. Currently, such intrusions are typically covered up or are accepted as the price of living in the modern era, even though there are ostensibly individuals responsible for cyber security in every organization. Stiennon calls for strict rules covering the oversight of government networks and the effort to defend data. Right now, there are dozens of key U.S. agencies that ignore the legal requirements to secure their networks, with little if any punishment for their lax attitudes. To force compliance, Stiennon would empower the Office of Management and Budget (OMB) to withhold federal

funding from agencies that fail to comply with cyber security requirements. He believes that decentralizing security
management for organizations would allow for a much
more secure system, although he also calls for a much
greater amount of cyber security sharing between law
enforcement, the military, and intelligence communities.
Stiennon believes that the government has wasted far too
many resources on cyber security awareness campaigns,
and would do far better to simply fix its flawed systems.
When it comes to cyber defense, measures should be
transparent, but not so onerous and expensive that the
United States relinquishes the advantages of the Internet.
Finally, Stiennon believes that defense should be the primary goal in preparation for cyber war, with the development of offensive measures a secondary priority.

Stiennon's work includes a large number of case studies
of cyber attacks that could very well be considered
cyber warfare activities. He begins with the Titan
Rain espionage campaign, discovered by Shawn
Carpenter at the Sandia National Laboratories. Titan
Rain and its discovery showed much of what was wrong
with the U.S. approach to cyber security. The Bush
administration refused to take the issue seriously, Sandia
refused to cooperate with the DoD and Federal Bureau
of Investigation, and Carpenter was fired from his job
for his efforts to track down the Titan Rain perpetrators. Stiennon methodically walks through many of the
worst cyber incidents in the nation's history, including
many early events that served as harbingers of later
Chinese espionage campaigns in the cyber domain.
He also shows a number of international examples
of cyber war, including the various conflicts between
Israel and its neighbors, the ongoing struggle between
India and Pakistan, and the constant cyber bickering
on the Korean Peninsula. He goes into great detail
about the Russian attacks on Estonia (2006), Lithuania

(2008), and Georgia (2008) and compares the Russian approach to cyber activism with the Chinese methodology. Thus, his work combines a theoretical discussion of the general concepts of cyberwar with a practical guide of recent examples of such activity.

Stocker, Gerfried, and Christine Schöpf. 1998. *Info War.* New York: Springer-Verlag.

Although this work is out of date in terms of its discussions of technology, it has more utility than simply seeing the state of the field in 1998, or showing the rapid obsolescence of works dealing with current technology that is in a state of flux. This work was one of the earliest studies of the potential of cyber operations in both war and peace. It shows that the notion of cyber war, even in a period without warfare in the physical world, may be a continual concern between nation-states. It also has an excellent discussion of the conceptual underpinnings of cyber war. The authors argue that a massive information revolution is currently underway, one that will change how societies engage in conflict and in peaceful relations. In their estimation, cyber war has made an entirely new position on the spectrum of conflict, where the existing assumptions about warfare do not apply. Interestingly, the authors also called for a cyber doctrine to be created by the United States, and they correctly predicted that the armies of the future that adopted networked operations could be much smaller than their non-networked peers, yet still project the same level of national power.

Ventre, Daniel, ed. 2011. *Cyberwar and Information Warfare.* Hoboken, NJ: John Wiley & Sons.

Ventre's book examines whether the term "war" should even be applied to any state conflicts that remain combined to the cyber realm. In his estimation, most cyber attacks should not be classified as acts of war, but rather as either espionage or sabotage. In the near future, he expects cyber forces to have four main functions, namely security, spying, ruses, and propaganda, none of which really constitutes an act of war. Currently, cyber is merely a facilitator of conflict, in much the same manner that early unarmed reconnaissance aircraft served to assist artillery gunners on the ground, but were not in and of themselves actual instruments of war. An essay by Francois Chauvancy examines the unique nature of warfare within Western democracies and how those nations might engage in cyber warfare. Joseph Henrotin's essay examines the way that intelligence services use any assets, but particularly cyber capabilities, to prevent strategic surprise, thus obviating the possibility of a "cyber Pearl Harbor." Ventre's essays within the volume examine the question of whether true domination in cyberspace is possible, and if so, whether it would be desirable. He also provides an interesting case study of a major example of cyber conflict during the Xinjiang province riots in China in 2009. Few Western media outlets paid substantial attention to the Xinjiang insurrection, in part because the People's Republic of China proved so successful in using cyber assets to censor information from the region and to prevent its own population from learning about the unrest. His final essay examines the nature of cyber capabilities in "special territories," specifically Hong Kong and North Korea, where the utilization of cyber is considerably different from that in most of the world. Ventre concludes with the argument that while cyber strategies may change, the fundamental principles of strategy, whether in the cyber domain or the physical world, remain constant.

Nonprint Resources

Defense Advanced Research Projects Agency (DARPA) website. http://www.darpa.mil/our_work/I20/.

The Defense Advanced Research Projects Agency (DARPA) aims to create revolutionary advances in technological innovation, largely by bringing together the resources of the U.S. military establishment and the research capabilities of industrial and academic thinkers. The DARPA website includes an overview of ongoing programs, personnel, and goals of each of the directorates within the agency. While certain researchers might aim for incremental improvements in cyber warfare capabilities, the purpose of DARPA makes it the most likely source of radical innovation in cyber capabilities.

Infosecurity Magazine. http://www.infosecurity-magazine.com. This electronic magazine (e-zine) targets information technology professionals but is very accessible to the general public and researchers interested in cyber security. In addition to its own native content, the website maintains a large archive of white papers and security resources, all available free of charge. These holdings supply guides to virtually every aspect of security within the network profession. *Infosecurity* also offers a number of Internet communications opportunities, including webinars and virtual conferences discussing issues of interest to cyber security professionals and academic researchers.

International Journal of Cyber Warfare and Terrorism. http://www.igi-global.com/journal/international-journal-cyber-warfare-terrorism/1167.

This online journal is published by the Information Resources Management Association. It is an academic publication, released quarterly, that focuses upon management, social, and government issues related to cyber activities. It was established in 2011; thus its published research tends to be extremely up to date. Its target audience includes researchers, cyber professionals, academics, government officials, military officers, and industry professionals.

Mandiant. 2013. "APT1: Exposing One of China's Cyber Espionage Units." http://intelreport.mandiant.com/Mandiant _APT1_Report.pdf.

In 2013, the Mandiant cyber security corporation did what the U.S. government could or would not do: it published a report documenting thousands of incidents Chinese cyber espionage, performed over years, by Unit 61398 of the People's Liberation Army. Mandiant designated the organization "Advanced Persistent Threat 1" (APT1) when it began monitoring the cyber intrusions on behalf of clients. Over several years, Mandiant investigators managed to determine the servers and IP addresses used by the organization, built profiles of individuals associated with the attacks, and managed to track a number of intrusions in real time.

In the report, Mandiant provides an enormous amount of specific data to bolster their allegations. It includes an overview of the targets of APT1, the chosen methodology of the attackers, the infrastructure that supports them, and the online identities of many of the key actors. In order to prove their case, Mandiant was forced to release many of their own techniques for tracking and monitoring APT1, a move that forced the enemy to change its tactics but that also made Mandiant's task of continuing its observations considerably more difficult. Nevertheless, the company decided that a public release of such information, and the benefits that might be gained from it, outweighed any selfish concerns about protecting only their own clients. Mandiant does not claim to have observed every attack carried out by APT1; far from it. Thus the report establishes a lower threshold for the total damage of the attacks conducted by APT1. Even with that caveat, its results are shocking—the Mandiant investigators found that APT1 exfiltrated hundreds of terabytes of sensitive information from 141 companies in 20 critical industries identified by the Chinese government as key to China's future economic development.

The Mandiant report ignited a firestorm of accusations by media outlets that found APT1 had infiltrated their networks. Not surprisingly, the Chinese government flatly denied all of the allegations and countered with accusations that the U.S. government is the largest supporter of cyber espionage in the world, based largely upon the leaks of Edward Snowden. Mandiant predicted the vehement denial in its reports, and declared its expectation that the company would be subjected to retaliatory attacks by Chinese state and nonstate hackers. Even with those considerations in mind, though, Mandiant released the report to enhance the security measures taken in critical industries to prevent further cyber espionage.

Network World. http://www.networkworld.com.

This website is designed to supply information to network and information technology executives. Unlike similar trade publications, it specifically targets key decision makers within Internet corporations, who would in turn be potential key targets in the event of a cyber war. One of the main goals of the publication is to ensure that CEOs and other company officers are more knowledgeable about cyber attacks than the current status quo, making their companies less vulnerable to at least some cyber attacks. It is primarily a news and opinion piece website, rather than a site for academic research, that tends to target the lower-ranking operators in the industry, although it does have occasional pieces of a technical nature. In many ways, this website is akin to reading the abstracts of academic articles—it provides the basic information about the deeper arguments and provides links to the in-depth studies for interested readers.

"Project CyW-D." http://www.projectcyw-d.org/resources.

This website serves primarily as a collection and distribution website that posts speeches, policy papers, war game outcomes, industry reports, pending laws, treaties, and books of interest to researchers investigating cyber warfare. It was created by Gina Bacon as a part of her master's degree project in communications at the University of Utah. While it serves as a one-stop shop for many primary documents of interest, it has not been updated on a regular basis since 2011. Many of the key resources created prior to that time are made readily available, though, which gives the site a substantial utility for at least the next few years.

RAND Corporation website. http://www.rand.org/topics/cyber-warfare.html.

This website is a resource center provided for RAND and other related organizations to make research on cyber warfare readily available to the public. It includes an enormous library of RAND publications, with most available for free download in PDF form. These free digital copies include entire books written on the subject by RAND senior researchers John Arquilla, Martin Libicki, and David Ronfeldt. In addition to providing almost unlimited resources, this is one of the most frequently updated and comprehensive cyber war sites on the Internet, and it includes an option for users to sign up for free emailed updates whenever new content is added to the site.

U.S. Army Cyber Command. http://www.arcyber.army.mil/org-arcyber.html.

This website is the organizational home of the U.S. Army Cyber Command, which is subordinate to U.S. Cyber Command. Each of the military branches has a dedicated cyber organization, and all of them have public portals detailing the operations and key personnel of the organization.

U.S. Cyber Command. http://www.stratcom.mil/factsheets/2/cyber_command/.

This website is the public face of U.S. Cyber Command, the overarching military cyber security organization that controls both the Department of Defense cyber efforts and the National Security Agency. The website provides an overview of the organization, including its stated mission, its leadership and key personnel, the components of the command, and fact sheets about its function.

Wired. http://www.wired.com.

Wired is a print magazine that focuses upon the effects of emerging technology on culture, society, politics, and the economy. It has been in print since 1993 and currently has a circulation of nearly one million copies per edition. *Wired* is best known for cutting-edge reporting on computers and related technology, and it was intricately involved in the Bradley Manning WikiLeaks scandal, with some critics blaming the editors of the magazine for releasing Manning's identity and contributing to his arrest and prosecution.

Wired has a companion website that includes content from the magazine and a much larger collection of web-only content. The website is updated daily, with new content on blogs added every few hours. Two of the regular blogs on the website are of particular interest to researchers studying cyber warfare. The first, "Threat Level," is produced by Kim Zetter and Andy Greenberg. It focuses upon security and privacy in cyberspace, with a particular emphasis upon how to protect oneself from cyber crimes. The second, "Danger Room," is the product of Robert Beckhusen, Allen McDuffee, Michael Peck, Michael Tanji, and Sharon Weinberger. It examines national security, with pieces on both the military's role in protecting the United States and law enforcement's approaches to domestic security. Each of these blogs frequently devotes attention to the issues of cyber security, conflict, and the possibility of using the Internet as a weapon.

ANK YOU,
WARD
OWDEN!

TAKE ACTION AT

YouEdSnowden.org

nip for Civil Justice Fund

This chronology chapter demonstrates the long history of human activities that might be considered cyber warfare, or that have contributed to the modern cyber conflict environment. It also shows that in recent years, cyber attacks have become both more common and significantly more dangerous. The relative sophistication of cyber attacks has also risen, and thus the most powerful cyber attacks to date have required the resources of nation-states for their creation, propagation, and eventual elimination.

1822   Charles Babbage designs his Difference Engine, a mechanical calculator capable of compiling mathematical tables.

1856   Charles Babbage describes the Analytical Engine, a far more complex mechanical calculator widely regarded as the first true computer. Most of the records are destroyed after the British government stops funding his experiments.

1917   The Cipher Bureau and Military Intelligence Branch of the U.S. Army is created, designed to provide codes for U.S. communications in World War I and, if possible, decode enemy signals.

Demonstrators affiliated with the activist group Anonymous protest government cyber surveillance of private citizens during a march at Capitol Hill on October 26, 2013. (AP Photo/Jose Luis Magana)

1940   John Atanasoff and Clifford Berry complete their design for the first all-electronic computer, demonstrating that such a machine can be built without reliance upon slower and less reliable mechanical means.

Members of the Ultra code-breaking project in Britain build an electronic computer nicknamed Robinson that is designed to decode German military encryption.

1941   Konrad Zuse completes the world's first programmable digital computer in Germany.

1943   The Ultra code-breaking project in Britain builds Colossus, a much-improved electronic computer that relies upon vacuum tubes for calculations. Later models of the same design remain in use until the 1970s.

1944   Howard Aiken, working for International Business Machines (IBM), designs the Automatic Sequence Controlled Calculator (ASCC), which allows new programming through paper tapes and relies upon vacuum tubes for calculations. The machine incorporates many of the separate design components first tested in the preceding four years.

1945   The Manhattan Project completes and tests the first atomic bomb in history. Two versions are soon used to destroy the Japanese cities of Hiroshima and Nagasaki.

Physicist John von Neumann suggests that permanent stored programs for computers might be possible, if memory capacity can be improved.

1946   The Electronic Numerical Integrator And Calculator (ENIAC) is built. Although initially intended for calculating ballistic trajectories for the U.S. Army, it is soon pressed into service to solve complex mathematical equations confronted by the designers of the hydrogen bomb.

1947   John Bardeen, Walter Brattain, and William Bradford Shockley collaborate at Bell Laboratories to build the first transistor, triggering a microelectronics revolution. It allows for smaller, faster, cheaper, and more reliable computers.

1948   The RAND (Research And Development) Corporation is formed, creating a direct partnership between the U.S. Air Force and the Douglas Aircraft Company.

1949   The Armed Forces Security Agency is created, designed to combine all U.S. military intelligence agencies into a single organization.

The Soviet Union tests its first atomic bomb, largely relying upon information stolen from the joint U.S.-British Manhattan Project.

Maurice Wilkes of the University of Cambridge Mathematical Laboratory creates the Electronic Delay Storage Automated Calculator (EDSAC), the world's first stored-program computer.

The Eckert-Mauchly Computer Corporation builds the Binary Automatic Computer (BINAC) for Northrop Aircraft Company. The machine is the world's first commercial digital computer.

1950   The Universal Automatic Computer (UNIVAC) is completed, using magnetic tape for data storage rather than punched cards. It is the first truly commercial computer; the first model is delivered to the U.S. Census Bureau to consolidate the 1950 returns.

1952   The National Security Agency is established to oversee all U.S. government signal intelligence collection efforts, as well as signal counterintelligence activities.

1957   The Soviet Union launches *Sputnik*, the world's first artificial satellite, into orbit.

1958   The U.S. government creates the Advanced Research Projects Agency (ARPA), later renamed the Defense Advanced Research Projects Agency (DARPA), an organization dedicated to preventing strategic surprise through technological development.

Jack St. Clair Kilby invents the integrated circuit while working for Texas Instruments. It is the first great leap forward in miniaturization since the completion of the transistor.

Seymour Cray, an engineer for the Control Data Corporation, finishes the first supercomputer, a machine that pushes the limits of processing speed for any given technology. Cray's first model relies upon transistors, and will soon be surpassed by integrated circuit machines.

1960 The Defense Communications Agency is formed at Fort Meade, Maryland. Its purpose is to oversee and protect all U.S. military communications.

1965 Gordon Moore's "Cramming More Components onto Integrated Circuits" is published in *Electronics*. The article includes "Moore's Law," a prediction that the number of components per integrated circuit would double each year, triggering exponential growth in the speed and power of computers.

1968 Intel Corporation is founded in Santa Clara, California, and quickly becomes the world's leading producer of microprocessors.

1969 ARPANet is introduced, linking a handful of government and academic computer networks.

The first Request for Comments (RFC) is circulated, encouraging discussion of technical developments on the ARPANet.

1971 Intel Corporation releases the first commercial microprocessor, a four-bit central processing unit on a single chip.

1972 The Transmission Control Protocol/Internet Protocol (TCP/IP) system was created, providing a specific model for how data should be formatted, addressed, transmitted, routed, and received by computers on a network.

1975 The Church Committee hearings in the U.S. Senate reveal that the National Security Agency has engaged in illegal domestic surveillance, particularly against opponents of the Vietnam War.

1976 Steven Jobs and Stephen Wozniak found Apple Computer Corporation and begin to build home computers designed for ease of use.

1978 The Foreign Intelligence Surveillance Act is passed, limiting the ability of federal intelligence agencies to engage in domestic surveillance without court approval.

1979 The first computer worm is developed, but not released upon a network.

1981 IBM announces the development of a stand-alone home personal computer (PC), making computers available to the public for the first time.

1982 A Siberian pipeline, constructed using technical specifications stolen by KGB operatives, explodes with a force of three kilotons due to an intentional flaw introduced in the plans, which were deliberately left to be found by Soviet spies.

1983 The movie *War Games* is released, in which a young hacker nearly starts a nuclear war by accessing a Department of Defense computer system.

The Domain Name System (DNS), a hierarchical naming system for computers connected to networks, is created.

MILNet, the dedicated U.S. military network, is split from ARPANet.

1984 William Gibson publishes the science fiction novel *Neuromancer*, in which the term "cyberspace" is coined.

The term "Internet" is created, and the TCP/IP system is selected for communication upon it.

Congress passes the Computer Fraud and Abuse Act. Initially, it only criminalizes misuse of government computers, but its provisions are expanded to unauthorized use of any computer system in 1996.

Apple offers its first Macintosh desktop computer for sale, creating a viable competitor for IBM's personal computer.

1988 The Morris Worm is released from the Massachusetts Institute of Technology laboratory, where it was developed by student Robert Morris. It infects thousands of machines on the nascent Internet and reveals the lack of protections against such programs.

Donald Gene Burleson is the first American convicted for malicious use of software, after writing code to destroy the payroll data of his former employer, creating one of the first logic bombs in history.

The first Computer Emergency Response Team (CERT) is formed by DARPA at Carnegie Mellon University, in response to the effects of the Morris Worm.

1989 British computer scientist Tim Berners-Lee proposes the creation of the World Wide Web, a system of linked hypertext documents accessible via the Internet.

1991 The Defense Communications Agency is renamed the Defense Information Systems Agency and given responsibility for maintaining and protecting all military communications and information networks.

1993 The Mosaic web browser is released by the National Center for Supercomputing Applications (NCSA) at the University of Illinois at Urbana-Champaign. This web browser makes the Internet accessible for nonexpert home users.

1994 The Air Force Rome Laboratories are hacked by two individuals, Kuji and Datastream Cowboy. Kuji proves to be a 22-year-old Israeli hacker, who is not prosecuted because his actions did not violate Israeli law. Datastream Cowboy, a 16-year-old British student, pled guilty to cyber crime and was lightly fined.

1995 The U.S. Congress requires a national policy to protect information infrastructure from strategic effect, as part of the Fiscal Year 1996 Department of Defense budget authorization bill.

The Java programming language is released by Sun Microsystems, enabling programmers to write a single program and run it on multiple platforms without any reconfigurations.

Admiral Arthur K. Cebrowski publicly describes the U.S. military's new concept of network-centric warfare, an attempt to incorporate sensors, commanders, and operators into a single system, making for a reflexive, adaptive military organization.

Amazon is created, and it quickly becomes the largest marketplace on the Internet.

EBay is created, allowing individual sellers to auction goods in exchange for a percentage of the sales price.

1997   The U.S. Department of Defense conducts "Eligible Receiver," its first information warfare exercise. The 35-person "Red Team" easily demonstrates an ability to hack into power grids, government websites, and industry networks using off-the-shelf technology.

1998   Moonlight Maze hacking attacks begin against government, academic, and corporate networks. It is not discovered until 2000, and the culprits have never been identified, although the attacks have been traced to a server in Russia.

In the Solar Sunrise incident, two California high school students and their teenage Israeli mentor compromised more than 500 computer networks, but because they did not remove any classified data, the Department of Justice declined to press charges.

The U.S. federal budget includes $1.14 billion for critical infrastructure cyber security.

Larry Page and Sergey Brin incorporate Google while PhD students at Stanford University.

The Internet Corporation for Assigned Names and Numbers (ICANN) is founded in Los Angeles, California. It coordinates multiple databases to assign unique namespaces on the Internet, ensuring its smooth function.

The President's Commission on Critical Infrastructure Protection (PCCIP) is created.

Three thousand Chinese hackers attack Indonesian government websites to protest anti-Chinese riots in Indonesia.

The Digital Millennium Copyright Act (DMCA) is passed, an attempt to prevent piracy of digital media, including protection of software and entertainment encryption.

1999   The science fiction blockbuster *The Matrix* is released, in which the protagonist discovers that the entire human population on earth is living in a virtual reality world.

Serbian hackers take down the NATO main web server and e-mail server, disrupting NATO operations in Kosovo.

Chinese colonels Qiao Liang and Wang Xiangsui release *Unrestricted Warfare*, a book advocating unconventional strategies to defeat the United States or other technologically advanced nations, including massive cyber attack campaigns.

A NATO jet bombs the Chinese embassy in Belgrade, Serbia, during operations to oust Slobodan Milosevic. Several hundred U.S. government websites are attacked by Chinese hacker militias in the subsequent weeks.

2000   The I-LOVE-YOU virus spreads so quickly that it causes $10 billion in damages.

Cyber security expert Dorothy Denning testifies before a congressional oversight committee, warning the members that cyber attackers are constantly attempting intrusions against government, corporate, and private networks.

IBM estimates that online retailers lose an average of $10,000 in revenue per minute if knocked offline by DDoS attacks.

2001   Operatives of Al Qaeda seize four aircraft and deliberately crash them into the World Trade Center, the Pentagon, and a field in Pennsylvania. More than 3,000 U.S. citizens are killed in the deadliest terror attack in history. The incident is widely perceived as a major intelligence failure.

The USA PATRIOT (Uniting and Strengthening America by Providing Appropriate Tools Required to Intercept and Obstruct Terrorism) Act is passed, creating massive new opportunities for signal intelligence collection in both domestic and international locations.

The Code Red worm exploits a vulnerability in Microsoft's Internet Information Server software, allowing defacement of infected websites and possible theft or destruction of data.

The Nimda worm uses a five-method approach to spread, including through backdoors created by the Code Red worm.

The U.S. federal budget includes over $2 billion for critical infrastructure cyber security.

Wikipedia is released by Jimmy Wales and Larry Sanger, who intended to create a collaboratively edited reference work.

The European Convention on Cybercrime is passed and signed by 33 states.

The U.S. Department of Homeland Security is established.

A Chinese fighter jet collides with a U.S. military aircraft in international airspace, killing the fighter pilot and forcing an emergency landing by the American aircrew on Hainan Island. In the aftermath of the incident, 80,000 Chinese hackers launch attacks against U.S. government websites.

2002   NATO begins its Network Enabled Capabilities Transformation, adopting the network-centric warfare concept for the military alliance.

Russian special forces troops attempt a hostage rescue to free civilians held by Chechen terrorists in a Moscow theater. Russian hackers attack two Chechen websites at the same time.

The United States passes the Homeland Security Act, creating a new cabinet-level department tasked with defending the nation, including its cyber infrastructure.

2003   The U.S. government releases its first National Cyber Security Strategy.

Titan Rain cyber attacks target U.S. government and corporate networks, eventually exfiltrating more than 20 terabytes of data before being discovered. The attacks are eventually traced to China, which denies all culpability.

The SQL Slammer worm is released. It spreads so quickly that it completely shuts down the entire Internet for 12 hours. Ten years later, it remains one of the most commonly detected pieces of malware.

The MS Blaster worm replicates much of SQL Slammer's success, demonstrating the transitory nature of most security fixes.

The United States leads a military coalition to invade Iraq and depose President Saddam Hussein. In preparation, American cyber warriors conduct a massive information campaign, including personal e-mails and telephone calls to Iraqi military officers, demanding that they surrender and offer no resistance to the coalition advance.

The U.S. Federal Trade Commission sets up a national spam database, after receiving nearly 20 million complaints about spam messages the previous year.

John McAfee, creator of McAfee antivirus software, announces the identification of nearly 60,000 computer virus threats, with an additional 10 to 15 discovered daily.

The Department of Homeland Security announces the creation of the U.S. Computer Emergency Response Team at Carnegie Mellon University.

2004   Facebook debuts, revolutionizing the concept of social media.

The MyDoommailto:W.32.Norvarg@mm worm spreads throughout computers operating any recent version of Windows, causing $2 billion in damages worldwide.

2005   General Keith B. Alexander is named director of the National Security Agency, and the organization begins attempts to collect the full electronic communication stream of entire global regions.

2006   General Michael Hayden is named director of the Central Intelligence Agency, returning from retirement to assume the position as a four-star U.S. Air Force general.

Google begins censoring Chinese search results, as required by the Chinese government in exchange for doing business in the People's Republic of China.

The U.S. Air Force announces the creation of its Network Operations Command.

A U.S. Air Force officer publicly states that "China has downloaded 10 to 20 terabytes of data from the NIPRNet."

Hackers target U.S. military educational institutions. Cleansing infected networks requires weeks of downtime.

2007   Israel bombs a suspected Syrian nuclear facility, using a cyber attack to blind the Syrian air defense network in the process.

Estonia decides to move a bronze statue depicting a Soviet soldier, provoking a massive cyber attack by Russian hackers against the Baltic nation's cyber infrastructure.

The U.S. National Security Agency commences PRISM, a massive data-collection program that targets foreign communications that pass along the backbone of the Internet.

The Microsoft Vista operating system is released, the first Microsoft OS designed with security as a key priority.

The U.S. Air Force Cyber Command is announced.

Distributed denial of service attacks are launched against the Internet's core Domain Name Servers, essentially stopping almost all Internet traffic.

The U.S. Bureau of Industrial Security, an arm of the Commerce Department, is attacked, and its networks are taken offline for several months to halt the intrusions.

The National Defense University has to shut down its e-mail system due to foreign cyber intrusions.

The e-mail account of Secretary of Defense Robert Gates is hacked by unknown foreign attackers.

German chancellor Angela Merkel formally complains to Chinese president Hu Jintao about Chinese cyber attacks on German networks.

The Chinese government accuses foreign hackers of stealing information from Chinese corporate networks.

The National Security Agency begins a major covert campaign to infiltrate the networks of Chinese telecommunications giant Huawei. Details of the program are leaked in 2013.

2008   Russian hackers contribute to an attack upon the republic of Georgia, cutting off Georgia's access to news outlets and attacking Georgian government websites.

Chinese hackers attack CNN.com over coverage of Tibet, and encourage "militia" volunteers to voluntarily infect their computers with a virus that targets the CNN website.

The Lithuanian parliament passes a law requiring removal of Soviet symbols, provoking a massive Russian cyber attack against government and commerce websites.

A Pakistani computer engineer accidentally knocks YouTube offline by rerouting its entire traffic to Pakistani government servers, knocking the entire nation of Pakistan off the Internet in the process.

WikiLeaks publishes a State Department cable alleging that foreign hackers stole 50 megabytes of e-mail messages as well as usernames and passwords.

Oil companies ConocoPhillips, ExxonMobil, and Marathon Oil have their databases hacked, allowing foreign attackers to steal data on the location, quantity, and quality of global oil discoveries.

TJX Corporation reports a breach of its credit card information, a cyber attack that eventually costs the company more than $250 million.

Israel launches Operation Cast Lead against Palestinian militants in the Gaza Strip. A massive cyber war erupts between Israeli and Arabic hackers. Both state and nonstate hackers are involved on both sides.

U.S. Department of Defense computers are the victims of at least 40,000 cyber attacks over the year 2008.

The U.S. military bans the use of all flash drives due to the high incidence rate of worms and viruses on the devices.

2009   A North Korean cyber attack uses a botnet to bring down U.S. and South Korean government websites in response to a planned joint military exercise near the Korean Peninsula.

Five million machines participate in a coordinated attack against Israeli Internet infrastructure during Israeli attacks in the Gaza Strip.

French naval databases are infected by the Conficker worm, forcing the grounding of naval aircraft.

Google, the Internet's largest search engine, announces that it will no longer filter results in the People's Republic of China, largely because Chinese hackers have penetrated Google's software and used it to persecute religious dissidents.

Hamas hacktivists deface 800 American and Israeli websites.

North Korean government hackers launch attacks in response to UN sanctions over nuclear weapons testing.

Canadian researchers discover "GhostNet," a network of infected computers in 103 countries all connected to a single espionage effort against the Tibetan government-in-exile.

The Homeland Security Information Network (HSIN) is penetrated and loses significant data to hackers.

U.S. unmanned military aircraft downlink feeds are hacked, allowing Iraqi insurgents to see what the UAVs viewed. The hack requires only a laptop and cheap off-the-shelf file-sharing software.

Questionable returns from the Iranian presidential elections trigger protests on Twitter and Facebook. The Iranian government shuts down media channels and Internet access to quell the disturbances.

2010 U.S. Cyber Command is activated at Fort Meade, Maryland. It incorporates the separate cyber organizations of each of the military services as well as the National Security Agency.

The Stuxnet virus is first discovered and publicly reported. Earlier versions of the worm had already significantly damaged the Iranian nuclear program at Natanz.

Google reveals it was attacked as a means to track and hit Chinese subversives.

The "Iranian Cyber Army" hacks Chinese search engine Baidu and disrupts its service.

Indian missile system networks are hacked, purportedly by Chinese hackers.

2011   Secretary of Defense Robert Gates announces that the United States may consider cyber attacks to be acts of war and retaliate in any fashion it deems appropriate.

The Oak Ridge nuclear research facility is hit by a spearphishing attack. Hackers copy 1 GB of data but fail to reach the classified portion of the network. In response, the laboratories eliminate all Internet access to stop further penetrations.

The Georbot worm infects Georgian government systems, allowing both snooping and exfiltration of data. A Georgian CERT team reverses the attack and seizes control of the botmaster's computer, managing to film him with his own web camera.

Canadian government agencies are forced to disconnect from the Internet after sustained attacks attributed to China.

Japanese legislators and their staffs are targeted by a phishing attack that planted a Trojan on their computers and the servers of the Japanese Diet. The hijacked machines sent data to a Chinese server for a month before being discovered.

A computer virus places a keystroke logger onto U.S. Air Force computers at Creech Air Force Base. The targeted systems are used to fly unmanned aircraft.

The U.S. Chamber of Commerce discovers that its networks have been penetrated for more than a year by Chinese hackers, allowing access to members' communications.

2012   The Shamoon virus attack against Saudi Aramco renders 30,000 workstations unusable; a previously unknown group, "Cutting Sword of Justice," claims responsibility.

The Flame worm is discovered and publicized, and quickly regarded as the most complex malware ever developed.

The *New York Times* claims the U.S. government engineered the Stuxnet virus. The government refuses to verify the claims, but the Federal Bureau of Investigation begins searching for the source of leaks regarding Stuxnet.

The Gauss worm is discovered, targeting Lebanese financial institutions used by Hezbollah.

The British Broadcasting Company reports that Iranian hackers attempted to disrupt its Persian Language Service, in conjunction with an effort to jam BBC satellite feeds into Iran.

More than 100 Indian government websites are compromised and defaced by Pakistani hackers.

A spearphishing campaign targets U.S. gas pipeline servers with unknown intent.

Iranian oil production facilities are disconnected from the Internet after a series of disruptive attacks.

The head of the British Security Service announces that an unnamed British company lost more than $1 billion to cyber attacks launched by a foreign state.

Mahdi, a Trojan with Persian-language strings, is discovered on 800 infrastructure, government, financial, and academic networks in the Middle East.

The director of the U.S. National Security Agency declares that cyber attacks upon U.S. infrastructure increased by 1,600 percent between 2009 and 2011.

An Iranian hacker group, Izz ad-Din al-Qassam, launches Operation Ababil, a sustained DDoS attack against Western financial and corporate targets. The attacks continue throughout 2013.

Al Qaeda's recruitment and propaganda websites are attacked and knocked offline for two weeks.

2013 National Security Agency contractor Edward Snowden engages in a massive whistle-blowing operation, exposing an enormous domestic surveillance program undertaken by the NSA.

Target Corporation reports a data breach in which more than 50 million consumers' credit card information was stolen. The company had failed to engage in even the most basic security measures.

Major media outlets, including the *New York Times*, *Washington Post*, and *Bloomberg News,* announce that they have been under continual Chinese cyber attack for years.

The U.S. Department of Homeland Security announces that cyber criminals hacked at least 23 gas pipeline companies and stole data that would be useful in a sabotage attempt.

North Korean hackers release DarkSeoul, a malware program targeting South Korean media and financial corporations and specifically designed to evade South Korean antivirus software.

North Korea accuses the United States and South Korea of attacking its Internet access.

The Syrian Electronic Army hacks into U.S. and European media outlets that have urged intervention in the Syrian civil war.

Hackers encrypt elements of Al Qaeda's English-language website, making it unreadable.

Israeli cyber security experts foil an attempt by the Syrian Electronic Army to disrupt water supplies to the city of Haifa.

Edward Snowden releases documents demonstrating that the United States had engaged in cyber espionage against China.

President Barack Obama issues an executive order instructing the United States to aid allies being attacked by North Korean and Iranian hackers.

The United States and Russia sign a bilateral "cyber pact" that establishes communication hotlines for use in a cyber crisis.

China's country code top level domain, .cn, is taken offline by a massive DDoS attack. The outage lasts several hours.

The Chinese Central Bank is hit by a major DDoS attack shortly after issuing regulations prohibiting Chinese financial institutions from trading in Bitcoins.

Mandiant, a cyber security firm, releases a massive report detailing sustained Chinese cyber attacks, probably launched by PLA Unit 61398, against hundreds of Western private corporations and government agencies.

Apple becomes the most valuable company in the world.

2014   Admiral Michael S. Rogers is named commander of U.S. Cyber Command and director of the National Security Agency, continuing the pattern of one military officer commanding both organizations.

A U.S. federal grand jury returns indictments for five members of the Chinese PLA Unit 61398, who are accused of cyber espionage, cyber sabotage, and other computer crimes against private American corporations.

A member of the Islamic State of Iraq and Syria beheads American journalist James Foley on a live video feed broadcast through the Internet.

Hamas and Israel go to war in Gaza, with significant accompanying cyber attacks upon each others' websites. Both sides use Internet sites to post propaganda footage.

Glossary

The glossary provides a list of the key terms related to cyber warfare. It is not limited to terms that appear in this work; there are additional terms that are common to works of cyber warfare that are not necessarily included in this book.

AI: Artificial Intelligence.

Air-gap: A computer or network physically isolated from other networks, including the Internet, as a means of enhanced security.

Anonymous: A hacker organization with a large, multinational membership united by political ideology and vigilante actions.

APT: Advanced persistent threat, a cyber attack conducted over a long period of time against a very specific target. Usually requires the resources of a nation.

ARPA: Advanced Research Projects Agency, an American Department of Defense research organization founded in 1958, tasked with preventing strategic surprise through innovative technology. Renamed DARPA (Defense Advanced Research Projects Agency) in 1972.

ARPANet: The forerunner to the modern Internet, created by ARPA and designed to link military, government, and academic research institutions at a small number of locations.

Authentication: Computer protocols that attempt to verify that a network user is who he or she claims to be.

Backbone: The "Internet Backbone" is the collection of fiber-optic cables run by Tier 1 ISPs.

Back Door: A secret opening in a computer program, allowing easy access for unauthorized users.

Bandwidth: A communication channel's capacity to process data, usually expressed in bytes per second.

Bitcoin: A digital currency, designed to allow anonymous purchases regardless of nationality.

Black Hat: An unethical hacker whose goal is to exploit security flaws.

Bot: A computer that has been infected by malware and is subject to commands by an unauthorized user. Short for "robot."

Botmaster: A user who has established a collection of enslaved computer "bots" for any purpose.

Botnet: A collection of enslaved computer "bots." Typically used for DDoS attacks.

C2: Command and Control.

C4ISR: Command, Control, Communications, Computers, Intelligence, Surveillance, and Reconnaissance.

CDX: Cyber Defense Exercise.

CERT: Computer Emergency Readiness Team (U.S.) or Computer Emergency Response Team (Europe).

Certificate Authority: A network organization that digitally vouchsafes websites via security certificates.

CIA: Central Intelligence Agency (U.S.).

Cloud computing: Using networked systems to both store data and run computer programs, without storing information on the operator's computer.

Conficker: A computer worm detected in 2008 that sought to create botnets out of computers running Windows operating systems.

Cookies: Small programs inserted onto a computer to facilitate the use of larger programs or websites.

Cracker: A hacker engaging in criminal operations.

CSOC: Cyber Security Operations Center.

Cybercrisis: An emergency arising from cyber activity.

Cyberspace: The domain in which computers can interact with one another, both through the Internet and through smaller local networks.

Cyber War: A campaign of cyber attacks that might be construed as an act of war, rather than a criminal act, espionage, or sabotage. Traditionally reserved for nation-state actors.

Data: Information that can be processed by a computer.

DDoS: Distributed denial of service, an attack designed to render a website, server, or computer inoperative by overwhelming it with requests for information, usually conducted by a large number of computers making simultaneous communication attempts.

DISA: Defense Information Systems Agency (U.S.).

DMCA: Digital Millennium Copyright Act (U.S.), a law designed to prevent piracy of digital media by protecting software and entertainment from illegal copying via encryption methods.

DNS: Domain Name System, the system that translates written website names into IP addresses.

DoD: Department of Defense (U.S.).

Domain Name: A unique name for a computer, in a human-readable format.

DOS: Disk Operating System, the original program of the Microsoft Corporation.

E-mail: Messages sent via electronic means that are retained in a mail server.

EMP: Electromagnetic Pulse. One of the effects of a nuclear detonation is a pulse wave that can destroy electronic components.

Escalation: Responding to an attack in a disproportionately strong fashion.

FEMA: Federal Emergency Management Agency (U.S.).

Firewall: A digital filtration system that blocks data from entering a network or machine unless it conforms to certain preset limitations.

Flame: An extremely sophisticated piece of malware related to Stuxnet that was discovered in 2012. Computers infected with Flame can be externally controlled, to include the activation of their cameras and microphones.

GCCS: Global Command and Control System (U.S. Department of Defense).

GhostNet: A secret network of more than 1,200 computers in 103 companies discovered by Canadian researchers in 2009, reporting back to a server on Hainan Island in China.

GIG: Global Information Grid.

Hacker: An individual who writes computer code, and may use that talent to launch cyber attacks. In popular culture, an individual who gains or attempts to gain unauthorized access to a computer or network.

Hacktivist: A hacker who launches cyber attacks for ideological purposes rather than criminal gain.

Hardware: The physical components of a computer.

Honey Pot: A website designed to attract malignant users who will believe they have compromised a valuable network. Used by security professionals to allow computers infections, in order to study their behavior and prevent further damage.

IAD: Integrated air defenses.

IC3: Internet Crime Complaint Center.

ICANN: Internet Corporation for Assigned Names and Numbers, a private nonprofit founded in 1998 to administer the Internet.

ICS: Industrial control system, a computer network or machine that runs industrial equipment.

IDS: Intrusion detection system, sensors that search for digital signals of cyber attacks and identify suspicious behavior and data.

IM: Instant messaging.

Internet: The global network of computerized connections through which information and commerce flow.

IPS: Intrusion Prevention System.

ISAC: Information Sharing and Analysis Center, an organization for coordinating cyber security. Members are major hardware, software, and e-commerce firms.

ISP: Internet service provider, through which individual computers can access the Internet.

JWICS: Joint Worldwide Intelligence Communication System, the U.S. Department of Defense's highest classified network.

Keystroke Monitor: A program designed to record the computer keystrokes by a user, which can be useful in obtaining passwords.

LAN: Local area network, an access point for the Internet or for smaller internal networks.

Logic Bomb: A software program that causes a system or network to shut down or delete all data, usually by creating an illogical set of instructions that cannot be reconciled by the target computer.

Malware: Any type of malicious computer code, including worms, viruses, and Trojans.

MMORPG: Massive multiplayer online role-playing game. By far the largest in history is World of Warcraft, with an estimated eight million current subscribers and more than 100 million accounts created since its release in 2004.

Moonlight Maze: A massive series of cyber intrusions against U.S. government, academic, and corporate websites that began in 1998 and was traced back to Russia.

NATO: North Atlantic Treaty Organization, a military alliance formed in the aftermath of World War II and dominated by the United States.

NIPRNet: Nonclassified Internet Protocol Router Network, the U.S. Department of Defense unclassified network.

NIST: National Institute of Standards and Technology, a branch of the U.S. Department of Commerce that develops and applies standards for industry.

Nonstate actor: A group or organization that does not directly represent a nation.

NSA: National Security Agency (U.S.), the premier signal intelligence organization in the United States.

OSI: Open Systems Interconnection.

P2P: Peer-to-peer, computer software that allows direct communication between two computers, typically bypassing security systems of networks. This creates a major vulnerability for cyber attack.

Packet: A small component of data that can be easily delivered across the Internet, to be reassembled with other packets at the destination.

Patch: A software code update, usually provided to close security vulnerabilities or fix programming errors.

PC: Personal Computer.

PCCIP: President's Commission on Critical Infrastructure Protection (U.S.).

Phishing: A social engineering effort to trick a computer operator into supplying information, often by spoofing a legitimate website.

Phreaking: Using whistle tones to simulate an electronic telephone switching signal, allowing one to make free telephone calls.

PLA: People's Liberation Army, the Chinese military.

Pwn: A hackers' term, a deliberate misspelling of "own." A computer that has been taken over by a hacker or program is "pwned."

RFID: Radio Frequency Identification, a microchip emitting a specific frequency.

RMA: Revolution in Military Affairs, a fundamental change in the nature of warfare or how wars are conducted.

RSS: Real Simple Syndication.

SCADA: Supervisory control and data acquisition, a specific industrial computer system that controls and monitors a process, most closely associated with electric power generation and distribution.

Server: A computer accessed by many other computers, often a router that directs Internet traffic automatically.

SIGINT: Signal Intelligence, intelligence derived from electronic signals.

SIPRNet: Secret Internet Protocol Router Network, the U.S. Department of Defense classified network.

Social engineering: Manipulating individuals to coerce them into unknowingly providing information, usually in a digital forum.

Software: Programs designed to run on computer hardware.

Spam: Junk e-mail, notorious for containing malware or bogus financial offers.

Spearphishing: A phishing attack that targets a specific individual for exploitation.

Spoofing: Impersonating another user to gain unauthorized entry to a computer or network, or pretending to be a legitimate website to gain user credentials and information.

SQL: Structured query language, a type of programming language used to control data, often the mechanism used by malware to seize control of a computer.

Stuxnet: A computer worm created to sabotage the Iranian uranium enrichment program.

TCP/IP: Transmission Control Protocol/Internet Protocol. This is the method by which information transmissions are broken into small digital packets, routed across the Internet, and reassembled at the receiving computer.

TIC: Trusted Internet Connection.

Tier 1 ISP: The five largest Internet service providers (ISPs) in the United States.

Titan Rain: An extremely broad series of cyber attacks against U.S. government and corporate networks, almost certainly launched by Chinese government hackers.

Trapdoor: Software that allows an unauthorized user access to a network or program via a quick means.

Trojan: A computer virus that appears to be a benign program, but which contains malicious code that usually opens a backdoor for unauthorized access.

UCITA: Uniform Computer Information Transactions Act.

UDDI: Universal Description, Discovery, and Integration.

UN: United Nations.

Virus: A malware program capable of copying itself and spreading from one computer to another by embedding in an application or program, designed to prevent detection by the user of the targeted computer.

VSAT: Very Small Aperture Terminal.

White Hat: An ethical hacker whose goal is to improve security, rather than exploit its flaws.

Wi-Fi: A wireless local area network, allowing computers to connect to the Internet.

WikiLeaks: A digital organization determined to release any and all confidential information onto the Internet, made famous by the release of U.S. diplomatic messages in 2010.

Wiper: A particularly devastating malware attack that deliberately destroys all files on a computer or network, including the boot file necessary to start individual workstations.

Worm: Malware that spreads automatically over a network, potentially shutting down or clogging network traffic through its sheer size and exponential growth, which does not require embedding in a program or application.

WSDL: Web Services Description Language.

WWW: World Wide Web.

Zero Day Exploit: A cyber attack that uses a previously unknown security vulnerability. Discovered zero day exploits are sold on the digital black market for hackers.

Index

About the Author

Paul J. Springer is an associate professor of comparative military studies at the Air Command and Staff College. He teaches courses on leadership, strategy, military history, military technology, and the history of terrorism. His previous books include *America's Captives: Treatment of POWs from the Revolutionary War to the War on Terror*; *Military Robots and Drones*; and *Transforming Civil War Prisons: Lincoln, Lieber, and the Politics of Captivity*, coauthored with Glenn Robins. He holds a PhD in history from Texas A&M University. In 2014, Springer was named a Senior Fellow of the Foreign Policy Research Institute.